D1105878

RUSSIAN SHADOWS ON THE BRITISH NORTHWEST COAST
OF NORTH AMERICA

University of British Columbia Press Pacific Maritime Studies

Russian Shadows on the British Northwest Coast of North America is the third in a continuing series dealing with naval history and related maritime subjects published by the University of British Columbia Press. Other volumes in this series are:

1. *Russia in Pacific Waters, 1715-1825: A Survey of the Origins of Russia's Naval Presence in the North and South Pacific,* by Glynn Barratt.
2. *Distant Dominion: Britain and the Northwest Coast of North America, 1579-1809,* (a companion to *The Royal Navy and the Northwest Coast of North America, 1810-1914),* by Barry M. Gough.
4. *Gunboat Frontier: British Maritime Authority and Northwest Coast Indians, 1846-1890,* by Barry M. Gough.

RUSSIAN SHADOWS
on the
BRITISH NORTHWEST COAST
of
NORTH AMERICA, 1810-1890

A Study of Rejection of Defence Responsibilities

Glynn Barratt

UNIVERSITY OF BRITISH COLUMBIA PRESS
VANCOUVER

RUSSIAN SHADOWS ON THE BRITISH NORTHWEST COAST OF NORTH AMERICA, 1810-1890

A Study of Rejection of Defence Responsibilities

© The University of British Columbia 1983
all rights reserved

This book has been published with the assistance of a grant from the Social Science Federation of Canada, using funds provided by the Social Sciences and Humanities Research Council of Canada.

Canadian Cataloguing in Publication Data

Barratt, G. R. V., 1944-
Russian Shadows on the British Northwest Coast
of North America, 1810-1890

(University of British Columbia Press Pacific
maritime studies; 3)
Includes index.
Bibliography: p.
ISBN 0-7748-0165-4

1. Pacific coast (Canada) — History, Military.
2. Canada — Military relations — Soviet Union.
3. Soviet Union — Military relations — Canada.
4. Great Britain — Colonies — America — Defenses.
5. Federal-provincial relations (Canada) — British
   Columbia.* I. Title. II. Series.

FC3811.B37   971.1'3   C83-091143-X
F1088.B37

International Standard Book Number 0-7748-0165-4
This book is printed in Canada on acid-free paper.

Contents

Illustrations

Credits
Plates 2, 3, 5, 6, 7, 11, 12, 13, 14, and 15 are from the Provincial Archives of British Columbia, and Plates 4 (E6665-3), 8 (C-33482), and 10 are from the Public Archives of Canada.

Preface and Acknowledgements

Russia threw her shadow on the Northwest Coast of North America before the British came to what is now British Columbia; and Spanish apprehensions of a "Muscovite" advance on Alta California from outposts in Alaska were traditional and widely known in Europe by the later eighteenth century. For Britain, as the heir of Spain and as the would-be ruling Power on that coast, the very fact of Russia's interest and presence on the far fringe of America was pregnant with political significance and military and economic menace. To the frustration of affected interests in Montreal and London, British cabinets stored up much future trouble and compounded it in 1810–20, by declining to commit British resources — or prestige — to the defence of British interests or even sovereignty on the Northwest Coast. The problems flowing from the growing strength of the United States on the Pacific littoral and from the likelihood of Russo-American collaboration in an effort to resist the further spread of British influence, composed a legacy inherited by Canada. Inherent in *Canadian* reluctance to accept proper responsibility for the defence of the Dominion's west coast were both hostility between too many western residents and the authorities in Ottawa (in whose opinion the Russian threat was best opposed by means of railways and westward immigration) and a lesson for Great Britain and the world about the nature of the non-militaristic, unaggressive nationalism of a Canada forever overshadowed by the Russians' friend, the giant to the south.

In this survey of the longer term defence responsibilities, I have attempted to relate the work of recent specialists to one another and, by synthesizing pertinent material from several adjacent areas of study and from various archival sources, to present it in a way that pays no heed to compartmentalizing lines. The focus is of course on Russophobia, defence measures (and non-measures), and guns. Such is the nature of my book, however, that I touch on diplomatic, naval, military, and even local history. The need to do so leaves me deeply in the debt of writers on specific areas and topics: F. V. Longstaff, W. Kaye Lamb, and M. A. Wolfenden on earlier Esquimalt; A. Beliaev, F. Veselago, L. G. Beskrovnyi, R. Makarova and F. A. Golder on the Russian naval enterprise in the Pacific; N. Bolkhovitinov, A. L. Burt, R. W. van Alstyne, F. Merk, and S. B. Okun' on the flowering of Russo-American relations in the early nineteenth century; T. Armstrong, J. E. Caswell, B. Gough, and Glyndwr Williams on the Arctic and exploratory issues then, as earlier, connected with the Northeastern Pacific Ocean; W. E. Ireland, R. H. Roy, D. M. Schurman, G. F. Stanley, and C. P. Stacey on the earlier Canadian militia and defence questions and postures; D. and G. C. Davidson, J. S. Galbraith, J. R. Gibson, F. W. Howay, and E. E. Rich, on Britain's fur-trade in the far Northwest and West; N. Shrive, A. Berger, and A. P. Thornton, D. M. Farr, and R. Faber on the nationalistic and imperialist movements of the later nineteenth century; R. A. Preston and D. C. Gordon on "Dominion partnership" with Britain in "Imperial defence." If I have placed much emphasis on the significance to British North America in general and to its west coast in particular of Russo-American entente, real or otherwise, it is because I judge it central to this study as to any other study of the tensions that created and sustained the three-Power Pacific triangle of the United States, Russia, and Britain. By avoiding all discussion of the terms of the agreements reached in 1839 and subsequently by the Hudson's Bay and Russian-American Companies, I obviate the danger of repeating E. E. Rich's, D. C. Davidson's, C. Ian Jackson's, and, particularly, J. R. Gibson's work.

This essay largely rests on printed primary materials, British, Canadian, American, and Russian. These however have been complemented by a range of manuscript materials and by a few unpublished works, of which details are given in the bibliography. Chief of the British manuscript repositories used have been the Public Record Office and the British Library, in London; chief of the Canadian — the Public Archives of Canada in Ottawa and the Provincial Archives of British Columbia beside the harbour in Victoria. Some use was made of major libraries in the United States, including the Baker at Harvard University, the Bancroft in Berkeley, the Hawaii State Library in Honolulu. I have also used material on microfilm at the United States National Archives, Washington, D.C. In the USSR, I obtained microfilm or photostats of primary material in TsGADA and TSGIA and visited certain other central institutions, including the Geographical Society of the USSR and the Institute of History of the Academy of Sciences of the USSR, both in Leningrad. Exhausting and costly though these study-trips have proved, of recent years, they would certainly have been far longer and the costs prohibitive but for the readiness of numerous librarians (in Finland, England, and Hawaii) and of friends (in Australasia as in Canada) to send me photocopied or transcribed MS material. I here express my deep thanks, for assistance of one sort or another, to Irina Grigor'eva of the International Exchange Section, Saltykov-Shchedrin Public Library, Leningrad: the late S. B. Okun', of Leningrad State University; E. Häkli, Chief Librarian at the Helsinki University Library; Richard A. Pierce of Queen's University and Berkeley, California; Barry M. Gough, of Waterloo, Ontario; Donald W. Mitchell, of La Mesa, California; Patrick Waddington of Wellington, New Zealand; the staff of the Royal Commonwealth Society in London; and Viscount Palin, Rare Books Librarian at Carleton University in Ottawa.

Finally, I thank Carleton University for travel grants and, latterly, extended leave; the SSHRCC for study grants over a four-year period; and all my children, for their patience.

Introduction

This little book surveys the causes and development of British and Canadian awareness of Russia's presence on and by the Northwest Coast of North America during the nineteenth century and weighs the varied consequences, psychological, political, and military, of a reluctance on the part of the imperial, dominion, and regional authorities to face up to legitimate defence responsibilities on the Dominion's west coast. It is in part because the Russian naval menace to that coast was periodically so real in the age of ironclads, but more especially because the nature of the Russian threat was such that the Canadians alone *could* have controlled it, had they wished, and obviated scares that disturbed British Columbia in every period of Anglo-Russian tension of the nineteenth century, that study of Canadian reaction to the west coast's "Russian problem" is, *par excellence*, the case-study of Ottawa's unreadiness to take responsibility for federal defence against the likeliest of European enemies of the Canadians at large.

Consideration of Canadian reluctance to attend to the defences of the west coast, all alarums and excursions in Victoria or Ottawa or London notwithstanding, also offers a useful frame of reference for larger questions. It illuminates the non-militaristic nature of dominion nationalism (in Macdonald's National Policy and in the view of the Canadian electorate at large by 1870, no coastal battery could do as much to keep the Russian raiders off as the construction of the C.P.R. and westward immigration) and it shows inherent flaws within Canadian imperialist teaching *à la* Denison, Foster, and Mair. By extension, it illuminates two facts of wide strategic and political significance today, a century after the last of the Victoria-Esquimalt "Russian scares": that the growth of friction and disputes between the west coast and the government in Ottawa did not invariably have to do with money, but could stem from incompatible perceptions of the needs of the Dominion and province; and that nationalism came of age in that Dominion without the benefit of martial fervour thanks, essentially, to a Canadian awareness of U.S. military superiority so deep and lasting that it numbed the national will to render Canada secure even against Russia's hypothetical attentions.

British and Canadian awareness of Russia's shadow — naval, strategic, or commercial — on the fur-rich Northwest Coast of North America both reflected and itself contributed towards two major nineteenth-century political developments: the flowering of Russophobia in the United Kingdom and the British Empire including Canada and the dramatic shift of power in North America in

1863–1867 towards Washington. These processes in turn made British subjects, in the young Pacific province in particular but also in Ontario, the Maritimes, and Great Britain, conscious of the danger in an anti-British Russo-American entente for the Pacific. They did not result in measures which would have minimized or even shrunk that danger from the West. Despite the strain on dominion resources, British Columbia could have been made a far less vulnerable and attractive target for a Russian seaborne raid, whether or not the British taxpayers contributed towards, for instance, the development of the Esquimalt naval base which was the Royal Navy's major *point d'appui* in the North Pacific basin. The Canadian-American frontier was a hopeless proposition from the military standpoint, by comparison, and had been recognized as such even in London by the later 1850's.[1] This study assesses the nature and describes the results of that Canadian response to foreign shadows, a response largely inherited from Britain but matured in Canadian conditions of the post-Confederation period, which in itself turned Russia's presence in the North Pacific area into a bogey.

The first three chapters concern the pre-Confederation years. I consider, briefly, British unassertiveness west of the Rockies in and after the Napoleonic period, the Stikine River incident of 1834 and its protracted aftermath, and the Crimean War in the Pacific basin (1854–56). This emphasis on the events and attitudes of times when Hudson's Bay Company governors held sway on the Pacific, is deliberate. Political and military as well as economic patterns then established in response to Russia's presence on that littoral were in due course adopted or adapted by dominion authorities in Ottawa. Central to these patterns were a readiness to scorn and yet deplore that Slavic presence, but to pay no heed whatever to the changeable reality of Russian naval strength and policy in North Pacific waters till obliged to do so by the danger of an actual collision — and in any case to make no genuine commitment to defence of British property or sovereignty there. Chapters follow on the spectre of a Russo-American *entente* in the Pacific and the meaning of a changed balance of power on the continent to the Canadians in general and on the west coast in particular; on the panics of another time of Anglo-Russian crisis, 1877–78, with reference to local and dominion (as well as to imperial) responses to the evidently growing Russian threat; and to the west coast's needless and continuing defencelessness against that threat, the Royal Navy's fluctuating presence on the coast apart, throughout the 1880's and the 1890's. Certain of the "larger questions" mentioned earlier, including the political and military importance of the anti-militarists' victory over the likes of Major-General Sir Edward Selby-Smyth and his Canadian Militia officers, and over Colonel G. T. Denison and his imperialist Torontonians and ex-Canada Firsters, are addressed in brief concluding comments. They are raised, not with the idle thought of treating them exhaustively, but with a view to underlining the potential value for students of defence, politics, and even local history, of an assessment of Canadians' reluctance to defend their own strategically most vulnerable coastline.

Paradoxically, in the early nineteenth century, the British on the Northwest coast itself had shown far less overt hostility towards the Russians to their north, in what was then Russian America and is today Alaska, than did Englishmen in England. Hudson's Bay Company servants saw their Russian counterparts, hunters and traders of the Russian-American Company, as minor rivals and potential nuisances along the coast, indeed, but also as the enemies of Yankee gun-running and licence. Of the Russian Navy's recent grand ambition in the area, there was no sign by 1824.[2] Like the Nor'Westers who preceded them in what was then New Caledonia, the Hudson's Bay Company men drew comfort from the knowledge, hardly conscious though it was perhaps, that Russia's coastal interest was weak and could be further undermined at any time either by Royal Navy action or by British economic power. But of course it was essentially with trade, not sovereignty, that the Hudson's Bay Company servants and their Russian counterparts had been concerned, for all that Governor John Pelly or Admiral N. S. Mordvinov might contend in the negotiations that resulted in the Anglo-Russian Boundary Convention of 28 February 1825. Conversely, it was not with furs or profit but with sovereignty and imperial authority that students and exploiters of the first and only Anglo-Russian clash in North America to make the London headlines, the Stikine Affair, were concerned. Sir Herbert Taylor, David Urquhart, and other Russophobes allied with them were deeply annoyed that, notwithstanding evidence that Russians had in fact broken the terms of that convention and affronted British interests and dignity, the British government would not take up the challenge in the West. As in the years after the War of 1812 and at the time of the conclusion of the Treaty of Ghent with the United States, Great Britain showed marked unwillingness to demonstrate support either of British trading interests or of imperial assertions on the far northwestern fringes of America. Unwilling to become involved in a possible dispute or controversy in a distant area where, like Russia, she was none too strong and had no overriding national interest at stake, Britain chose a "soft" line on the sovereignty issue which Americans, like Russians, did not scruple to exploit.

On the commercial plane, relations between Russia and Great Britain were correct and even cordial during the 1840's, and the two fur-trading companies collaborated to the limits of expediency. Had the Anglo-Russian rivalry which marked the age been only on that level, accommodation would no doubt have been arrived at in the 1830's and, despite some Russian naval patriots' annoyance over clauses of the 1825 convention which (they rightly held) debased the economic value of the Russian *lisière* in North America, it would have been preserved. But from the first years of the century until the 1830's and the rule of Ferdinand von Wrangel, an imperialist element was intermittently injected into trading competition by ambitious, patriotic Russian officers from whom the governors of Russian North America were chosen. Well controlled and even well exploited while only Pelly had confronted them, the basically imperialist aspect of the situation on the

coast became more obvious and dangerous in 1839–40. Servants of both companies were told of clauses, in an agreement signed in Hamburg, that related to
procedures on the Northwest Coast in the event of war erupting between Russia
and Great Britain. Nor, by 1850, were the War, Colonial, or Foreign Offices in
London, or the company officials or the members of the infant Legislative Council
on Vancouver Island, in the slightest doubt — when they could bring themselves
to think about such matters — that the threat posed to the new Pacific colony by
Russia did not lie in her potential as an *economic* force but in her military and naval
capability, imperial ambition, and above all in the possible strategic value of her
settlements and bases round the North Pacific rim from Sakhalin to Sitka. That the
British government would make no costly effort to defend Vancouver Island
against Russian or any other troops in the event of war, if it in fact made any effort,
had been spelled out to the company in 1847. All in all, the situation was not rosy
for the British Northwest Coast.

Regional Russophobia came into its own at Fort Victoria and on Vancouver
Island, as in many other isolated portions of the Empire, as a result of the Crimean
War. Because that war happened to coincide both with the hesitant beginnings of
the Hudson's Bay Company's organized colonization of Vancouver Island and
with Russia's recognition of the military and economic promise of Amuria,
mistrust of Russia, in the North Pacific context and in general, was the unques-
tioned birthright of the two Pacific colonies that were to form British Columbia.
Both exercised it fully, with encouragement from British settlers and from the
Russophobic London press, until in 1867 they were shaken by the black news — as
they viewed it — of the sale of Alaska. Russo-American entente and possible joint
action against Britain's interest in the Pacific were dangers that had weighed on
politicians, naval officers, fur-traders, and Pacific colonists for many years, the
more oppressively since 1854 and the arrival at Victoria of rumours that a Russian
privateer had been fitted out at San Francisco with a view to raiding British or
colonial (Pacific) commerce. Now, by purchasing Alaska from the Russians, the
United States had "sandwiched" British Columbia, in preparation, colonists
feared, for digesting it in the enormous body politic of Washington. Over the next
two decades, local Anglo-Canadian hostility towards an ill-defined conflation of
the Russian military, Crown, and populace came fully into bloom. The imported
propaganda of the British press added to local causes for concern: the growth of
Russian naval strength in the Pacific and the continuing neglect of the militia and
coast defences of the province by the governments in Ottawa and London.

Ottawa and London had recognized by the late 1860's, that the outcome of the
Civil War in the United States, so closely followed by the purchase of Alaska, left
British Columbia quite indefensible in any war in which Americans were openly
involved. The British Admiralty, which was tending to describe Esquimalt naval
base and depot as "essential," grappled with this truth for half a century, while
Ottawa acknowledged it by inactivity congenial to the Canadian electorate at

large. ("Outright hostility to military preparations of any kind came from many sources — from the French Canadians who said that they would defend *their* country . . . [from those who did not believe that war was imminent, and from others] who thought the security of Canada ensured by the Monroe doctrine.")[3] Expenditure for Canadian defences after 1870 went almost wholly on the inland forces, west coast batteries especially being neglected by authorities, Conservative and Liberal alike, whose view it was that in extremis Mother England would protect British Columbia — and that, if she did not, the very fact would serve to justify their prudence in not wasting hard-earned dollars on a task beyond the means of the Dominion. It was a popular, illogical position to adopt. Because British Columbia was indefensible against the strength of a belligerent United States, successive cabinets in Ottawa implied, they were unwilling to enable that far-off fringe of the Dominion at least to ward off the aggression of the other naval power in the North Pacific, Russia. Mackenzie's Liberals, indeed, had a genuine depression in 1874–79 to give a pretext for the attitude — one cannot dignify it with the label "policy"; but the Conservatives' attitude proved more or less identical from 1878 to 1896.

Ottawa's dilemma also concerned London, and specifically the Admiralty Board, from which Canadians resident far from any ocean still expected rather more than they could pay for and considerably more than could be justified by the importance of the seaborne trade and sea-lanes to and from the Northwest Coast of North America.[4] As a result, much hinged on British judgments of the value of Esquimalt as a naval base and coaling depot. After weighing the imperial importance of Vancouver Island and the coast against the weakness of Esquimalt as a base and *point d'appui*, the Royal Navy stayed. British Columbia continued to be sheltered by its guns and so, to some extent at least, secure notwithstanding Ottawa's indifference. What if Russians *did* attempt to shell Victoria, asked politicians in Ontario and eastern Canada whose federal commitment was as sketchy as their Cobdenite distaste for spending money on (no doubt unnecessary) armaments was powerful. Both John A. Macdonald and Alexander Mackenzie felt that any such misfortunes would be pinpricks, quickly healed, hardly worthy of the notice of Canadians at large.

Mackenzie, Macdonald, and their numerous adherents would have been correct in their assessment of the meaning of a few burned ships and stores to the Dominion, had they been soberly considering and planning for a war involving Russians and Canadians and doing so in terms of *wartime* strategy. But neither Conservatives nor Liberals were, in reality, considering the west coast's problems in those terms. During Macdonald's terms of office Russia caused two grand alarums, but he consciously declined to make dominion defences and preparedness to hold her borders any part of his expansive National Policy. In his opinion, nationalism had no need of martial instincts of the sort provoked by the imperial positions at Esquimalt or Halifax; nor were imperialists needed to instil a sense of pride in the Dominion. More important were the settlement of prairies, a stiff protective tariff, and a railway which, in emergencies, could carry armaments and troops as well as settlers and food to the Pacific coast.

On the coast itself, both official and unofficial evidence points to a widespread consciousness of the inadequacy of the land defences and militia and a correspondingly extensive nervousness, frustration, and annoyance with the government in Ottawa in times of Anglo-Russian crisis. Anti-Russian sentiment transcended social barriers and was the property of British Columbians *en masse* in 1890 as it was a quarter-century before and after. Troubled by the obviously weak defences of the Lower Mainland and Vancouver Island, yet aware that they had no voice in Ottawa or London on the subject, even influential colonists, including editors, militia men, and wealthy merchants, turned their eyes away from Russia's strength and interest in the Pacific. While relations between London and St. Petersburg were civil, they could do so and absorb themselves in the quest for wealth from natural resources and for pleasure in their immediate surroundings. In 1870, moreover, they still regarded the Americans as their most likely future adversary, though increasingly they chose, like Ottawa and London, not to think about that grim eventuality. But Russia too had always to be borne in mind: for added to the memory of the Crimean War was the reality of Russo-American *entente* in the Pacific. By the early 1870's few summers passed without the visit of at least two Russian warships to a Californian port. Then came the large-scale Russian naval exercises of the later 1870's (see chapter 5 here), the panic and appeal for assistance to the government in Ottawa. In sum, suspicion of the Russians, deeply tinged by a protective coat of scorn, was widespread in the province and conducive to alarms when Anglo-Russian relations were not good, but conducive to a tendency to ignore the realities of growing Russian strength and foreign policy at other times. If British Columbians had to face expansionism of another power, paradoxically they aligned themselves and their provincial *partis pris* with anti-militarist ministers in Ottawa and regarded the United States as a growing threat that Russia could not equal. Thus, the Russian factor in the North Pacific stood aside in quiet times, ready to leap in times of international tension and alarm especially those men who had been striving hardest to ignore it. The Russian factor was transformed into a bogey less by anything the Russians did to reinforce their naval presence in the 1870's, significant enough though Russian ironclads in North Pacific waters were, than by Canadians themselves.

Nonetheless, Ottawa, as represented by Mackenzie and Macdonald in the 1870's and 1880's when the Russian naval threat was least ephemeral, neglected to discharge its constitutional and moral duty to the new Pacific province where defences were concerned. Russia's Far East Squadron may or may not have been strong enough to have delivered an effective blow against provincial property and shipping and morale during the 1880's. In the present writer's view, it was. Coastal batteries around Esquimalt might or might not have deterred a raider or invasion party, had the Anglo-Russian crises of the age ended in war, and measures might or might not have been taken to decrease the likelihood of an attack on an unguarded and unpopulated section of Vancouver Island's coast. In any case, the authorities in Ottawa were less informed of Russian strengths (and weaknesses) in the Pacific, and of Russian policies and projects that affected the provincial interest or outlook, than they should or need have been by 1880. Almost automatically, successive cabinets shrugged off responsibility for the protection of the province — not only against possible attack by the United States, which they regarded in a fatalistic light, but even against Russian raids. Not only was the growing Russian fleet in a position to give trouble to the Northwest Coast; the government in Ottawa, for reasons different from those of west coast residents but with essentially the same result, was not much interested in the fact, to which, it felt, the Royal Navy should continue to address itself on the behalf of all Canadians. Esquimalt was a British base. That being so, it was not difficult to view Vancouver Island's, even the entire coast's security, as an exclusively imperial responsibility.[5] That it was not, both the dominion and the provincial governments had recognized, officially and publicly, in several agreements reached with London since Confederation; but in Canada the very cause of adequate defences had been tarred by the imperialist brush and was accordingly to suffer.

Not till 1906 did the Dominion reluctantly assume responsibility for even the Esquimalt garrison, nor even then would it create a separate, Canadian-financed and managed naval force to guard British Columbia by sea or buy more powerful and modern long-range ordnance for the Provincial coastal batteries. By word and action, the dominion authorities thus demonstrated yet again that, short of means for an effective system of defence though Canada might be, she was more seriously lacking in the *will* to meet the fundamental challenge to a properly self-governing community or state: that of defence against a past and likely outside enemy.

List of Abbreviations

ABTP	*Alaska Boundary Tribunal Proceedings* (Washington, 1904)
AGO	Arkhiv Geograficheskogo Obshchestva SSSR (Archive of the Geographical Society of the USSR, in Leningrad)
AHR	*American Historical Review*
AVPR	Arkhiv Vneshnei Politiki Rossii (Archive of the Foreign Policy of Russia, in Moscow)
BCHQ	*British Columbia Historical Quarterly*
BL	British Library, London
BLB	Baker Library, Harvard University, Boston
BT	Board of Trade
CHSQ	*California Historical Society Quarterly*
CO	Colonial Office Records
CHR	*Canadian Historical Review*
DAB	*Dictionary of American Biography*, ed. Johnson, Malone (NY, 1928–36)
DCB	*Dictionary of Canadian Biography*, ed. W. S. Wallace (Toronto, 1963)
DNB	*Dictionary of National Biography*, ed. Stephen (London, 1885–1900)
EHR	*English Historial Review*
FO	Foreign Office Records
HAHR	*Hispanic American Historical Review*
HBCA	Hudson's Bay Company Archives, London and Winnipeg
JRAHS	*Journal of the Royal Australian Historical Society*
JRUSI	*Journal of the Royal United Service Institution*
L	Leningrad
M	Moscow
MM	*Mariner's Mirror*
OHQ	*Oregon Historical Quarterly*
Op.	*Opis'* (inventory or account)
PABC	Provincial Archives of British Columbia
PAC	Public Archives of Canada, Ottawa

PHR	*Pacific Historical Review*
PRO	Public Record Office, London
razr.	*razriad* (class or category)
SEER	*Slavonic and East European Review*
St.P.	St. Petersburg
SpAGI	Archivo General de Indias, Seville, Spain
SpAHN	Archivo Historico Nacional, Madrid
TsGADA	Tsentral'nyi Gosudarstvennyi Arkhiv Drevnikh Aktov (Central State Archive of Ancient Acts, Moscow)
TsGIA	Tsentral'nyi Gosudarstvennyi Istoricheskii Arkhiv (Central State Historical Archive, in Leningrad)
TsGAVMF	Tsentral'nyi Gosudarstvennyi Arkhiv Voenno-Morskogo Flota CCCP (Central State Naval Archive of the USSR)
USNA	United States National Achives, Washington, D.C.
WHQ	*Washington Historical Quarterly*
WO	War Office Records

1

Early Patterns: British Unassertiveness and Sovereignty on the Northwest Coast

Almost by tradition, British governments paid scant attention to the enterprise of Englishmen and Scots west of the Rockies or in North Pacific waters. The success of the New Englanders in ousting British traders from the Northwest Coast-to-China fur-trade by the late 1790's, the immense journeys of Fraser and Mackenzie, representatives of a dynamic North West Company yet to succumb to competition from its rivals, even the birth of the Columbia enterprise itself, in 1807, had produced few ripples of concern or interest at Westminster. Such insouciance vexed leading figures of the North West Company, whose very enterprise, they argued with increasing passion, both facilitated and necessitated an officially acknowledged westward movement of the western bounds of British North America or, better still, some formal statement or re-statement of Great Britain's sovereignty over lands west of the Height of Land. By 1810, when it was certain that Americans financed by J. J. Astor of New York were to erect a trading outpost on the banks of the Columbia, thereby forestalling Britain's claims there and undermining her position in "a vast and fur-rich" country which could easily "be made dependent on the British Empire,"[1] Nor'Westers' irritation touched on anger. Scornful of suggestions that the British Northwest Coast was a strategic liability, practically indefensible in view of warfare and imperial commitments nearer England, and in any case of relatively modest economic value, William and Simon McGillivray and other "Interested Merchants" did their utmost to prevent the British government from standing idly by as Astor's people gained control of the enormous hinterland of the Columbia. It was, they noted in appeals to the Foreign Office, then under Lord Wellesley, the Foreign Office that would certainly address itself to their concerns when the Americans and British traders clashed on the Pacific slope.[2]

The McGillivrays' and their adherents' choice of government department symbolized a situation facing the Nor'Westers and the British trading interest in its entirety west of the Rockies. For the first time since the struggle for dominion that had apparently been settled on the Plains of Abraham, further extension of the British fur trade to the west involved the prospect of collision with, in Franklin's words, "another and . . . perhaps a hostile Power."[3] A new age was beginning for the fur trade in the Northwest of America.

As the McGillivrays might have foreseen if they had judged him by his record, Wellesley was out of sympathy with that new age and ready to ignore it. He was preoccupied with the Napoleonic Wars, in which Astoria, the fur trade, and the North Pacific Ocean played no part, and he knew little of the workings of the trade. And he had little interest, if any, in a wilderness ten thousand miles off.[4] Theoretically, as he and Castlereagh had recognized in 1810–12 when the McGillivrays, McTavishes, and other Nor' Westers had petitioned and lobbied for a charter for themselves, such men deserved encouragement — for they were justified in the assertion that, henceforward, to control the fur trade in the lands west of the Rockies was potentially at least to win possession (or perhaps re-state possession) of them for the Crown.[5] In practice, neither had sufficient time or interest to back the North West Company in its attempt to win the race to the Columbia or in a policy that took account of the contingency of clashes with Americans, or Russians, on the coast. The North West Company's petition for a charter of November 1812 well summarized the matter:

> It is the peculiar nature of the Fur Trade to require a continual extension of its limits, into new Countries; because the number of Animals diminishes in those Countries where the Trade has been for any considerable time established, and if the Trade cannot be occasionally extended . . . the returns of it will not long be sufficient to support the expense of the requisite establishment. . . . The Country beyond the Rocky Mountains is the only outlet by which it can be so extended with advantage and success. . . . Your Memorialists also humbly conceive that the Territorial Possession of the extensive Country bordering on the North West Coast of America will ultimately accompany the Trade.[6]

In short, the government should view the presence of Americans at Fort Astoria, if not of Russians on more northerly reaches of the coast, both as a menace to the British trading interest (which it indubitably was) and as a threat to British sovereignty.

In particular, this threat lay in plans that J. J. Astor was developing with a view to domination of the North Pacific fur trade. Thanks only to the outbreak of hostilities with the United States in 1812, the British cabinet was that November thinking of dispatching one small brig to Fort Astoria, to burn it and to capture vessels found there and sent by Astor. The frigate *Phoebe* was in due course readied for the mission.[7] The Nor' Westers did not look on Russia as a comparable threat to British trade or future jurisdiction on the shores northwest and north of Fort Astoria. Americans, not Russians, were their chief concern. Nevertheless, there were many brief allusions to the Russians in the North West Company reports and correspondence for the period. The two McGillivrays and the McTavishes and Frasers at their table were aware, as the cabinet was not thanks to the pressures of the European struggle, the beginning of the War of 1812, and a traditional indifference and ignorance where lands west of the Rockies were concerned, that Russians, Britons, and Americans were building outposts on the same, extensive coast. Its very length indeed somewhat decreased the risk of meetings, and Nor'Westers and Astorians alike well knew where Sitka was. But as the North West Company itself observed, the trade demanded an "occasional extension"; and as Fraser, Black, and others had already shown, the limit of that trade might be advanced five hundred miles in a single season.[8] J. J. Astor too had shown awareness of the political significance, as of the economic threats (and promises) of Russia-in-America: Russo-American contact on the coast had not been severed by the outbreak of the War of 1812. In sum, the North West Company saw the necessity of taking Russia, and Russo-American entente, into account. Its London agents, Inglis, Ellice & Company, agreed to emphasize the point to the appropriate authority. Accordingly, they suggested to the Foreign Office that it was essential that the *Phoebe* or another man-of-war should take their principals' small vessel, *Isaac Todd*, from England to the Northwest Coast where the two craft might collaborate in seizing the Astorians' vessels. More than this, it was essential that the North West Company's representatives should make official, friendly contact with Chief Manager Baranov and the Russians. Bathurst, the secretary of state for war and for the colonies in 1812, did not demur; but he declined to raise the matter with the Foreign Office that same week as Edward Ellice wished. Three weeks went by. Simon McGillivray, who was in London, became restless and sought an interview with Bathurst. He insisted on the need for rapid action: if Astoria grew strong, so would an American trade link with the Russians that would work to Britain's detriment, in one way or another. In itself, the state of war between the United States and Britain made it prudent to improve relations with the Russians. Nor' Westers might be given documents making that point, in case an unexpected Anglo-Russian meeting should occur on the Pacific Coast while Britons and Americans were still at war.[9] Bathurst agreed. McGillivray discussed the point with Henry Goulburn, under-secretary of state for war, who sent the relevant material to J. W. Croker at the Admiralty Board and to the Foreign Office. Notes were drafted with a view to oiling contacts between Russians and Nor'Westers on the coast.[10]

It was one matter to send a frigate to support the North West Company while the United States and Britain were at war, however, but another to press a claim to British sovereignty on the coast north or south of the Columbia in 1814, as the company discovered shortly after British possession of Astoria was confirmed and the fort renamed Fort George (by Captain Black of the *Racoon*).[11] England had been at war almost uninterruptedly for more than twenty years. War-weariness worked to the benefit of the United States in the discussions that resulted in the Treaty of Ghent (December 1814). Again the British government chose not to press the sovereignty issue or, indeed, to dwell on the Pacific slope at all. Trade, after all, hardly depended on exclusive territorial control; and by accepting a return to the pre-war status quo on the Columbia, a most unpopular and costly episode could be concluded. Furthermore, Bathurst observed, demands for formal "recognition or guarantee of His Majesty's rights" west of the Rockies might "cast doubts upon a title . . . sufficiently strong and incontrovertible."[12] In short, the government preferred to take a soft line on the question of control of lands west of the Height of Land. The contest for the "Old Oregon Territory" thus began.

After the war, the North West Company continued its vain petitions for a charter, argued for a formal British claim to sovereignty over countries north of the Columbia, and fully recognized the Russian presence on the Northwest Coast, by word and deed. Starting in May 1815, its London agents, Inglis, Ellice & Company, three times pressed Goulburn for a statement of the government's official attitude towards American pretensions. The North West Company, they noted, still considered all the lands between the Rockies and the coast as British property; but confirmation of the fact would ease investment. Meanwhile, Nor'Westers were about to press beyond the Fraser River in the general direction of the Russian settlement of Novo-Arkhangel'sk.[13] The British government declined either to issue statements on the matter or to pay further attention to the fringes of America. The Congress of Vienna filled the newspapers and politicians' thoughts. It was enough that Britain was again at peace with the United States, on honourable terms.[14]

In 1817 the North West Company again drew the attention of the press and government to the activity of Russians on the Northwest Coast and to the likelihood of Anglo-Russian contact on it, in the near future. That eventuality, announced a pamphlet printed privately in London and entitled, *A Narrative of Occurrences in the Indian Countries of North America*, was being planned for. The partners were "extending their inward trade . . . northward to the [outpost of the] Russians at New Archangel." [15] "The restless, hostile spirit" of Americans towards Great Britain and the prudence of arriving at a friendly understanding with the Russians on the Coast were once more urged on Castlereagh, the foreign secretary.[16] But again the latter listened to the counsels of conciliation and restraint. The cabinet declined to make assertions of exclusive territorial control and sovereignty on the coast north of Astoria, preferring peace to confrontation and an easier relationship with Washington to a triumphant North West Company.

The Russian edicts of 4/16 and 13/25 September 1821, by which exclusive rights were claimed for Russia to all commerce, whaling, "fur-hunting and fishery and every other industry" within an area extending south from Bering Strait to 51°N.L. on the American Pacific coast,[17] showed that the Castlereagh position on the sovereignty issue at Astoria-Fort George and Britain's failure to assert full rights of ownership had been unfortunate. As Russia might effectively have backed her new and grandiose pretensions by establishing an outpost south or east of Sitka Sound by 1820, so might Britain have averted argument over the sovereignty issue by a firmer policy in 1812–17. British readiness to take a "soft line" on that question and unwillingness to strengthen London's hand by (costly) military measures were alike to be reflected in the policies of the dominion authorities towards Vancouver Island in the later nineteenth century.

RUSSIA, THE UNITED STATES, AND BRITISH SOVEREIGNTY ON THE COAST

Russia's claim to sovereignty over North Pacific shores and waters stretching to a line 115 miles offshore on the American and Asian side alike, was a dramatic response to pressure long applied by Russian naval officers. They had been reacting to the Russian-American Company's inadequacies, as the agent of the Russian state, as a monopolistic trading company, and as the guardian of Russian national interests against the long-term and increasing "pilfering" of Russian peltry by New England traders. Paradoxically, that "pilfering"[18] and the ukases it had finally provoked were to result in closer Russo-American collaboration on the Northwest Coast, to the concern and detriment of British national interests.

"The trade conducted by our subjects . . . on the Northwest Coast of North America," it was observed in a preamble by Alexander I, "has been suffering from secret and illicit traffic, and has thereby been impeded." Foreign craft were in future to approach the shores of Russian North America only in emergencies. By the ukase of 13/25 September, the ill-managed and beleaguered Russian company was given a monopoly of fur-hunting and trading in those waters, on the Kuril and Aleutian islands, and on "every other northern island" situated between Asia and America north of the 51st degree of latitude for twenty years. Necessarily, since the intention was to stop Americans and Britons from continuing to hunt and trade in regions claimed by Russia, the edicts mentioned reprisals. Such imperial ukases had inevitably to be backed by hints of strength:

XIV Foreign vessels are forbidden to conduct any traffic or to barter with natives on the islands and northwest coast of North America in the whole extent hereabove mentioned. A vessel convicted of such trade shall be confiscated.

XXV   The commander suspecting a foreign vessel to be liable to confiscation shall inquire and search the same and, finding her guilty, take possession of her. Should the foreign vessel resist, he should first use persuasion, then threats, and finally force. . . . If the foreign vessel employs force against force, then he shall consider the same to be an enemy and shall oblige her to surrender according to naval laws.[19]

No less arresting than the sweep of such pretensions was the fact of the assertiveness itself. For half a century, Russian activities about the Northwest Coast had been supported circumspectly by the Russian court. The prudent wish not to alert Britain or Spain to the extent of cossack voyaging and fur-trading beyond Kamchatka, which might provoke reactions harmful to the Russian interest in Europe, had induced it to proceed with caution. Not till 1821 however, and assertion of imperial authority "commencing from the north point of the Island of Vancouver," [20] did the problem of forestalling the reaction of "affected" Powers to an open demonstration of the Russians' jurisdiction over North Pacific coastlines seem intractable even to ardent naval patriots who had inherited Baranov's mantle. Theoretically, no doubt, it was as easy for the company and Navy to defend their joint position on the Northwest Coast as for Americans or Englishmen to press it. In reality, the decision was deeply flawed; it not only paid no heed to the United States, but also overlooked the fact that danger could approach the Russian posts from the interior of North America itself. By boldly alerting the United States and Britain to the latest Russian movement on the Northwest Coast, the two "Pacific edicts" of September 1821 cost Russia what Empress Catherine II had avoided so successfully in other years: a collision where the weakness of the Russians made withdrawal or defeat too probable.[21]

However, Britain hardly *hastened* to defend her national interest on the Pacific littoral. Quite to the contrary: she rose unwillingly and slowly to the challenge of the edict of 13 September, which was handed to the British cabinet, as represented by Lord Castlereagh, on Wednesday, 12 November, and provoked a blend of scorn and incredulity.[22] The cabinet had other, more immediate concerns to occupy it at the moment, so decided to await the next despatch from the ambassador, Charles Bagot, in St. Petersburg. In short, nothing was done. Bagot's despatch duly arrived, and then another. From them, the cabinet deduced that the Russian edicts that related to the North Pacific fur trade were almost certainly directed more at the United States than at Great Britain; but in any case clarifications were required. Prime Minister Canning decided not to answer Russia's "challenge" — as the London press now viewed it — for another week or two. In fact, eleven passed before he acted.[23] In the interim it fell to members of the Opposition in the Commons, headed by a Scot, James McIntosh, and to the *Quarterly Review* to keep the matter in the public eye. McIntosh, who had connections with the fur trade, asked the government what it proposed to do about the Russians on the coast if protest led to nothing. He was told that a discussion of the issue had been started with the Russian minister. Negotiations were still pending.[24] McIntosh and his supporters were dissatisfied. It was impossible, they urged, to overlook the double threat to British interests posed by the edicts: the commercial, based on maritime pretensions, and the territorial, based upon references to the 51st degree of latitude.[25] In their opinion and in the *Quarterly Review's*, it was inevitable that Great Britain take the tsar to task for his presumptuous assertion of "a principle which he will hardly be permitted to exercise."

> Whether this wholesale usurpation of two thousand miles of seacoast, to the greater part of which Russia can have no possible claim, will be tacitly passed over . . . we pretend not to know; but we can scarcely be mistaken in predicting that his Imperial Majesty will discover at no distant period that he has assumed an untenable authority.[26]

The Times of London and the *Mercury* of Liverpool, among other important daily papers, likewise waxed indignant about the edict which, they argued, was an insult, an infringement of the principle of open navigation on the high seas, and a challenge. Canning's response in Parliament let them down. Russia had already been requested to explain her grand pretensions. It was necessary to await the answer. Mr. Canning had no need for extra international crises in the early weeks of 1822; and he refused to raise the diplomatic temperature further in response to agitation in the press or in the House.[27] No protest would be sent off prematurely even though Britain had unquestionable rights of sovereignty on the Northwest Coast between the Fraser River's mouth and 60°N.L. and from the Rocky Mountains to the ocean.[28]

John Henry Pelly, Hudson's Bay Company governor, was in a difficult position in these circumstances. Unlike Canning, he felt bound to take prompt measures to defend company interests along the coast. Since the merger of the Hudson Bay Company and North West Company in 1821, the troublesome activities of Russians and Americans in New Caledonia and the Columbia Department seemed certain to increase. On the other hand, the coalition had been finalized so recently that he himself was initially unsure of how commercially and politically important those new interests might be and how effectively they could be guarded by the company, with or without the Crown's support.

Pelly's and the Hudson's Bay Company's attitude towards the problem posed by Russia was significantly influenced by the uncertain economic situation, and the more uncertain future, of the Columbia Department. By the terms of an Anglo-American convention of October 1818, lands west of the Rockies to which either state laid claim were to remain open to citizens and vessels of the other. Both Nor' Westers and Americans, in consequence, had founded posts along or near the

Columbia. At Fort Astoria/Fort George they even traded cheek by jowl. Both had outposts in the valleys to the north, northeast, and east. Title to trade and land alike, in short, was open to discussion in the future and could very well be forfeited by Britain. Competition from American free traders was continuous in the Columbia Department. There were rumours that American free colonies were to be planted there. And again, the Canton beaver market was notoriously fickle. All in all, it seemed to Pelly and his colleagues that a modest trading loss was to be looked for and, indeed, that the department might be treated as a buffer zone, protecting territories to the north from the encroaching competition of Americans. New Caledonia, by contrast, offered rosy prospects, and in view of the contentious situation in the Fort George area, he was obliged to reach for them. Governor Pelly calculated that the cabinet would, in the end, support a policy designed to counter Russian territorial pretensions on the mainland by extending Britain's interest and influence northwest from the interior and northwards up the Northwest Coast itself. Early in February 1822, accordingly, he took a risk, instructing George Simpson and his council in the west to found new trading posts as far as practicable north and westward of the Fraser River valley and to act without delay. "It is probable," he added, "that the British Government would support us in the possession of the country which may be occupied by trading posts."[29] George Simpson threw his weight behind the letter of instruction. In his own view, the ukase was "sweeping and absurd." So he told John Dugald Cameron, chief factor in the difficult Columbia Department.[30]

Over the following twelve months, company servants pushed the far north-western limit of its influence beyond the route of Ignace Giasson's exploratory voyages of 1821, erecting Fort Kilmaurs in the so-called Babine Country. Other parties pressed on north towards the Liard River and the empty lands beyond. How far the company would push "to keep the Russians at a distance" now depended more or less on Simpson and on what was practical, given his limited resources and his people's energy. As he already knew, a naval party led by Franklin had for months been pressing west along the Arctic Ocean shore towards the mouth of the Mackenzie River. Fundamentally, therefore, since it was late for Russian interests to challenge either British influence or British sovereignty over Arctic North America east of the Rocky Mountain range, it was a question of a westerly expansion of the Hudson's Bay Company's influence, that is, along the Rockies and across the Height of Land.[31]

Pelly took a nicely calculated risk, arguing strongly for such westerly expansion and accepting the attendant possibility of a collision with a Russian hunting party, for he recognized that Canning and his ministers had little interest in company profitability. He judged, in other words, that pertinent non-economic factors that related to the Russian edicts and the cabinet's response to them would bring the government to view New Caledonia as an essential part of British North America, as he and Simpson did already. One factor was strategic commonsense;

another — national pride. It was a curious position for the senior official of a trading enterprise to take; but then, the company had always functioned as an active or potential arm of empire. The risk was quickly justified. As is apparent from the cabinet and Board of Trade files dealing with North Pacific trading matters for the period, the British government did not appreciate how probable it was that economic concentration on the Fraser River valley and the virgin Babine Country would itself produce a change in the direction of the trade route on the coast, bringing the Hudson's Bay Company servant to an area where Russians might be looked for.[32] Traditionalist servants might repeatedly assure members of a special House Committee that the company could very well continue to export its skins to European Russia, at a profit and without the risk of diplomatic struggles.[33] But inexorably pressure grew on Canning and his ministers; and it could hardly be denied that control of an enormous territory was at stake. That fact having been granted by the cabinet, it was an easy step to government support of Pelly's arguments. Next came the news that Secretary of State John Quincy Adams had protested in the name of the United States against the Russians' economic and imperial pretensions in the far northwest and west of North America. The intention to exclude all foreign shipping particularly offended the United States.[34] The point was noted in the British daily press. At length, the cabinet declared — with the company — that access to New Caledonia by sea as from the east was indispensible if promising new trade was to develop.[35] Thus encouraged, the committee and Pelly pressed ahead with their containing policy towards the interloping Russians. North West Company positions, for example, Fort Alexandria which had been built beside the Fraser River eighteen months before, were reinforced. Another outfit made its way to Babine Lake under the leadership of William Brown and scouted further north beyond the fifty-fourth degree of latitude. Pelly himself composed a forceful "Memorandum on the Claims of Russia to the North West Coast of America," and sent it off to Canning (25 September 1822) with an accompanying letter. "It appears to the Directors of this Company," he wrote, "that the claim of Russia [to sovereignty on the Coast] is *not well founded* and . . . that the interests of the British fur trade would be essentially and greatly injured, should the claims of Russia be admitted by the British Government."[36]

Never, insisted Pelly, had Chirikov, Bering, Steller, or any other servant of the Russian Crown or Russian trading company taken possession of the Northwest Coast or built an outpost on the mainland of America. When Cook had paid his visit to the Russians on Unalaska Island in October 1778, the Russians' settlements had all been off the coast, on islands. They remained on offshore islands as of 1822. Pelly was wrong here, but he was arguing *à thèse* and had no reason to take Iakutat or other coastal forts into account. Meanwhile, as he knew, Hudson's Bay Company servants were enhancing Britain's claim to territory north of 54 N. east of the Rockies. Not for another eighteen months or so would Sitka be regarded as the "proper" northern limit of the company's authority west of the Rockies.[37] Even by the autumn months of 1822, conversely, company officials were considering the prospects for an Admiralty-Company entente, where the expansion of the national interest along the Arctic was concerned. It was from personal discussions between Pelly and officials of the Admiralty in the early part of 1823 that there emerged a formal offer by the company to aid the Navy in an effort to avert all Russian claims to still uncharted Arctic coasts at the expense of British interests.[38] To what extent Franklin himself had felt the company's considerable influence in London when, in late November 1823, he lobbied strongly for a survey of the Arctic shore west from the mouth of the Mackenzie River, is not certain.[39] It is evident at all events that, faced with Russia's challenge on the coast, he and officials of the company alike thought in imperialist terms, and that his summary of the position in a letter to John Barrow of the Admiralty might have come from Pelly's pen. "The objects to be gained" by fresh activity on the remote northwestern shores of North America, he argued with the news of Captain Otto von Kotzebue's major geographical discovery (the modern Kotzebue Sound) and with the 1821 edicts in mind, were "important to the Naval character and the Commercial interests" of Britain. More specifically, it was important to "preserve" vast tracts of country "rich in Animals" from "the encroachments" of "another and, at some period, perhaps a hostile Power" — Russia.[40]

THE SPECTRE OF A RUSSO-AMERICAN ENTENTE

Insofar as the political and economic interests of Britain on the Northwest Coast were separable in the first years of the nineteenth century, the former were more obviously menaced than the latter by the Russian presence in America.[41] New Englanders offered the greater economic threat on those remote Pacific shores. Bostonians (as Russians called New Englanders) however had collaborated profitably with Chief Manager Baranov and his native Aleut hunters in the lucrative sea-otter trade for many years.[42] In fact, by the late 1790's, the American and Russian factors in the North Pacific fur trade and along the coast itself were inconveniently linked (from London's viewpoint) and could hardly be assessed in isolation from each other. British governments and trading interests, and in due course elected governments in Ottawa and British Columbia, were to be faced repeatedly by the American predisposition to support the Russian cause in North America to the extent that it restricted the *Imperium Britannicum*, and so augmented the political, if not the economic, value of the Russians' modest presence on the continent.[43] From the vantage point of Montreal or London, it was a pity that the trading rivalry that had potentially existed between Russians and Americans on the Pacific Coast had, broadly speaking, been outweighed by their co-operation. That co-operation, London merchants knew, extended to joint fur-hunting or, more accurately, poaching expeditions on the undefended shores of California where sea-otter continued to abound.[44] Such ventures, it appeared, made considerable profits. In the eight-year period from 1803 to 1810 in fact the value of the so-called "Boston trade" with Russians on the Northwest Coast exceeded half a million dollars.[45] City men and British politicians had no accurate statistics, to be sure, to be used as ammunition in campaigns to force the cabinet to recognize and shelter the beleaguered trading interest of Britons in the North Pacific; but the volume of the trade involving Boston and adjacent ports, the Russian settlements in North America, Canton, and otter-skins, was not in doubt. And to the large City investor, in particular, the exploitation of the skills of Aleut hunters in their kayaks, cossack foremen, and New England crews seemed menacing. Russo-American commercial understanding posed a threat to British-registered or British trading enterprise and shipping; and political entente rested more commonly than not on economic understanding. New, regular supplies of first-grade sea-otter and other wanted skins would permanently depress the Canton mart, which had been shaky since the late 1790's.[46] Then came news of J. J. Astor's venture and proposed collaboration with the Russian settlement at Sitka (Novo-Arkhangel'sk). To the McGillivrays and others, it was obvious by 1810 that such collaboration was itself a threat to British trading interests in the Pacific, more particularly to their own.[47] Of its resilience there was no doubt: strains caused by the unwillingness or inability of Congress to suppress the gun-running long practised by Americans among the Northwest Coastal Indians had not, as hoped in Montreal, ruined the prospects of continuing relations between Astor's new American Fur Company and its Russian counterpart.[48]

The British government took little interest in these events. Pressures were such that neither time nor money could be spared for remote parts of America, even if policy had argued for increased investment of resources there.[49] It was thoroughly improbable at all events, argued the Board of Trade, that Russo-American collaboration in a small, lucrative sector of the fur trade in Canton would cut out competition between Russians and Americans. New England shipmasters were known to be continuing to trade in firearms and spirits on that portion of the Northwest Coast that Russians treated as their own. It could be hoped that private interests or national pride or both would stretch entente to breaking point.[50]

So long neglected by a British Parliament preoccupied with European crises, the political significance of understanding between Russians and Americans in the Pacific and, potentially at least, between St. Petersburg and Washington, became too stark to be ignored on the outbreak of hostilities between Great Britain and the Anglophobe United States. To the Nor'Westers and their friends, Russian neutrality in such a conflict was irreconcilable with Russo-American co-operation in the North Pacific Ocean — or in any other. For at least six months, however, the Colonial and Foreign Offices declined even to see the hypothetical Pacific aspect of the war. When forced to do so at the close of 1812 by the consideration that the tsar was an important ally, whose relations and associates held shares in the company with which John Jacob Astor traded, both were quick to recognize that, neutrals' rights apart, it might be foolish to harm that trade ostentatiously and so affront the Russians' pride. In the event, matters went better for the Russians on the Northwest Coast than they themselves could have anticipated. Month by month Baranov and his men pursued a policy of pro-American "neutrality" that was not only in their interest, but also in accordance with their feelings. Several New England shipmasters had dealt with them, correctly, for a decade. By the time news reached the coast from European Russia, war could have erupted between Russia and another power. The alliance that existed between London and St. Petersburg could have dissolved three months before Baranov knew of it. Under the circumstances, prudence argued for a policy responsive to immediate realities. Using New Englanders then on the coast as messengers, Baranov passed the word that if Americans would risk the passage north to Sitka from Canton or other ports where fear of capture by a British warship was detaining them, they might proceed under the company's flag, carrying Russian furs to China with their own. By mid-December 1812 five "Boston" shipmasters had made the move. So little did the war impinge on company activity that by the following July Baranov had not only bought two Yankee vessels outright, but had hired both another English shipmaster, George Young, and two Bostonians.[51] By March 1814, thanks to that war, he had a half-a-dozen ocean-going craft at his disposal — an unusual state of affairs.

Russia's commonsensical neutrality remained a minor irritant to British admirals in the affected areas, the North and South Atlantic and the China Seas, as to the Admiralty Board and certain sectors of the British press. Still, such overtly pro-American neutrality was vexing, never more so than when Russian and American co-operation was against the British economic interest, yet countenanced on British government instructions. Despite the feeling in the British squadron on blockade, J. J. Astor's trading vessel *Lark* thus left New York and made her way towards the coast on the explicit understanding that the Russian port of Novo-Arkhangel'sk would be her only destination.[52] Russo-American entente was yet again throwing a shadow on the British national interest north of Astoria, to the apparent unconcern of the authorities in London. After the edicts of September 1821 and the resultant international counter-bargaining over the future terms of trade and future areas of sovereignty on the coast, it was reluctantly recognized that the problem had to be confronted.

Distinguished students of the controversies born of the imperial ukases have asserted that the Canning government inclined to emphasize the territorial dimension of the matter, while the government of the United States, as represented by Bostonians like Adams, from the first focused on trade and on the freedom of the seas.[53] There is indeed convincing evidence that Adams showed no interest in future boundaries along the Northwest Coast ("it is," he noted in November 1822, "quite immaterial to us whether Russia comes to 55 or 51 degrees — that is a question particularly for Great Britain"),[54] till he recognized the need to have pretensions that could be abandoned — in return for a concession by the Russians.[55] Even so, such distinctions between Washington's and London's attitudes are too simple. In reality, the British cabinet was by September 1822 prepared to concede the justness of the argument advanced by the McGillivrays in 1812: that on the coast, control of trade and the possession of the country were essentially connected. More than this, it saw the need to pay more serious attention to the maritime and trading aspects of the Russian claims. Six months before, it had refused to do so. Why the change? Because the government of the United States had paid attention to those aspects and, moreover, seemed disposed to scrutinize them at the possible expense of British interests. In short, the cabinet had grown aware of the spectre of a Russo-American entente or understanding that must surely work to Britain's economic and strategic disadvantage.

Bagot and Nesselrode had brief preliminary discussions on the matter of an Anglo-Russian boundary in August 1823. "I have," wrote Bagot on the 31st, "explained to Count Nesselrode that, the United States making no pretensions to territory so high as the fifty-first degree . . . the question rests between His Majesty and the Emperor of Russia alone."[56] Bagot had challenged Russia's claim south of the fifty-ninth degree on his own responsibility. Canning, he later learned, would have preferred 57°N. as the initial stand-off point. As grew apparent in discussion with Poletika, however, there were problems inherent in the drawing up of demarcation lines along a line of latitude: for south of Iakutat the coast lay on a northwest-southeast axis, and an east-west boundary would make it necessary for another, north-south, line to be negotiated, which would probably result in an impasse. Turning this problem over in his mind as he awaited further orders on the demarcation question, Bagot saw a possible solution. Canning learned of it in late October:

> I have half a mind to exceed my instructions and try if I cannot get a degree of longitude instead of latitude for our line of demarcation. It appears to me that if we take a degree of latitude, we leave Russia with undefined pretensions to the eastward and in the interior of the continent, whereas a degree of longitude would describe both the boundary on the Coast and that within the continent at the same time. I do not know whether Russia would listen to such a proposition.[57]

All indifference to the precise nature and area of Britain's sovereignty in the far Northwest of North America was gone at last. It was "intolerable" now that any foreign power should obtain even a shadow of authority east of the Height of Land. Hudson's Bay Company interests alone made it essential that whatever north-south boundary was drawn should not lie east of it.

All Bagot's plans were altered, at this juncture, by the news that he and Canning had been ignorant of the United States' and Adams' true objects and pretensions on the Northwest Coast and that the British Government had been misled by Stratford Canning's facile remarks to the effect that Washington had no ambitions north of 51°N.L.[58] In fact, Bagot gathered, the United States asserted equal rights with Britain to that coast in its entirety, resting its case on a "prerogative" inherited from Spain, on the activities of Captain Gray the trader and Lewis and Clark the explorers, on provisions in the Treaty of Ghent, and, in effect, on the assurance that Henry Middleton, the minister plenipotentiary of the United States in Russia, had been given quietly by Capodistrias in August 1822: that the ukase of 13/25 September would not be enforced.[59] This revelation, which invalidated much of Bagot's work of the preceding seven months, changed the relationship of the United States and Britain in negotiations pending or in progress in St. Petersburg. American and British interests remained the same *vis-à-vis* Russia's maritime pretensions on the coast; but with regard to territorial pretensions, the United States and Britain were at odds. Bagot suspended his discussions with the Russians till a fresh set of instructions came and, in despatches and in private correspondence of the next several weeks, expressed disgust with, and suspicion of, Americans in general and in particular.

His awareness that the Americans, uncouth though they might be,[60] were diplomatically astute and now discussed the coastal difficulty from a relatively strong position formed the heart of that disgust — as of the British newspapers' contempt for the American volte face over the sovereignty issue. It annoyed the British press and even ministers, unwilling though the cabinet remained to view the controversy as of any moment or deserving of an outburst of emotion (or resources) that Americans could place Great Britain at a disadvantage, simply by playing certain cards that they possessed by chance. It vexed even the cabinet of 1823 to recognize that "scoundrel" Monroe and "Squinzy Adams" might arrive at understandings with the Russians that were positively harmful to the British interest in the Pacific and could reach them through concessions that would cost them almost nothing, for example, withdrawing their "preposterous" assertion of authority to 61°N.L.[61] For it was plain that the Americans *would* reach an understanding with St. Petersburg, rather than London. Anglo-American relations were as brittle in the early 1820's as those between the Russians and Americans were cordial. Disputes over the Maine-New Brunswick boundary, over the "Armbrister-Arbuthnot controversy," over Oregon, and over Cuba had increased the likelihood that as St. Petersburg and Washington came fully to appreciate the benefits that might accrue from a concerted anti-British policy in the Pacific, they would follow one. By early 1823, London began to perceive that it was a significant and long-term threat to British interests on the Pacific slope.[62]

It was especially regrettable, from London's viewpoint, that the diplomatic contact between Middleton and Nesselrode was actually heightening the Russians' and Americans' awareness of their increasing power to contain the British in the Northwest of America, and doing so from week to week. Fresh evidence of this arrived at frequent intervals in letters and despatches from the irritated Bagot. Deeply conscious of an anti-British bond with the Americans, the Russian government was on the one hand prudently sustaining good relations with the British Court while, on the other, taking pleasure from the mutual suspicion and contempt with which the Cannings and the Adams viewed each other.[63] Larger common interests in fact made it improbable that Russo-American frictions would produce more than a diplomatic spark, glimpsed and forgotten. Few Americans were even conscious of the Russian presence on the far rim of their continent, in 1822–24, but many recognized the possible utility of friendship with the Russian tsar.[64] Conversely, lack of sympathy between the British and Americans made it quite probable that friction would continue both in Oregon and in adjacent territories to its north.

For Canning as for Bagot, the discovery that the United States was, as the former put it afterwards, "prepared to accommodate" the tsar "at the expense of Great Britain,"[65] was disillusioning. John Quincy Adams' diatribe against Great Britain on the Fourth of July in 1821 and certain of his yet more recent broadsides were remembered and reciprocated publicly.[66] Both pondered the effect of the discovery on the negotiations, now suspended, in St. Petersburg, and on the xenophobic patriotic party in the Commons, who could use it as an argument for sending warships to the coast. Bagot himself, indeed, was more than once to point out in despatches of the next twelve months that, though the Russians' and Americans' decision to combine to weaken Britain's economic and political position might make it difficult to reach an understanding with the tsar, the Royal Navy was at sea, and Britain's strength in North America was greater — and more likely to increase — than Russia's.[67] All such thoughts were soon suppressed. In 1823–24, as ten years earlier at Ghent, the representatives of a Britannia exhausted by a period of wars and essentially reluctant to embark on new campaigns or confrontations on the distant Northwest Coast, even if British national interests *were* suffering, closed ranks against the sabre-rattling Russophobes.

Avoiding Middleton and swallowing his anger, Bagot asked Poletika what Russia would consider an acceptable frontier. Poletika suggested 54°N.L., 140°W. Such demarcation lines, Bagot replied, were very different from those that London had in mind: approximately 57°30′N.L. (to make Cross Sound the east-west boundary) and 135°W. Such a meridian, replied Poletika, would give Great Britain Novo-Arkhangel'sk, which was inequitable. Russia might withdraw her southern limit on the coast to 55°N.L.[68] November and December passed, and still no new instructions came for Bagot. Henry Middleton then struck, observing that his government had stronger claims than Russia or Great Britain to the coast between 51°N. and 60°N., but that if Russia would retract exclusive maritime and trade pretensions and be flexible on certain other matters, the United States was ready to discuss questions of territory — notwithstanding presidential comments about colonizing in the New World by European powers.[69] Fresh negotiations between Bagot and Poletika began in January 1824. There was a lack of cordiality and easiness in the discussions from the start; all knew that Middleton was meeting Nesselrode, and Bagot was frustrated by the fact that, while the Russians had agreed that commonsensical "convenience" and not "strict right" should be the basis of discussion, they regarded the retention of the 55th degree of latitude as Russia's border on the coast as crucial. Middleton's remarks of recent weeks were thus already being used by Russia as a lever by which Britain could be eased along that coast. Bagot unhappily accepted 55°N.L. as the potential east-west line. Emboldened by their tacit understanding with the government of the United States, the Russians next refused to treat the sovereignty aspect of their difficult discussions with Sir Charles, that is, the future longitudinal, inland frontier, separately from the maritime and trade aspects. The shadow of that understanding fell on Bagot, and Great Britain, unmistakably in 1824. In angry letters written weeks or even days before resigning from his post in Russia, Bagot vented his frustration: "The Russians . . . must be dealt with as you would deal with a horse dealer . . . huckstering and peddlarlike character . . . told roundly that, if they will not arrange the matter equitably, they shall not be allowed to settle anywhere . . . south of Sitca."[70]

By the early weeks of 1824, the British government was following a more conciliatory line over the sovereignty issue in the Northwest of America than Bagot, the ambassador, John Henry Pelly, or the Admiralty Board. Faced with the fact of Russia's presence on the Northwest Coast and with the need to end the prospects of increasing Anglo-Russian competition for a limited supply of furs west of the Rockies,[71] Pelly emphasized the trading and, especially, political significance of any north-south boundary and the importance of establishing an inland line at least as far as Mount St. Elias. ("Russia's *only* fort is situated on Sitka Island which, consequently, can give her no title to the opposite continent . . . Russians not to trade in the interior south of the boundary.")[72] In short, the governor made much of territorial control. Even the notion of a Russian outfit east, or northeast, of the Rockies was intolerable; and the Russian *lisière* on the mainland, if conceded, should be nothing but a strip, less than a hundred miles wide, "south of the head of Lynn Canal."[73] For want of an extensive *lisière*, the Russian-American Company would find it hard to draw a profit from its southern settlement; and in the territory south of Sitka, which the Russian Crown could not abandon easily in any case, having already claimed it by ukase, lay the essential *point d'appui* for the settlement, the trade, and "the solidity" of Novo-Arkhangel'sk.[74] Loss of the coastline south of 56° by Britain, on the other hand, was loss of access to at least two British outposts from the sea, and so it could not be countenanced.

As Bagot had become impatient with his Russian counterparts, Admiral

Mordvinov and Count de Lambert of the Russian-American Company, and out of tune with Canning's own conciliatory policy towards imperial ambition and commercial enterprise on the remote northwestern fringes of America,[75] so too did Pelly grow increasingly impassioned on that subject and increasingly uncomfortable with Canning's cool approach. The truth, as both men recognized in private, was that Canning had no interest in the mechanics or the prospects of the fur trade, and the problem of the Northwest Coast was wholly overshadowed in his mind by South American and European issues. In his lighter moods, he even found amusement in the picture of Poletika, Bagot, and Middleton "bobbing for whale" in a far-off region none of them had seen, or ever would.[76] It was without enthusiasm that, on sending Bagot's orders of mid-January 1824, he followed Pelly's lead in stressing territorial concerns as much as maritime or "purely" economic ones; nor did the cabinet know anything of Pelly's difficulty in conceding that the Russo-American convention of 17 April 1824 ended the hope of keeping Russia further north than 54°40'N.L.[77] Three more months were quite sufficient to persuade that cabinet to end a deadlock that the Russian government seemed willing to protract, now that agreement had been reached with Washington, and to present a new draft treaty to St. Petersburg.[78]

In spite of Stratford Canning's efforts, Britain finally conceded almost everything on which Poletika and Nesselrode had been insisting, on 28 February 1825. Russian obtained her *lisière* and extensive territories north of it to which her claims had not been strong. Britain, however, gained commercial rights within the new limits of Russian North America which undermined its economic viability. Realization of this truth produced dramatic but belated outbursts of annoyance, both at the company main office in St. Petersburg and in affected naval circles.[79] Nesselrode and Alexander I proved unrelenting. Russian America, Mordvinov of the company was told, had gained political security and international guarantees of territorial integrity that more than compensated for concessions made to Britain on the economic front, to wit:

VI: It is understood that the subjects of His Britannic Majesty, from whatever quarter they arrive, whether from the ocean or from the interior of the continent, shall forever enjoy the right of navigating freely, and without any hindrance whatever, all the rivers and streams which, in their course towards the Pacific Ocean, may cross the line of demarcation. . . .

VII: It is also understood that, for a space of ten years from the signature of the present convention, the vessels of the two Powers, or those belonging to their respective subjects, shall mutually be at liberty to frequent, without any hindrance whatever, all the inland seas, gulfs, havens and creeks on the Coast mentioned in Article III [that is, north of

54°40′N.L.], for the purposes of fishing and of trading with the natives.[80]

It was paradoxical. Initially, the Canning government had stressed the territorial as much as the marine and trade dimensions of the 1821 ukases, notwithstanding Britain's proper and traditional concern for freedom on the high seas. In so doing, it had been responsive to the Hudson's Bay Company interest and to the spectre of a Russo-American entente. Diplomatic setbacks and reflection showed, however, that the Russian acquisition of a narrow strip of shore, even to 54°40′N.L., was of slight significance compared with Russian renunciation of pretensions in the North Pacific basin. Russia had obtained her *lisière*, but the heart of the convention lay in articles that dealt not with that issue, but with British trading privileges in a country that was formally acknowledged to be Russian.

RUSSIAN OPPOSITION TO CONCESSIONS ON THE NORTHWEST COAST (1824–25)

British government reluctance to adopt a forward policy along the Northwest Coast, or even to defend effectively large territories that had long been viewed as British on the basis of discovery and Acts of Territorial Possession, pointed to the future. So too did the pain with which the sixth and seventh articles of the convention of 28 February 1825 were heard by patriots, particularly Russian naval officers. Already, patterns for the future were discernible — up to a point — in latent pressures on the governments of Russia (to advance in North America as feasible) and of Great Britain (to avert the very prospect of an international conflict on the Northwest Coast through policies of caution). In the Stikine River incident of 1834, these early patterns were dramatically, if not predictably, confirmed to the annoyance of St. Petersburg and the frustration of the British trading interests and Russophobic press.

As naval minister, N.S. Mordvinov had no role in the negotiations held between Poletika and Henry Middleton in 1823–24; and yet he was abreast of them. As spokesman for his company, he felt obliged to warn against extreme conciliation. The convention of 17 April 1824 confirmed his fears; the Americans had gained far more than had been necessary. He protested both in private and officially to Nesselrode, while company directors sent their own, heated objections to the minister of state finance, E. E. Kankrin, under whose jurisdiction they held office.[81] Nesselrode sent Admiral Mordvinov's protest to the tsar, who struck a small committee to investigate the matter.[82] In response to Kankrin's obvious reluctance to commit himself in the unwelcome controversy, the directors sent another, more explicit memorandum-cum-petition, spelling out their apprehensions for the future if the emperor's "new favour" were "bestowed upon" them.[83] The petition had been drafted and was signed by K. F. Ryleev, poet, radical, company manager based in St. Petersburg, and an important figure in the protest against Nesselrode's and Middleton's convention.[84] It placed the question in a dark perspective. "Once the foreigners have acquired a legal right to compete with the Company domains, and even at its posts . . . many others will hasten there and . . . will soon enough inspire a distaste for their dependence on our Company in natives now attached to Russia. We may well anticipate . . . ruin, and within ten years."[85]

The committee formed to weigh Mordvinov's and the company's objections met but once, in mid-July. It was the view of the majority that the convention of 17 April should be ratified. With only minor reservations, the committee also publicly accepted the interpretation that Poletika and Nesselrode had placed upon it. Foreign traders had been active in the company domains for years, and the company, though representing state and Crown, had lacked the power to prevent it. The United States now formally acknowledged Russian rights and powers, one of which was to refuse any extension of the ten-year trading privilege on Russia's coast (Article IV).[86]

The risk inherent in discussions between Nesselrode and Bagot now being alarmingly apparent to Mordvinov and to others with an interest in Russian North America, they did their best to stay Nesselrode's hand. Young naval officers who had themselves been in Kamchatka or in North America were prominent among the group of patriots around Mordvinov who, like him, thought it essential to forestall the consequences of concessions in America, if not the actual concessions.[87] D. I. Zavalishin, N. P. Romanov, and Baron V. I. Shteingel' were such officers.[88] Among employees of the company and their associates also concerned lest Nesselrode deliberately jeopardize its future were Ryleev, G. S. Batenkov, and O. M. Somov.[89]

All these critics of imperial withdrawal were to some extent disgusted with the workings of autocracy and serfdom and were either on the path to confrontation with autocracy, or soon to find it. For Ryleev, involvement with the secret anti-autocratic cause that climaxed on 14 December 1825 in the Decembrist Revolution, led to early and heroic death; for Zavalishin, Shteingel', Batenkov and many others, to disgrace and retribution.[90] Their associations with the company and their fate ruined all prospects of reversing the official Russian policy towards the company's possessions on the Northwest Coast and cast a shadow over Russian North America. For Nicholas I, now emperor, the company's very existence had deplorable connections with sedition.[91] Individually and in general, in any case, these youthful liberals and patriots had lacked political importance in St. Petersburg and true perception of the nature of the Alexandrine *Realpolitik*. Even Mordvinov's day of influence had long since passed, so far as moulding Alexander's views on major issues was concerned.[92] Nevertheless, it would be wrong to think that 1825 and the Decembrist insurrection put an end to aspirations that such officers had vainly entertained, leading Ryleev among others to insist in memoranda to the ministry of state finance of 1825 that Russian forts be built "at once" along the Mednaia or Copper River to the foothills of the Rockies. ("We *must* do so, with our future interests and their stability in mind. . . . Those same mountains can and ought to be the boundary . . . Potential benefits, justice, and nature all demand it.")[93]

Students of the "empires in conflict and cooperation" on the Northwest Coast in post-Napoleonic years have, in general, made much of the inherent difficulty of the Russians' position in America, for example, the failure of the oceanic system of provisionment from Northern Europe, which was certainly not obvious to London at the time.[94] Much has also been made of certain factors that contributed to actual withdrawal of assertions to control and would assuredly have militated against Russian territorial designs on what are now British Columbia and Washington.[95] It has been stressed that serfdom and the nature of the Russian passport system certainly made recruitment by the company a problem and would have done so even if the edicts of September 1821 had not been promulgated, and that many other problems made the Russian government conciliatory even in the late summer of 1822, where North American pretensions were concerned. Among the factors that would have had negative effects on any programme of imperial expansion south of Sitka, it is said, were long-term conflict between naval officers and "merchants" in the company possessions and their different objectives; inefficiency at company main office in St. Petersburg; communications and supplies problems stemming directly from the distances involved and the remoteness of the company possessions; the impossibility of keeping "poachers" from the long indented coastlines claimed by Russia; Alexander's reluctance to endanger good relations with the government of the United States; and the importance of Anglo-Russian trade, which might have suffered as a consequence of diplomatic conflict to the economic detriment of landowners in European Russia.[96] The validity of all these factors in the policy equation for the Russian Northwest Coast of 1820-24 cannot be doubted. Their comparative or relative significance is arguable.

Basically misguided though the 1821 ukases were and soon though Alexander was instructing Nesselrode and Capodistrias that he was "ready to settle by negotiation the limits of the Russian and British possessions on the Northwest Coast,"[97] scholars have paid little attention to the forces that had lately *been* at work to bring such edicts into being. And those forces, which resided most conspicuously in the "North Pacific section" of the Navy,[98] did not suddenly evaporate in 1824-25. Whether or not a British cabinet would, under pressure from those forces at some future date, be willing to identify the British trading and the British national interest, and both with national honour on the coast, and to defend them all by strength of arms, remained uncertain in the later 1820's. Early precedents, of 1810-12, 1814, and 1822-24, were not encouraging for patriots of an imperialist bent or for the Hudson's Bay Company servant. Nor was Pelly's inclination to conduct an independent "foreign policy" north of the Fraser River mouth and west of Great Slave Lake, presenting ministers with *faits accomplis*,[99] calculated to encourage the conflation (or confusion) of "imperial" and "economic" interests — and a resultant call to arms.

2

The Stikine River Incident

The full cost of a ban on trade with foreigners in Russian North America, made absolute in 1821–22, had grown apparent to the Russian-American Company's shareholders by 1825. It was a cost reckoned in terms of human suffering and, more persuasively for most, by the account-book.[1] Undeniably, the spectre of starvation had receded on the Northwest Coast by 1825–26: New England traders, who were once more fairly numerous at Novo-Arkhangel'sk, brought foodstuffs to the Russian settlements.[2] But it was pointless to provision men in a locality where sea-otter were vanishing and when perforce a high percentage of the company's fur-seal skins — of which at least there was an adequate supply despite the overkilling and mismanagement of half a century — was bartered to Americans for foodstuffs and supplies.[4] It was certain that the supply even of fur-seals would soon shrink. As for the Tlingit Indians of Sitka and its area, to whom New Englanders brought guns and liquor as before, they were more threatening in 1823–26 than they had been for twenty years.[5]

Governor of Russian North America in these unhappy years was a naval officer of modest means named P. E. Chistiakov. Lacking his predecessor Murav'ev's connections in St. Petersburg, and totally dependent on his salary, Chistiakov was loath to take immediate initiatives on any front. But action was necessary even so, if the conventions lately signed were not to undermine the company's commercial viability disastrously. With the latitude that extreme remoteness from the capital afforded, he personally supervised or ordered the development or even the establishment of mainland forts.[6] He hoped to initiate a trade with other coastal tribes, thus competing with the British and Americans directly and avoiding middlemen. But to the governor's misfortune, the rival British company in

London was resolving to push harder on the coast north of 51°N.L. when Russian North America was weak and struggling to come to terms with economic and political realities that threatened it as never previously. Thanks to Simpson's energy, Fort Langley was erected at the Fraser River mouth in record time. Fort Simpson followed, and by 1828–29 it was becoming evident to Chistiakov that Hudson's Bay Company posts would soon extend from the Columbia right to the tip of the Alaskan (Russian) panhandle. Already Indians were making journeys from the Russian to the nearby British territory, bartering their furs for better goods better adapted to their needs. Liquor and guns with ammunition were among these goods, despite an undertaking given formally in the convention of 28 February 1825 that they would not be sold.[7]

In Pelly's and Simpson's view, the Hudson's Bay Company shareholders had more to gain from peaceful co-existence with the Russians on the Northwest Coast, at least till all Americans had been eliminated from the trade by competition, than from taking quick advantage of their evident superiority over the Russians. Such Americans as Pierce, Meek, Blanchard, and Cotting were dependent on their regular supply sales to Russia, and so they could easily be hurt by Anglo-Russian understanding on the question of provisionment. As for the Russians' competition, unimpressive though it was, it could be dealt with when the larger menace had been met. New circumstances called for new approaches; for the moment, Russian shadows on the coast were not unwelcome. Such was ·Simpson's basic message to the company in March 1829:

> In reference to our intended opposition to the Americans on the Coast: we expect to injure them very materially, by depriving them of the benefits arising from their dealings with the Russians. To this end, we have it in view to propose furnishing the Russian Fur Compy. regularly with all the British Manufactures they require, deliverable at New Archangel, at whatever we can get above 33% on prime cost. . . . The transport . . . will occasion no material expense and will interfere very little with our other operations.[8]

Shortly afterwards, Lieutenant Aemelius Simpson, R.N., carried to Novo-Arkhangel'sk the brief but seminal proposal that the British company supply the Russian settlements with fifty to a hundred tons of goods brought out from England every season, plus a fixed amount of beef or pork and wheat. The British would accept a modest profit level. The authorities at Novo-Arkhangel'sk were favourably struck by the immediate and long-term possibilities of the arrangement, but declined to make commitments on the subject. They themselves, Lieutenant Simpson was assured, lacked the power to engage in such activities: all contracts would perforce be signed in European Russia.[9]

THE STIKINE AFFAIR

Thwarted by the workings of a cumbersome Russian bureaucracy and by the remoteness of St. Petersburg from Russian North America, Simpson and Pelly pressed ahead with plans to spread the Hudson's Bay Company's trade into the areas of formally acknowledged Russian influence. A survey was conducted and a site found for a new company post near the Anglo-Russian border on the coast, to which, George Simpson calculated, many groups of Indians might be attracted from the north and east. Whether the survey party truly thought that the selected site lay on the Skeena River which flowed into the ocean at the head of Chatham Sound in British territory, as they later claimed, or whether they and Simpson were aware that the river was the Stikine, not the Skeena, and so entered the Pacific quite two hundred miles north in Russian territory, has been discussed by generations of historians. The extant evidence is contradictory but ample.[10] It is plain at all events that the mistake, if it was one, was viewed in London as at Fort Vancouver with an equanimity that verged on actual approval. After all (argued proponents of expansion to the gates of, and behind, Russian America), article VI of the recent convention entitled British subjects to ascend all streams that crossed the Anglo-Russian border south of Mount St. Elias. The company could therefore build an outpost on the Stikine River, so long as it was far enough inland, and then provision it and reinforce it from the ocean in accordance with the terms of the convention. What was privately admitted on the coast even in 1831–32 was acknowledged in official correspondence two years later. The object of the Stikine River post, Simpson conceded in the late summer of 1834, was "to cut off the Russians from the valuable trade they have hitherto enjoyed without interruption, drawn from the British territory." It was highly likely, Simpson added, that the governor at Novo-Arkhangel'sk would try to stop the move, as "we are now striking at the very root of their trade."[11] The governor in question was no longer Chistiakov, but a politically astute and far more influential officer, Baron von Wrangel, whose command of the mechanics of the fur trade was as firm and comprehensive as Simpson's.[12]

In preparation for the struggle he regarded as inevitable, Wrangel had in fact taken precautionary steps even in 1833. With Hudson's Bay Company pressure on the Stikine area in mind, he had sent Captain A. Etholen (Etolin) of the company-owned vessel *Chichagov* to make a survey of the Stikine River mouth and to trade with Indians he encountered on a broad, generous footing. Etholen reported that the local tribe would welcome Russians, but they welcomed any foreigners with suitable supplies, and British traders, who had made a deep impression, were expected to return with trading goods of better quality than those that Russia could supply, if not with guns and spirits. Wrangel had already drawn attention to this aspect of his problem in despatches to the company main office:

The excellent quality and abundance of the merchandise of the English constitute an attraction to the Kolosh [Tlingit] which we have no means to compete with; and there is no doubt whatever that if the Board of Directors does not find means to supply the colonies with merchandise of such quality and in such quantity as to be able to hold out against the Hudson's Bay Company, that company will be in possession of the whole fur trade in North-Western America.[13]

He could move against American free traders, who continued to bring rum and firearms to Tlingit bands and to abduct the Aleuts' women and steal their fuel; and their ten-year trading privilege, granted in 1824, was not renewed. Against the British, he could make no comparable move until the early part of 1835, because the relevant convention was more recent. Even so, Wrangel was prepared to anticipate the abrogation of their rights under its sixth and seventh articles, that is, to take some action to prevent their moving freely up the waterways of Russian North America. If he deliberated and delayed, it was inevitable that the Russian national interest would be considerably, if not irretrievably, affected for the worse. In short, the rapidly evolving situation on the coast made it expedient to bend a treaty. Like Simpson, Wrangel judged it right to risk collision by the early weeks of 1834. "Until further instructions," he accordingly informed his directors on 28 April, "I will hinder the British by force from sailing up the Stakhin [sic] River." [14] He did so, or the British claimed he did, some six weeks later.

Led by Dionisii Zarembo, a lieutenant of the Russian Navy on secondment who was also in command of *Chichagov* brig, which had brought them there, a Russian party wintered on the Stikine River (1833–34) with a view to raising a stockaded fort as soon as practicable. By early June 1834, stockade and ditch were taking shape around a group of rough-hewn cabins. The "establishment," as Hudson's Bay Company visitors referred to it, was named Fort Dionisii after Zarembo.[15] On the morning of 18 June, the Hudson's Bay Company trading vessel *Dryad*, commanded by Chief Trader Peter Skene Ogden, also anchored just below the fort or strongpoint. Ogden's orders from Chief Factor John McLoughlin were explicit: he was to proceed along the Stikine River and erect a new company post on British territory. The Russian and British eye witness accounts of what actually occurred do not quite tally. The essential point, however, on which all accounts agree, is that Zarembo stopped the Hudson's Bay Company party from proceeding any further up the river:

On the 18th June [Ogden reported], we came in sight of the Russian Establishment on Point Highfield, within a distance of 15 miles, when a Russian boarded us, and the officer not understanding the English or French language, we could only comprehend a few words of no import: he handed me a proclamation signed by Baron Wrangell and shortly after took his leave. About two hours after, as we were casting anchor, another Russian boat with a Russian officer boarded us, and by signs and with the assistance of an Indian interpreter gave us to understand that we must not cast anchor but immediately depart. To this order I paid no attention. Having invited him down to the Cabin, all I could comprehend from him was that they were determined to use force against us and requesting me to write a note to their commander.[16]

Also in the *Dryad's* cabin at this meeting was her captain, Alexander Duncan, of "North Britain, in the service of the Honourable Company." He too leaves an account in which the Russian threat of force is stressed. "The Russian officer," states Duncan, "stated most peremptorily that . . . *Dryad* must not proceed up the Stikhine . . . and that the Russians would use force to prevent it."[17] Shortly after these unsatisfactory encounters, yet another "Russian officer" boarded the vessel, with a "Spanish linguist" in his wake. By chance, the surgeon with the Ogden party, Mr. Tolmie, knew some Spanish; but the Russian officer, it soon transpired, had no more to say to Ogden than the others.

Next morning, at 6 A.M., the "Spanish linguist" and this Russian officer returned in a baidarka to ask their unwelcome visitors to disembark and to attend a conference ashore. Yet another warning against pressing upriver and trading with the local Indians was given. Tolmie and others duly landed and by 10.15 A.M. were in the "Russian Establishment," where they remained for ninety minutes. Here is Ogden again:

> They found a Russian Brig mounting 14 guns with a crew of 84 at anchor in front of the Establishment. . . . Captain Sarembo the commander gave them to understand. . . that he would make use of the force he had, against us, if we attempted to proceed. . . . He did not deny that we had a right to erect an establishment in the interior, on English Territory, but we had no right to navigate these straits, and his orders were to prevent us . . . and he would not deviate from them unless he received contrary instructions from Baron Wrangell.

The thwarted Ogden asked to send a note to Wrangel, and Zarembo readily agreed. Ogden's heated protest to the governor was entrusted to the "Spanish linguist," who set out for Sitka that same day. He was expected to be gone about a week.

To judge by Hudson's Bay Company evidence, which cannot yet be balanced by the proper Russian source, it was now that local chieftains showed their hand. For the past several months these Indians had been bartering with Russians, but they had not been cowed by them. Here, the Tlingit were completely independent. They could choose their foreign allies and suppliers, and they meant to make their choice judiciously. They did not know what strength, or goods, the *Dryad* had, and so delayed a day or two till all the Hudson's Bay Company men had shown themselves and *Dryad's* armament — and wares — had been noted and compared with the Russians'. Neither Ogden nor his people were accustomed to such treatment and resented it, the more acutely because Ogden and the Indians well knew, by 20 June, that *Chichagov* outgunned the *Dryad*. Two "principal chiefs" named Seiks and Anacago who came aboard the *Dryad* now "assumed a tone" that Ogden "was not in the habit of hearing" and asked him frankly if he planned to build a strongpoint in the area. "They had no objections to our building also in the Sound, but were determined to prevent us if we attempted to proceed up the River."

All in all, the situation was fraught with danger. One more evening came and went. Russians and Indians met and conferred ashore, observed by Duncan through his telescope. Next day the chiefs returned and asked for liquor. They were given some, "reduced two thirds" and therefore stronger than the spirits that Zarembo could provide; but they again asserted that the *Dryad* would not move upstream without a fight. As Duncan saw, they were not lacking guns and powder, thanks to *Chichagov* and Wrangel: "the Indians who were in the redoubt and also afloat were armed with muskets and with rifles and fowling pieces, and were provided with ammunition. The said muskets were long bright muskets of large calibre, very different from those in use by the Hudson's Bay Company in their trade with Indians." Long days of watchful inactivity began to tell on Ogden's men. Ogden himself gave up all thought of risking battle, since the Russians were so well entrenched and the many Indians were so well armed, but his sense of outrage grew. Time seemed to drag. Nevertheless, "the threats of the Russian Commander . . . the opposition evinced by the Chiefs . . . and the state of alarm" of his men "determined" him to "await the return of the Express from Sitka." Next, regaining his composure, he himself called on Zarembo on 21 June. He was received politely, and the Russian struggled briefly to express himself in English, words of which he understood, before abandoning the attempt. Ogden reiterated all his protests and referred to the convention of 1825. At this, Zarembo simply stated a reality that his behaviour itself had been implying: "My instructions are to prevent you, and by these, and not by the Treaty, shall I be guided." Ogden hurriedly withdrew to *Dryad*, where the natives had been "numerous and trouble-some," demanding liquor. They returned again next day, and every single day thereafter, often brandishing their "long bright" Russian muskets. Finally, at mid-day on 29 June, "two Russian boats" arrived from Sitka with a note from Wrangel's deputy, Etholen. Zarembo was instructed to persist with the resistance, and the British were emphatically advised to sail away:

> My situation [noted Ogden at the time], is becoming not only more unpleas-ant, but I find myself most critically situated and assuredly at a loss how to act. If I attempted to act conformably with the Treaty, I am aware I should be

justified; but I am firmly of opinion . . . that it would be attended with a loss of lives . . . I have no alternative left but to leave this quarter without making any further attempt . . . however galling it is to be obliged to yield.

So ended an unprecedented Anglo-Russian confrontation, which had lasted just eleven days. Zarembo celebrated his victory, such as it was, by further strengthening his post and his entente with local chiefs by judicious distribution of adulterated spirits. In the light of later arguments about the true aims of the *Dryad* expedition, it is noteworthy that Ogden did not make for Fort Vancouver from the Stikine, as he might have done despite the loss of trading time in summer had he genuinely not expected an encounter with the Russians, but instead continued north, spending another fourteen weeks about the coast. In mid-July, indeed, he faced a second international incident. While men from *Dryad* were ashore and cutting timber, they were seen by Russians and obliged to leave their work unfinished and to re-embark immediately. Coming finally to Sitka, on 7 September, Ogden was received by Wrangel, who contended that the 1825 convention's second article completely justified Zarembo's actions.

Dryad returned to Fort Vancouver in December, and McLoughlin wrote to London straightaway about the Stikine incident. Nevertheless it was nearly seventeen months after the event by the time a preliminary account of it reached Pelly and the company committee.[18]

NON-COMPANY REACTIONS TO A "VERY SERIOUS INJURY"

Pelly viewed the Stikine River incident as a Foreign Office matter from the moment that he knew of it. While it was the company and not the Crown which sought indemnity for things intangible and tangible that had been lost: furs, cash, and dignity, it was nonetheless an international treaty that had been broken. Great Britain was involved; and should the cabinet or press so view the issue, national honour was at stake. Even while lobbying for government assistance in an effort to extract apologies and an appropriate indemnity from the imperial authorities, Pelly remained just as attracted to a policy of mutually advantageous good relations with the Russians in America as he had been in 1826. He wrote à thèse, in short, when in October 1835 he made his case to Palmerston:

> Your Lordship is aware that a Convention was entered into between His Late Majesty George IV and the Emperor of Russia . . . I have now to complain of an infraction of the terms of that Convention, to the very serious injury of the commerce of the Hudson's Bay Company, by Baron Wrangal, Post Captain in the Emperor's Navy . . . who opposed an armed force to our expedition [of May 1834] and thereby prevented the object for which it was outfitted, being carried into effect.

In so doing, the Russian Fur Company have violated the 6th Article of the Convention, which provides that the subjects of His Britannic Majesty, from whatever quarter they may arrive, shall forever enjoy the right of navigation freely . . . in all the rivers and streams which in their course towards the Pacific Ocean may cross the line of demarcation. . . . They have thereby violated moreover the 7th Article. . . . And I have further to complain of a violation of the 11th Article . . . subjecting the Hudson's Bay Company to a considerable pecuniary loss, [expenses incurred in outfitting the expedition,] independent of the injury which our commerce in that quarter has sustained by being thus lowered in the estimation of the natives.[19]

Palmerston read Pelly's hand. By making much of such an incident, indignant though the governor might truly be and on good grounds, the Hudson's Bay Company hoped to gain unqualified support from the Colonial and Foreign Offices and from the cabinet in its attempt to gain a permanent advantage over Wrangel. Twice already, Pelly reasoned, company attempts to reach a long-term understanding with the Russians whereby they would provision Novo-Arkhangel'sk had come to nothing. Now, the company could try again for such a contract, reinforcing British rights of navigation through the Russian *lisière*. In reality, perhaps, it felt no threat from the Russians that it could not meet, given some limited assistance by the Royal Navy. Since the early 1820's, Hudson's Bay Company men had taken comfort from the knowledge that that *lisière* was not only weak, strategically and economically, but also vulnerable to external pressure. Hence the company did not try to inspire a movement on the Northwest Coast to take advantage of the Stikine River incident to "teach Russia a lesson." But what, politically, was to be gained by minimizing the significance of Anglo-Russian rivalry and conflict? Hudson's Bay Company economic strength vis-à-vis Russian North America, which was a function of superior supply-lines both from Europe and from food-producing regions of America, had major psychological importance for the company; but this was something of which Pelly did not speak to Viscount Palmerston. What was significant about his public presentation of the Stikine River incident was that, together with the fact that an infraction of an international treaty had indeed occurred, it opened up the way for others to make use of it. And much could certainly be made of the Zarembo-Ogden face-off by a man who had some reason to inflate its international implications and to see it, in the context of the 1830 Polish insurrection and more recent Russian military moves in the Near East, as symptomatic of essential bellicosity and of expansionist ambition round the world.

Pelly fully recognized that soured Anglo-Russian relations made it probable that government support would be forthcoming for his protest and demand for an apology and adequate indemnity from Russia. Still, his thoughts revolved round company advantage as the thoughts of many other would-be users of the Stikine

River incident, notably members of the nationalistic, Russophobic party led by David Urquhart[20] and certain Royal Navy officers, did not.

Urquhart, linguist, traveller, and specialist in Ottoman affairs was also an essentially lifelong Russophobe. He and his followers reacted to the Stikine River incident with virulent campaigns against Russia in the Urquhart *Portfolio* and such other journals of the 1830's as *Foreign Quarterly Review, British and Foreign Review, Blackwood's Edinburgh Magazine*, and *Westminster Review*; and their comments were illustrative of the rising tide of anti-Russian feeling in the Britain of that day.[21] The 1830 Polish insurrection marked a change of attitude, towards the martinetish Nicholas I in person and towards the Russian state at large, in England and her colonies alike. Russia's quashing of the Polish patriots and liberals had fully reawakened anti-Russian sentiment, for it was nothing new. The Anglo-Russian understanding of Napoleonic years dimmed the national memory, so that the Ochakov and other eighteenth-century alarums caused by Russia were not well remembered by a British public which was not disposed, in any case, to dwell on the reality of Russia's growing military power. News of Russian victory over the Turks and of concessions won at Unkiar-Skelessi led *The Times* at least to wonder if the "Muscovites" were shortly to command the East Mediterranean. "How long," it asked rhetorically on 19 March 1833, "is Europe to be exposed to the ambitious designs of this barbarous Power?" It was time to make a stand, "to drive the Muscovite back to his Asiatic wilderness." The moment passed. *The Times* cooled down and, with it, other papers of the day.[22] For David Urquhart, it was intolerable. He had more than once before stirred up widespread feeling against Russia. He resolved to give repeat performances. Since 1830 he had made the Polish cause his own. What other ammunition was at hand?[23] Sir Herbert Taylor, private secretary to King William IV and David Urquhart's supporter in the anti-Russian cause, was only one of those who seized on news of a collision on the Northwest Coast of North America towards the close of 1835. He wrote to Urquhart, proposing that he use the event in the next *Portfolio* and so incite "the British nation" to an overdue "uncompromising stand" against the hateful Nicholas.[24] The press took up the cue, and Aaron Vail, the American chargé d'affaires in London, thought it necessary to inform the U.S. government of the increasing heat of anti-Russian sentiment in London:

> Among the means daily employed to popularize this feeling, the pretended views of Russia upon British India have been, however absurdly, held up to excite the ignorant fears of the people. Some territorial dispute between British subjects and Russian authorities on the Northwest Coast of America has come at a very opportune time to operate upon the public mind.[25]

Vail thought it hardly likely that the British would resort to war as a result of this "incessant" propaganda, which "distingished Polish exiles" were feeding;[26] and the Stikine River incident could not, in his opinion, be inflated further even by the anti-Russian bigots. As he emphasized, however, the United States should note the possibility that Anglo-Russian friction on the coast might, in the end, be a contributory factor in the outbreak of an Anglo-Russian war fought over Turkey and the Bosphorus. Vail's remarks were given substance by the texts of *Hansard* (House of Commons) for 1 and 18 March 1836, and by sabre-rattling in several of London's daily papers during the following weeks.[27] In short, the Northwest Coast could play its part in European politics, as it had done before during the Nootka Sound Affair. The United States, he suggested, might exert more pressure on events than had been possible when Spain had lost her struggle for that coast.

British Admiralty servants also noted rising Anglo-Russian tensions on the Northwest Coast and in Europe and sent reports of them to Valparaiso and Halifax to be digested by the admirals commanding. By the early part of 1836, McLoughlin's version of the Stikine River incident had been received at Valparaiso by Rear-Admiral Sir Graham Hamond, Commander-in-Chief on the Pacific Station, with a packet of related papers. As was customary, London periodicals were also sent to Chile, so that Hamond and his staff could keep abreast of home developments. In short, the admiral was made aware of the incident, and of alleged Russian designs to push the limits of a giant Russian empire yet further, so "pressing against Britain's far possessions" that all "neutral space" would soon be "wiped out of the map."[28] Under the influence of well-informed and energetic Russophobes like Captain (later Admiral Sir Charles) Napier, Captain H. W. Craufurd, and Palmerston himself, the Royal Navy took due notice of the Urquhartite winds blowing in London. Craufurd's thoroughly alarmist little book, *The Russian Fleet in the Baltic in 1836* (London 1837), was complemented by "a Flag Officer's" (Napier's) frightening *Letter to His Grace the Duke of Wellington upon the Actual Crisis of the Country in Respect to the State of the Navy*. Hamond undertook to keep the Russian traders on the North Pacific rim, if they were actually that and nothing more, under surveillance.

Of necessity, the Lords Commissioners had for the past half-century shown interest in the extreme northeastern reaches of the North Pacific Ocean in two contexts only: Arctic exploration and foreign menace to the British interest on the Northwest Coast. The Stikine River incident did not indeed directly bear on Navy efforts such as Captain Beechey's north of Alaska.[29] It would scarcely militate against the work of Beechey's probable successor. But it plainly represented, or was seen to represent, a Russian challenge to the growing British interest west of the Rockies. In itself, Beechey's *Narrative* published in 1831, with its accounts of *Blossom*'s work in Russian waters off Alaska and of vain attempts to rendezvous with Franklin in the Arctic, had increased public awareness of the activity of Russia on the far rim of America. Now, in the early part of 1836, another voyage of inspection of the North Pacific shores of North America was starting — that of *Sulphur*. Thanks to comments made by Beechey to the Admiralty hydrographer,

Beaufort, his new orders had required him to work in San Francisco Bay and off the Farallones Islands, where the Russians kept a post, before proceeding up the coast to the Columbia and so northwest.[30] In the end command of *Sulphur* went to Edward Belcher, not to Beechey; but her mission and expected route remained the same.[31] What more desirable, given the Stikine River controversy and the Admiralty's lack of recent information about Russian naval strength in the Pacific, than that Captain Belcher call at Sitka and perhaps at other Russian trading posts, for instance, Kodiak, Port Etches, and Ross in California? For want of solid information from a naval source, unhappy rumours flourished: while at Mazatlan in Mexico, for instance, Rear-Admiral Sir Graham Hamond's son, then in the *Rover* sloop, heard of renewed Russian expansion down the coast from "a grand settlement at Nootka Sound."[32] Such rumours were the fruit less of the Stikine River incident itself, perhaps, than of contemporary anti-Russian sentiment in general — and of a lack of British subjects in the area of Nootka. Nonetheless, a full report on Russia's bases in America was plainly needed.

Captain Belcher duly visited the Russian settlements of Kodiak, Port Etches, Novo-Arkhangel'sk, and Ross. He paid two calls indeed at Novo-Arkhangel'sk (September 1837 and July 1839) and was hospitably received on both occasions by the governor, now Kupreianov, or his deputy.[33] In his reports, as in his *Narrative* of 1843, he took due note of the defences and the shipbuilding facilities and harbour of the place. He saw no evidence either of warlike preparations or of strength such as might reasonably trouble Hamond or the Hudson's Bay Company governor. Still, rumours persisted to the general effect that Russian forces were about to make a move along the coast despite conventions that had stabilized frontiers. Nootka Sound was named again, early in 1841, as the great springboard for renewed Russian advance towards the south. Here are extracts from an Admiralty Board instruction of 21 August 1841 to Hamond's successor on the huge Pacific Station, Richard Thomas:

> As it has been represented to us that the Russians have not only established themselves in Nootka Sound, but also much lower down on the Coast of California . . . in the Bay of St. Francisco, with the ostensible purpose of curing fish, but that the Buildings said to be there erecting have much more the appearance of a strong stockaded Fort . . . you will instruct the Commander of the Ship to be employed to call off this part of the Coast, and also at Nootka Sound, to examine as well as he may be able and without exciting the suspicion of those who may be stationed at those places, what is the nature and extent of those Establishments as to Forts, Guns, and Men; and also whether there be any and what Armed Vessels or craft of any kind.[34]

There proved to be no Russian fort at Nootka Sound in 1839–41. Had there been one, we may think, McLoughlin, Finlayson, and others would have known of it and would have sent the news to London, to be used by Captains Napier and Craufurd in the anti-Russian propaganda effort of the day. But rumour has no need of confirmation. Thanks to cumulative efforts by the Russophobes of many years, not a few of whom were serving naval officers, and thanks to faint lingering memories of Ogden's trouble with Zarembo on the coast, many were ready to believe such whispers as would not have been misplaced in Padre Torrubia's anti-Russian warnings of a century before.[35]

COMPANY AND GOVERNMENT RESPONSES

In correspondence with the government, John Henry Pelly did not hesitate to place Zarembo's words and attitudes of 1834 in as invidious a light as possible, or to exaggerate the "injury" sustained as a result of Russian policy. In cash terms, that "injury" amounted to exactly £22,150. 10s. 11d. To glance over the Ogden text of 1834 and that submitted to Lord Palmerston is to appreciate Pelly's determination to present as strong a case as he could manage, even if he had to omit unhelpful portions of the evidence. Gone, for example, were descriptions of the native opposition to the *Dryad*'s passage up the Stikine River. In the text that Palmerston was shown, full blame for Ogden's setback rested with the Russian officers — as though the Indians, if in the area at all, had played a wholly passive part in the misfortune. To the governor's frustration, and despite the widespread anti-Russian feeling of the day (which he had counted on to help him force the government to act in concert with him), Parliament was not disposed to make a feast of Ogden's morsel; nor was Palmerston, intensely Russophobic though he was, impressed by Pelly's public sighs. Not till 13 November was the Hudson's Bay Company told that "certain papers" would be forwarded to the ambassador in Russia, who would be instructed on the matter of the company's complaints. The message was extremely plain: what was important to the company was less important to the Crown, whose interests were global. Britain's interest on the Pacific slope was too peripheral and too remote to justify commitment of resources there or espousal of a policy that would result in open conflict with the tsar. It was the same attitude that Castlereagh and Wellesley had held in 1810, updated for the different yet basically unaltered circumstances on the British Northwest Coast of the mid-1830's.

Pelly wrote to Palmerston again without delay, seeking an explanation of official policy towards the breach of the convention on the coast, so that "instruction" might be sent to Fort Vancouver with a view to obviating further crises. Silence was the answer until January 1836:

In reply to Lord Durham's representation, Count Nesselrode has stated that he received no official information on the subject but declared that he would institute an immediate inquiry, adding that any violation of the Treaty would be a matter of great regret to the Emperor, and should be redressed, if it had occurred.[36]

Frustrated, Pelly sent another letter to the Foreign Office, this time openly referring to the danger that "a serious collision" might occur in North America before the British government had had an answer from St. Petersburg. He wondered if a document, in which the emperor's "regret" was mentioned, might be forwarded to Sitka from St. Petersburg by way of London in a Hudson's Bay Company vessel.[37] If collision did result from lack of action, it would be a national, not a company, affair; and the government would have no choice but to defend the national interest and honour. The suggestion was acknowledged briefly, then ignored.

Finally, there were developments: the Russian government, so Pelly learned, had disavowed Governor Wrangel's reading of the 1825 convention. Russian traders would in future not impede the Hudson's Bay Company servants, or other British subjects, as they went about their proper business on the Northwest Coast. The Russian government did not admit however that the *Dryad* had been stopped either by force or by the threat of it and claimed that there had been language difficulties. In reality, Zarembo had not menaced Mr. Ogden and his people, but had "struggled to acquaint them" with the fact that, if they went upriver, they would act "without permission or consent." At least, the Foreign Office noted, it was now certain that Russia would not bow to the "demand for compensation" at the level fixed by Pelly and had given grounds.[38] It was moreover obvious that Baron Wrangel would dispute the British version of events of two years earlier. In sum, the Foreign Office showed a lukewarm sympathy with the affronted company, whose interests, significantly, it did not officially and forcefully identify with Britain's.

Pelly returned to the attack, stung by suggestions that his men had shown "excess of caution" when confronted by Zarembo. He collected Ogden's first report, Governor Wrangel's proclamation, and the later Ogden-Wrangel correspondence and immediately sent them on to Palmerston. "It is," he added, "fitting that the Hudson's Bay Company should be indemnified. . . . If Mr. Ogden *had* resorted to forcible measures in the face of these hostile demonstrations, he would have been acting in disobedience to, and in contravention of, the 11th Article."[39] There followed a protracted and extraordinary discussion of the ways in which the Foreign Office, Hudson's Bay Company governor, or both, might make their cases in St. Petersburg with greatest chances of success.[40] As a consequence, Durham did not put his case to Nesselrode until February 1837. By then he had collected bulging files on the normal costs of fitting out an expedition on the Northwest Coast, on *Dryad*'s work since 1831, on Ogden, Wrangel, and Zarembo, and on gun-selling and bartering (because the Russians charged that Ogden had been trafficking in spirits, arms, and powder in the Stikine Territory).[41] The Russian government responded three weeks later by observing that no new facts had emerged from the voluminous material presented and insisting that the Indians themselves had shown more forceful opposition to the *Dryad*'s enterprise than had Zarembo.[42] Yet another round of quasi-diplomatic correspondence was begun. Progress was nil. Early in 1838, Pelly addressed the Privy Council on the subject of the Stikine River incident, again without result.

Even by 1836, however, Pelly and the company had grasped the need to cope with Russia-in-America without the government's assistance, since the government would not risk war with Nicholas I yet, Russophobia and Russian military adventures by the Black Sea notwithstanding. Competition with the Russians on the coast was stepped up and the company-owned steamer, *Beaver*, was instructed to present herself at Novo-Arkhangel'sk. Ogden himself was now chief factor in New Caledonia, so Duncan Finlayson, chief factor managing the coastal trade, was told to call on Baron Wrangel. After he did, he made a factually full and sound report on the conditions, strength, and trade prospects of Sitka.[43]

Finlayson found three Americans in port on reaching Novo-Arkhangel'sk, and a fourth arrived during his stay. He took the opportunity presented by this show of "Boston" enterprise to stress to Kupreianov, Wrangel's successor and his host, that the New Englanders could only be excluded from the Northwest coastal trade if Russian and British trading interests co-operated; and he spoke explicitly about a possible commercial pact between the two affected companies. The governor admitted that American free traders would hardly be missed, being so troublesome as dealers in weaponry and spirits, but he observed that such a pact would have to be concluded in St. Petersburg if anywhere. However, he requested samples and a price-list, and agreed to write to his directors on the matter.

To McLoughlin, who had recently been arguing that further efforts should be made along the Stikine River with assistance from the Royal Navy, Finlayson's reception by the Russian governor and Kupreianov's sensible reaction to the notion of a companies' agreement were of deep significance. He told his people not to venture into Russian country until further notice. Not long afterwards, Pelly was openly alluding to the prospects for direct negotiations between British and Russian fur-trade interests, thereby opening a second diplomatic front. He met both Durham, who was then in London preparing for his major work in Canada, and Palmerston to get advice about the proper ways of managing so delicate a meeting, if the Russians proved amenable to the approach. Even in May, the thought of visiting St. Petersburg in person had been taking shape in Pelly's mind. By mid-July he was resolved to go with Simpson, not as an official delegate to any prearranged and formal conference but as an unofficial visitor. Company business might be mixed with sightseeing, and he arranged to take his wife and sons. The British party travelled to St. Petersburg by way of Scandinavia in August 1838. Simpson and Pelly both left full accounts of their activities in Russia. Simpson's first impressions show that he was predisposed to view the empire as semi-civilized and dangerous:

> Monday, August 27. Arrived at Cronstadt at ½ past 9, a perfect Gibraltar in strength. Batteries of the largest calibre in all directions . . . and about 20 men of war. Three fourths of the people afloat and ashore in uniform. Well dressed and efficient for active Service. This is quite a *warlike* nation.[44]

Pelly and Simpson quickly realized that they had overestimated the degree of independence enjoyed by the Russian-American Company. In fact, it seemed, it was a private joint-stock company in name only and was widely treated as a branch of government. Nesselrode, not the company's own board, would voice the company's (and Russia's) policy towards the Stikine claims. That being so, the "tourists" thought it best not to discuss indemnity but to confine themselves to talks with Wrangel and the company directors "having for their end the establishing of intercourse . . . likely to be productive of advantage to the interests of both concerns."[45] Wrangel himself was out of town until 7 September. Sightseeing and shopping palled after a while and delay made the important visitors increasingly short-tempered and impatient of the meeting that they had in view, with Wrangel. Fortunately, that meeting had been easily arranged by A. I. Severin, now chairman of the board, for the earliest possible moment after Wrangel's return. Simpson, at least, found the ex-governor unprepossessing when at last he saw him:

> Found Baron Wrangal, an extraordinary looking ferret eyed, red whiskered and mustachioed little creature in full Regimentals. . . . The Baron, on behalf of the Company, said they would be most happy to establish a good understanding with the H. B. Coy. They had half made up their minds to have no further dealings with the Americans. But . . . with any professed desire of doing business with us, he stated numberless difficulties: such as the scarcity of goods with us . . . our want of shipping to carry grain, etc. We left our Book of Invoice prices with them, for comparison.

Another meeting was arranged for the following week. Days passed too slowly, and the visitors saw less of the directors of the company than they had wished. Little by little, they developed a distinct antipathy towards the Russians and distaste for all things Russian. Simpson's diary is eloquent: " Slaves are a saleable commodity. . . . The poor Devils cannot run away because no one can quit town without a passport. . . . The police and soldiery have a great deal too much power." Finally, 14 September came around. Wrangel was waiting, was polite, again made difficulties; but the visitors threw out a "Bait" that he could not pass by: "that of selling them our Fort Simpson furs which they could import as the produce of their own Colony on the N.W. Coast and thereby be admissible to entry for home consumption or sale to the Chinese, free of Duty. This threw a new light on the subject, and the little baron opened his eyes as if wakened from a dream." The Hudson's Bay Company attitude, said Simpson, was that any such arrangements should be taken as a package. There should be no haggling over minutiae, "a liberal and friendly compact" should be treated "as a whole" by large concerns, indeed, imperial concerns. Pelly and Simpson left for London shortly afterwards without a contract or official agreement to supply, but fully confident that they could get one, given patience and a free hand by the government. They were right. Negotiations were again protracted — in the end, an ultimatum signed by Simpson, who was shortly to return to North America (he said), proved necessary. But a contract was obtained, and signed in Hamburg (January 1839), which embodied economic understanding between Russia and Britain on the Northwest Coast and ended the Stikine controversy. The Hudson's Bay Company rented the coastal *lisière* between Cape Spencer and 54°40′N. for a ten-year term and in consideration for a fixed payment of otter skins. It also undertook to feed the Russian coastal settlements, to drop all claims for damages dating from 1834, and to persist in the attempt to drive Americans out of the trade. Such was the basis for a mutually advantageous, strictly mercantile pact that Russophobia, in Britain and her colonies, proved powerless to undermine. Inevitably, even so, political developments of 1836–39 involving Turkey, and the generally worsening relations between Russia and Great Britain, found reflection in that pact. Appended to it, at the instances of Pelly, was a section covering responses to, and conduct in, a future Anglo-Russian war. A few days in St. Petersburg had proved sufficient to impress upon the governor and Simpson equally that, given an uncertain international situation and the likelihood of Palmerston's retaining power, they were bound to make allowance for such warfare — and for the possibility of its affecting British interests in North America more painfully than had the War of 1812.

But was the coast, on which the British and the Russians both had settlements, to which both nations brought a civilizing influence, inevitably to be dragged into a European war? Was Fort Victoria, founded in 1843, to be attacked by men from Novo-Arkhangel'sk because of crisis on the Bosphorus or in the Persian Gulf? The very harmony prevailing on the coast during the 1840's as a consequence of Anglo-Russian understanding on the economic plane encouraged Simpson, who had even offered to submit reports to London on the mercantile and military activity of Russia in the North Pacific area in January 1841 (though the United States remained his major bogey),[46] publicly to speak of the advantages of quarantining it and thereby saving it from ruin thanks to European strife.[47] It was a point of view that even Russophobic naval officers and patriots, a good many of whom visited "Squirnal" or Esquimalt on Vancouver Island's southern tip during the 1840's, found congenial. Strategic factors and the monetary cost of waging war in such an area apart, the peace and beauty of Esquimalt and Victoria were eloquent. Lt. Richard Mayne, R.N., fondly recalled the visit of *Inconstant* frigate in the early part of 1849, when local Indians offered a threat to Fort Victoria that Russian sailors never had.[48] Three years afterwards, the same great forests kept the outside world at bay, lending an air of unreality to Anglo-Russian tensions over Turkey and the "Holy Places question." Only briefly, in the summer months, did Royal Navy axes send metallic echoes "ringing down the glades" around the track between Esquimalt and Victoria that was about to be "macadamized, after a fashion." [49] Yet, politically and in its actual relation to the Crown, Vancouver Island had completely changed. The very presence of a European settlement at Fort Victoria to which a road could *be* constructed, and that settlement's continuing expansion, made it plain — to British subjects in the area, at least — that British governments would be unable in the future to dismiss its small but genuine defence needs as they had so often in the past. In the event, the 1840's had *not* seen more open conflict between Hudson's Bay Company servants and the Russians in the coastal trade. Company vessels had been civilly received at Novo-Arkhangel'sk, to which they carried British foodstuffs as required by the 1839 pact; and, in the spring of 1849, a second pact had been concluded: the monopoly and lease were to continue for another ten-year term, but the provisionment arrangement was to lapse.[50] Free of annoying competition from American free traders, who no longer spread their spirits, guns, and tensions up the Coast, both companies reduced their buying prices. Coastal Indians with peltry faced an ever-falling market.[51] Every reason for an Anglo-Russian conflict on the Northwest Coast appeared to have been fore-stalled. But, then, future collisions could result from and indeed might be required by new warlike policies adopted in, or orders sent from, Europe. It was supposed in the affected trading circles both in London and especially on the Pacific that the British government would do its duty by a British colony,[52] in that event.

3

The Crimean War and the British Northwest Coast

Hudson's Bay Company servants, like their Russian counterparts, deplored the prospect of a North Pacific, regional extension of a European war. Partly no doubt because relations between London and St. Petersburg were worsening in 1838–39 as a result of Russian military activity in Central Asia and the Near East,[1] but more particularly because Pelly and Simpson saw that Anglo-Russian tension was unlikely to decrease so long as Palmerston held power, certain measures had already been adopted with the grim eventuality of war in view by early 1839. Pelly himself was Palmerstonian in outlook where imperial relations were concerned.[2] His very office, on the other hand, made him responsible for quasi-diplomatic efforts to anticipate an international crisis on the Northwest Coast of North America. Hence a significant insertion was made in the first companies' pact: should war break out between Russia and Britain, the authorities at Novo-Arkhangel'sk would give Hudson's Bay Company servants three full months from the arrival of the news in which to take themselves, their goods, and other British property out of the countries leased from Russia.[3] With minimal assistance from, or even reference to, government, the company thus strove both to ensure its trade and other interests against the overall disaster of a war and to obtain quasi-political control over a large stretch of the coast.[4]

In the event, the Hudson's Bay Company's international problems in the west of North America throughout the 1840's, and by extension, Britain's, were with citizens of the United States, not Russia.[5] And, though Russia drew some satisfaction from the crackling renewal of the Old Oregon question and of strains between the English-speaking governments, she made no effort to exacerbate them. She had much to lose in North America from a deliberately meddlesome policy and was more or less committed to expansion in Amuria and to a military withdrawal from the New World, where she was weaker than her rivals. Temporarily, to seal the matter, all was friendly between London and the tsar, who had in 1844 visited England and discussed the Turkish crisis inter alia with an obliging Aberdeen and civil Peel.[6] Thus the company and Britain had no need of any "three months' grace" provision while the first companies' pact remained in force. As for the actual provision, it had psychological rather than military significance for all its frank and simple reference to war.

To say all this is not, however, to detract from Simpson's, Pelly's, and the company's achievement of *inserting* such a sane provision in the pact: in 1840, even 1841, it seemed more probable that Russia and Britain would in due course fight a war over the Near Eastern question than that peace would be maintained.[7] And it was difficult to say that the hostilities would not, in one way or another, touch the North Pacific area. Again, if Simpson had been right to work with Wrangel and Etholen between 1839 and 1841, hoping to quarantine the Northwest Coast from the infection of a European war, how could he reasonably not repeat the effort when, in 1848–49, another companies' accord was being sought by Pelly?[8] Palmerston was back. "Blustering" Polk and the Americans were pressing hard along a new Anglo-American frontier on the coast, one almost visible from Fort Victoria. The Russian presence in the East and on the Asian shores of the Pacific were acknowledged to be growing by the British government.[9] And even casual acquaintance with that government's negative attitude towards the question of defences for the new and semi-agricultural Vancouver Island threw these international factors into menacing relief.

For eighteen months starting in January 1847 the Colonial Office and the Hudson's Bay Company had held discussions of terms on which a charter might be granted, so that full colonization of Vancouver Island might proceed and agriculture be developed as in Oregon.[10] For eighteen months, opposing principles and interests had clashed: those of Colonial Reformers, Little Englanders, fur traders, and the advocates of large-scale settlement. At length the secretary of state for war, Sir George Grey, found a compromise. The company itself would colonize the island, but it would make no profit from the process and would not expect assistance from the government against the warlike Tsimshian and Haida Indians. A British governor would be entrusted with the overall political direction of the colony, in which the Royal Navy's presence would be minimal, and a distinction would be drawn between aggression offered to the colony by Indians and by, for instance, the United States or Russia. "The said Company," as it was ultimately phrased by Under-secretary Stephen, "should defray the entire expense of any civil and military establishments which may be required for the protection and government of such a settlement . . . except, nevertheless, during the time of hostilities between Great Britain and any foreign European or American Power." [11]

From the company's perspective, it was something to have squeezed even this undertaking from a government so thoroughly unsympathetic to colonial expansion overseas. Cabinet recognition of these circumscribed defence responsibilities however, and appropriate expression of the fact within the Royal Grant of 1849,[12] hardly affected the reality that Britain was exceedingly unwilling to commit herself in public to the longer-term defence of another, remote Pacific colony.[13] Pelly's and Simpson's own encounters with the "Little England" party in the course of the discussions held since 1847 and their dealings with Sir George Grey and James Stephen fully convinced them of the prudence of attempts to place the British Northwest Coast in quarantine as far as Russia was concerned. The local Indians and the Americans were enemies enough, without the Russians on the coast, in any hypothetical scenario involving war at Fort Victoria.

Negotiating with their Russian counterparts over the terms of a revised companies' pact early in 1849, therefore, Pelly and Simpson made no bones about their wish to see the modest wartime safeguards in the 1839 agreement kept in place and somewhat strengthened.[14] They were gratified but not surprised to find the Russians sympathetic to this wish. As a result of mutual perceptions of advantages to be obtained and risks to be reduced without expenditure, in fact, there were few difficulties over wording what were ultimately sections four and five of a new contract, signed at midday on 3 April 1849:

4th   It is further agreed that, in case of rupture between Great Britain and Russia, all the transactions for the preceding time between the contracting parties must be fulfilled without contradiction, as if their respective nations were in friendly relations.

5th   It is further agreed that, in case of rupture between Great Britain and Russia during the existence of this agreement, the Russian American Company shall guarantee and hold harmless the Hudson's Bay Company from all loss and damage arising from such hostilities, insofar as to enable the Hudson's Bay Company to evacuate and abandon their possessions or trading stations within the Russian territory quietly and peaceably and to remove their goods, furs and other property within three months.[15]

All parties were satisfied with this arrangement. It was simple, in accord with commonsense, and cost no money. Whether trading companies could in reality conduct their business with an "enemy" concern as if their governments were not at war was, of course, yet to be seen; but there was nothing to be lost by including such articles in international contracts, on the very texts of which global diplomacy threw shadows — as the signatories knew.[16]

Almost immediately on the outbreak of another in the long series of Russo-Turkish Wars, in 1853, and on reception of the news that British warships had been sent into the Black Sea, the directors of the Russian-American Company turned their attention to the problem of defending their, and Russia's, interest in North America from an attack. War with Britain seemed inevitable, though the start might be delayed. Even at Novo-Arkhangel'sk, the shore defences were "inadequate," "to be relied upon only in warfare against natives," "almost useless in the case of proper war," while the position in the lesser outposts was considerably worse. There was no chance that any French or British raid on, for example, Kodiak, could be forestalled or driven off.[17] Such were the hard realities when, in the early days of 1854, the company's governing board resolved for want of other and more promising expedients in an emergency to make a play on observations made by Simpson to Etholen when he had been at Sitka, almost thirteen years previously. Simpson's frank remarks about the foolishness of either company's mauling the other on the coast because a war was being fought out over issues quite remote to coastal interests, it seemed, had been recorded verbatim by Etholen. They could therefore be presented to the Russian government, and so they were. Would the Crown permit the company to meet the Hudson's Bay Company board and, on the basis of the Simpson comments, to suggest that they induce Britain to recognize the full neutrality of both companies' servants, goods, and vessels on the coast, or even in the North Pacific area? The Russian government encouraged the approach, which was immediately made by Major-General F. Politkovskii (14 February 1854).[18]

The Russian-American Company, in short, took the initiative where the prospective quarantining of the Northwest Coast and North Pacific fur trade were concerned. To make the point is not, however, to imply that the Hudson's Bay Company "board" was not well pleased with the neutrality proposal: it received it with enthusiasm. Copies of the Politkovskii letter and related documents were sent immediately to the Admiralty Board and Foreign Office for discussion and response. No hidden menaces were found, although the Admiralty had specific reservations about placing certain reaches of the North Pacific Ocean out of bounds in such a war as was expected to begin.[19] The British government, Pelly and Simpson were accordingly informed by Henry Addington, permanent under-secretary of state at the Foreign Office (22 March), was prepared to recognize not the complete neutrality of the extreme northeast of the Pacific Ocean, but something fairly close to it. As far as Britain was concerned, the open seas around the Northwest Coast might see hostilities, and Russian vessels caught in them might be attacked or seized, together with their cargoes. Russian outposts on the Northwest Coast or the Aleutian Islands would be subject to blockade, under some circumstances, but would not be shelled or otherwise molested, from the seaward or by land. And Russian shipping in a Russian harbour on that coast would not be fired on.[20] The Russian company accepted the agreement on the stipulated terms, as it had reason to do, knowing its military position on the coast to be so shaky. On the other hand, the Hudson's Bay Company's welcome of the

Politkovskii note also reflected a correct perception of the military realities obtaining on the Northwest Coast and in the North Pacific basin on the eve of war. One of these realities was that even the immediate proximity of British men-of-war, which could actually be expected to arrive and leave and so could never constitute a fixed defence or watch off Fort Victoria, would not protect the Hudson's Bay Company outposts on the coast against a Russian seaborne raid, if it were carried out with secrecy and energy. Another was that any raid launched on a Russian outpost would not only indirectly harm the British coastal trade, but also call for adequate retaliation.[21] All in all, the British too had much to gain from the neutrality agreement.

JAMES DOUGLAS AND PREPARATIONS ON VANCOUVER ISLAND: 1854

Henry Addington and Clarendon, his minister, took various precautions in the early weeks of 1854 against the "possible eventuality" of an attack on allied (that was, French or British) citizens or property in the Pacific or in "other distant quarters of the globe," once the expected hostilities with Russia had begun.[22] Russia was, after all, entrenched on the Pacific rim, and it was known that she had warships in the East, albeit unimpressive ones.[23] The British government planned no attack or operation in the East or the Pacific. On the contrary, it was envisaging a more or less localized struggle round the Black Sea. Even so, it was impossible to overlook the Russian presence on the far side of the world and the importance of ensuring that colonial officials understood that France and Britain stood together, for the moment, and that French military forces should be given all assistance wanted, if they called.

James Douglas, governor of Vancouver Island, was among the many officials who received a circular despatch from Clarendon to that effect, dated 23 February 1854.[24] Clarendon knew, of course, that Hudson's Bay Company posts on the Pacific shore would soon be rendered safe from all aggression from the sea, if they were not already safe: he had himself approved of Addington's communication on that subject to the company's committee of 21 March.[25] But there remained the possibility that French or British warships would arrive at Fort Victoria or in Esquimalt Harbour on their way to, or returning from, an action. Rear-Admiral David Price, the Commander-in-Chief, Pacific, had instructions to co-operate efficiently with French forces at hand against the Russians in the East and the Pacific, should hostilities begin as now seemed virtually certain.[26] And in that case allied warships would presumably attempt to sweep the whole Pacific Ocean clear of Russians, more especially the waters of Kamchatka and the Northwest Coast of North America, where Price might well look to the company for aid. Moreover, wrote the Duke of Newcastle to Douglas in a despatch sent with the circular from Clarendon, signed on 24 February, it seemed reasonable to suppose that such a company, with agents on Oahu and at San Francisco, might assist the allied fleet in other ways. Possibly Douglas would tell the minister what steps were to be taken to protect the French and British national interests in the Pacific and, particularly, how the company intended to assist the Royal Navy in its hunt for Russians?[27]

Clarendon's and Newcastle's despatches reached the governor only in May. Six weeks had already passed since Britain had declared war on Russia. Not till mid-July however did official news to that effect reach Fort Victoria; nor even then did full particulars of the neutrality arrangement that the companies themselves had reached in Europe calm the governor and people of an outpost now, they thought, open to raids at any time.[28] Douglas hastened to reply to the orders sent in February and to state that, in his view, aid should be given to rather than looked for in the colony. Vancouver Island lacked not only modern armaments but also earthworks and a proper garrison. Victoria itself had only wooden palisades that any broad-side would destroy, if fired from a reasonable range. Company servants were of little use as infantry, and Europeans were extremely few. He lacked authority to raise a force, in any case.[29]

Douglas was unwittingly repeating observations made to Clarendon by Andrew Colvile, Pelly's successor, on 28 February and again more recently.[30] And indis-putably both men were right to stress that, militarily at least, Vancouver Island was a liability to Britain. Having made his point however, Douglas focused calmly on the future and on opportunities presented to him by the war. In the circumstances, he reasonably assumed that an attack was to be made on Novo-Arkhangel'sk with the assistance of the allied warships that were on their way and turned his thoughts to the construction of barracks for their companies, and to the arming and equipping of a temporary levy. He advised the Duke of Newcastle that an attack on Russian outposts in America would certainly succeed, if the attacking force were adequately armed. Would the imperial authorities despatch equipment for five hundred men, also four hundred muskets and a hundred rifles, and an ample store of Army victuals, and four light guns with carriages, and heavy ordnance for new emplacements at Victoria? And would the Admiralty undertake to keep a warship at Esquimalt for the present? In the light of the unfortunate experiences of his predecessor, Governor Blanshard, where attempts to have Vancouver Island garrisoned and guarded were concerned,[31] even James Douglas could hardly have expected to receive all the assistance he requested from the government. His letter met with frigid disapproval, even scorn, in London. His "uncalled for" requisi-tion for supplies for an extraordinary colonial militia was rejected. His request for guns, which had been sent on to the War Office for comment, prompted cutting observations from such officers as Colonel Manby and Colquhoun Grant, whose notations on official memoranda show not only private animus against the Hud-son's Bay Company's influence abroad, but also a professional contempt for local nervousness about a Russian raid in "such a place" as Fort Victoria.[32] G. C. Manby went so far as to imply that Douglas had hopes of sloughing off responsibility for the protection of his colony by fusing Indians and Russians in the War Office's mind — a simple trick to which the government was wise. In any case, why should the British government be much concerned about his militarily dispensible "outlying settlement, even supposing it to be seriously threatened"? Captain Grant, recently back from Fort Victoria, concurred with Manby, making much of the lack of troops at Novo-Arkhangel'sk who could attack Vancouver Island and of sea defences on the Russian Northwest Coast.[33] Had Grant been less impatient with the company and had he had a better grasp of Douglas's attitude towards the Russian settlements, he would have realized he was supporting it, and not as he supposed attacking it, by dwelling on the feebleness of Novo-Arkhangel'sk. Here is Douglas, considering a para-military operation on the coast and still quite ignorant of any "quarantine" arrangement, on 16 May:

> A very serious injury might be inflicted on Russia by taking possession of all settlements on the American Coast north of Queen Charlotte Islands; they are all upon the sea board and accessible to shipping. Their defences are on a scale merely calculated to cope with savages, and could not be maintained against a regular force.[34]

It was not Douglas's fault that he was far behind the current of events. Given his limited resources and scanty information, he was rising with considerable sense to the strategic challenge of the day.[35] Nor were Andrew Colvile or the company committee to be blamed if understandings reached in March had not been broadcast through the colony by May. Such was the tyranny of distance. That a company official, let alone a British governor in the Pacific, should be ignorant of them in mid-July, reflected badly on the company and government alike.

Simpson, in the meantime, had been offering suggestions to the Western Department's Board of Management, and anyone in London who would listen, about how best to protect company property along the Northwest Coast from the attentions of a Russian privateer. In his view, it would be "sensible" to send all "personnel" unfit for military duties, and the company-owned steamers, down the coast to the Columbia. "We may rely on the neutrality of the Americans at the very least, if not on their support." Furs too might safely be removed to the Columbia, where Russian raiders would not find them and, in all events, could not take them away as booty. He supposed that Douglas foresaw the possibility that Russia might attempt to raise the Indians, so numerous and forward in the colony, against the British; that the fur-trade might be thoroughly disrupted on the island and adjacent littoral as a result; and that the chiefs, egged on by Britain's enemy, might "seek to gratify their savage passions."[36] Such remarks did not alleviate the tensions that were growing pronounced at Fort Victoria by June when, unofficially, the colony discovered that the Russians and British were indeed at war. Still, it seemed, no single measure had been taken by the Home authorities to reinforce Vancouver Island, which lay open to attack. Under the circumstances, Douglas felt bound to write to Colvile to express his disappointment and concern. He did so, on 15 June:[37] but his sense of isolation was not eased.

In mid-July, in an atmosphere of rising apprehension, the Legislative Council of the colony considered the defence measures that Douglas had been proposing for the past ten weeks. The delay was caused in part, no doubt, by timetable exigencies, and in part by the impropriety of council's acting on suggestions of the sort until officially informed that Britain was at war, but more essentially, one thinks, it was because the council as a whole faced a dilemma in the governor's basic proposal, and was conscious of the fact. It was important, Douglas insisted, that militia be raised for the colonial defence; and since whites were all too few, it was inevitable that the force include some loyal Indians. The council would not hear of any Indians being provided with arms and ammunition by the government: it was not long since groups of armed, migrating Indians had threatened Fort Victoria itself, disrupting life on every plane.[38] The governor gave way. To the proposal that the company-owned steamer *Otter* should be armed and manned, however, council gave assent. No one imagined that a British warship would be stationed in the colony throughout the war, and some defence was plainly needed. As to costs, they would presumably be met by London since the enemy was now a European power. It was therefore ordered that the *Otter* and a crew of thirty be commissioned, at an estimated cost of £600 per month, till Britain made more suitable provision for the colony's defence against a Russian man-of-war or privateer. Her duties as a guardship would begin without delay: rumours were current and were now, in mid-July, almost believed, that one or two small Russian warships were in California and might attempt a raid either on Fort Victoria itself or on a British merchantman. Most councillors, indeed, looked on the Tsimshian and Haida Indians as a more serious and lasting threat than any Russians, but such rumours were increasingly disquieting.[39]

How ineffectual the *Otter* would have been if offered battle by a single man-of-war intent on shelling Fort Victoria or any other outpost of the British Northwest Coast, need not be laboured. As it happened, there was not a Russian ship in the Pacific Ocean ready and available to challenge her, and privateer rumours were discounted by the colonists and governor by mid-September on the basis of a reassuring message from the San Francisco consulate and of a half-a-dozen items in the Honolulu press.[40] The message was repeated six weeks later by a British naval officer well placed to know the truth about a Russian raider lurking on the West Coast. Commodore Charles Frederick, of *Amphitrite* razée frigate, had investigated the "Russian privateer" rumour, looking in at San Francisco and a number of the bays and harbours north and south of it. There was no reason to believe that any Russian man-of-war or privateer was in California or was about to enter an American Pacific port, asserted Frederick.[41] But, fairly obviously, *Otter*'s presence was important to the colony in psychological not military terms; and given his position in July, when the Russians might in fact have been about to raid Victoria, Governor Douglas was justified in chartering a guardship. True to form, the Home authorities later objected to his supposition that the cost of *Otter's* service would be met by the Exchequer. On 18 December indeed, Sir George Grey roundly criticized him for acting precipitately and not awaiting orders from the government before incurring such expenses.[42] Not till August 1855 was Douglas informed that the amount in question would, unwillingly, be paid by London. He received the news in mid-December.[43]

VANCOUVER ISLAND AND THE WAR IN THE PACIFIC: 1854–55

Starting in October 1854, Esquimalt Harbour and Vancouver Island played their full, albeit very minor, parts in the Crimean War. So long deprived of news, the company employees and others on the Island found themselves at last in closer contact with events, thanks to the intermittent presence of Royal Navy vessels in the colony. It is not necessary to repeat the details of the Anglo-French attack on Petropavlovsk-in-Kamchatka of September 1854 and the retreat with heavy losses from Avacha Bay. The story has been told, in English, recently, and on the basis of original materials.[44] Suffice to say that when the *President*, 50 guns, *Pique*, 40 guns, and *Virago*, 6 guns, with the captured Russian schooner *Sitka*, 10 guns, came to anchor at Esquimalt on 3 October, they had eighty wounded men aboard and there were vivid memories of gunfire and death.[45] The war's appearance in the colony was as dramatic as belated.

News of Price's failure in Kamchatka caused a stir at Fort Victoria; nor was the presence of so many wounded men, for whom no medical facilities or hospital existed in the place, without effect. And yet, to judge by the surviving evidence, the main colonial response to the arrival of the ships was of relief. No Russians could attack while such a force was in the offing. It was thus from mingled motives of self-interest and patriotic pleasure at the sight of British ships and guns that Douglas and all his people did their utmost to assist the naval visitors, and to extend the visit as was customary when the Royal Navy called.[46] No one doubted that the recent setback at the Russians' hands would be avenged, and soon.

Captain F. W. Nicholson, now commanding the Pacific Squadron by default, Admiral Price having removed himself forever from the scene, was not impervious to the effects of hospitality. His men were weary from defeat and the 3,000-mile passage from Kamchatka, and his ships needed attention. At Esquimalt there was wood, water, provisions from adjacent farms, and peace in which to put the ships to rights. Coal had been ordered from Nanaimo, where there were large and first-rate seams. Any kindness that the company employees or settlers might offer was a bonus. Such however were the circumstances that the captain, who must surely have anticipated the displeasure of the Lords Commissioners at the debacle of the previous month,[47] remained no longer at Esquimalt than was necessary to recuperate, revictual, and water. In a subsequent report he did at least direct the government's attention to the value of the place as a potential naval depot and revictualling point. The squadron and its Russian prize sailed for San Francisco on 16 October. From the strictly naval point of view, its two-week sojourn at Esquimalt had been clouded by the lack of hospital facilities and limited supply of certain foodstuffs. Such deficiencies, however, could be remedied without great trouble. From the standpoint of the colony itself, only the briefness of the naval visit cast a shadow.[48]

Four months later, in February 1855, Commodore Frederick met Rear-Admiral Sir Henry Bruce, Price's successor as the Commander-in-Chief, Pacific, at the station headquarters, Valparaiso.[49] Within two days of his arrival, which had been by way of Panama, the latter was deploying ships and stores with an attack on Petropavlovsk in mind. After so leisurely a winter, in the course of which morale had dipped again at Fort Victoria for all James Douglas's signalling that it was "in a state of perfect tranquility,"[50] the war in the Pacific and the East moved to a brisker rhythm.

Bruce's plan of action called for an assembling of French and British forces at Oahu. Such a rendezvous was calculated to impress the king and resident Americans alike and to support the principle of monarchy by demonstrating that the European powers disapproved of the continuing expansion of American political and economic influence at Honolulu — and could make their point by force, if pushed too far. The rendezvous was to be followed by an allied sweep towards Kamchatka, an attack, a mopping up of Russian vessels caught at sea, and a methodical retirement to good surveillance and patrolling points, Hong Kong and San Francisco for instance, so that any Russian shipping bound for Sitka, Kamchatka, or the Amur River could be bottled up, if not destroyed. Also part of Bruce's plan was a visit to Esquimalt by at least three of his ships, after the action at Kamchatka, for refitting, revictualling, and recoaling if the price charged by the company were not too steep.[51] He wrote to Douglas from Valparaiso, on 14 February 1855, to put him fully in the picture.

Sir,

I have the honour to inform you that the Service upon which the Allied Squadron will be employed during the present year, will bring to the Island of Vancouver three of Her Majesty's Steamers of War, and perhaps a fourth, in the month of July next. It will therefore be of the utmost consequence that a quantity, not less than a thousand tons, of coal should be retained in store for Her Majesty's Service; and I therefore beg the favour of your giving the necessary directions.

In all probability an opportunity will be afforded me of visiting the Island about the same time in my Flag Ship, the *Monarch* 84, and bringing with me other Ships of war. I am therefore led thus early to express a hope that arrangements may be made with a view to obtaining a full supply of fresh meat and vegetables, to prevent the inconvenience to which Her Majesty's Ships were subjected during their recent visit.

Your Excellency will probably be able to provide a building upon the arrival of the Squadron, that may service as a temporary Hospital for the sick and wounded: the want of which was seriously felt last year.

I have the honour to be, etc.,

H. W. Bruce, Rear-Admiral & Commander in Chief.[52]

As a patriot, Douglas welcomed the approach that would enable him to play a part in the avenging of defeat at Petropavlovsk. He recognized that action, of the sort that Bruce now needed on the company's own part, would boost morale across the colony. And as the agent for that company, he was delighted to do business with another large concern, the Royal Navy. He accordingly informed Bruce that his wishes would be met. Only the hospital presented certain difficulties which, however, could be overcome by money:

Instructions have been sent to the superintendant of the Coal Works at Nanaimo, to secure the quantity of Coal ordered for the use of the Squadron. Secondly, I have sent instructions to the Agent of the Puget's Sound Company at Nesqually to forward to this place 2,000 head of sheep and as many beeves as he can manage to purchase. Thirdly, I have issued a notice announcing to the public at large your intention of visiting this Colony . . . and exhorting them to use every exertion in raising vegetables . . . It has occurred to me that it would be only a proper and necessary step, more particularly during the continuance of hostilities, to appoint an officer to act as Commissary for the Fleet.

I have to inform you that in reference to the building required for the accommodation of the sick and wounded, that . . . finding on enquiry that no disposable building in the Colony was perfectly adapted for that purpose, I resolved, with the advice of a majority of the Members of my Council, to take immediate steps for the erection of decent and comfortable buildings to serve as a naval hospital . . . In taking that step, I have assumed a responsibility beyond the limit of my instructions from Her Majesty, and entirely of a personal nature, but . . . I am in hopes it will meet with the approval of Her Majesty's Government, and I feel assured that you will not hesitate to share the responsibility with me.

James Douglas, Governor.[53]

At once the servant of the Crown and of the company, the governor made ready for a naval visit. While construction of the hospital proceeded at Esquimalt, he himself went to Nanaimo to see that coal was set aside. He was quick to see that Bruce was vague about the question of payment for the hospital accommodation mentioned, but he chose to take the risk that, after lengthy correspondence with the central government, the colony itself would foot the bill, in whole or part.[54] The point deserves some emphasis: for the immediate and visible reality of the Esquimalt Naval Base sprang from his attitude — and that of the majority of members of "his" council, as he properly described them — toward Bruce's broad request. Much has been written by Canadian historians and journalists about the solid wooden structures to be known as "the Crimea huts," that is, the hospital so speedily put up on Duntze Head, Esquimalt.[55] What must be noted here is the readiness with which the colony itself gave body, in the form of "decent," "comfortable," and anything but temporary structures, to a notion that so many naval officers had entertained since the mid-1840's: that Esquimalt should become the Royal Navy's base and depot in the Northeastern Pacific.[56] True, such early advocates of its development as Admirals Sir Fairfax Moresby and Sir George F. Seymour and Commander Henry Kellett of the *Herald* would have preferred that any monies to be spent on it should go on quays and wharves and water-conduits, rather than sick-quarters; and all had thought of it in terms of counterbalancing a more or less American Hawaii, not of checking Russian influence.[57] But since the Admiralty would not spend one shilling on the Island, at least without great grumbling, such preferences were academic. And, predictably, those naval officers who gave their personal opinions of the three "Crimea huts" found much to praise in the behaviour of the governor and council.[58] Psychologically, they understood, hospital huts could serve as well as conduits to reinforce the Navy's presence in the colony and give it permanence. The huts had after all been built with Navy men in mind. They were *there* and were publicly connected with the squadron under Bruce, which was expected any day. As seen, Governor Douglas himself was highly conscious of the profit that the company and colony alike would almost certainly be reaping from the 1855 and, he supposed, subsequent visits by the Navy. Even so, he had more fundamental reasons for completing the "Crimea huts" and gathering a thousand head of sheep in seven weeks.[59] For Victoria was troubled as at no time since its origin in 1843 by its remoteness from the ships on which, essentially, it must depend for its security in wartime. Possibly the Russians were unable to attack it now; but what of future complications with the Russians or Americans? Both were building fleets and had their bases on the North Pacific.[60] The security not only of the colony but also of the British Northwest Coast in its entirety, the company and settlers now recognized, lay in the government's perception of Esquimalt as a future "naval Depot" for the whole "Pacific Fleet."[61]

A dozen French and British warships had been suffering repeated disappointments and frustrations, meanwhile, in their vain search for the Russian vessels known to be at large or, rather, lurking in the North Pacific: the *Avrora*, a 44-gun frigate, and *Dvina*, a 12-gun sloop.[62] Petropavlovsk, where the allies had been looking for a fight, had been abandoned by the Russians. An American free trader on the spot is said to have remarked, "I guess you're rather late, Admiral," to Bruce who, lacking better targets, burned a mastless bark found on the shore, then razed three barracks and a set of gun emplacements.[63] Frustrated in Kamchatka, Bruce next sought his enemy along the Asian shore, around the entrance to the Straits of Tartary, and at Ayan, whence, he was told, the Russians had again made off. He pressed on south.[64] The Russians took advantage of their better knowledge of the regional geography to give the slip again to the pursuing allied force, stealthily sailing to the estuary of the Amur River from de Castries Bay and vanishing.[65] Bruce was deeply embarrassed. Suspecting that the vanished ships had somehow made their way across the ocean to the Northwest Coast where they might shelter unmolested, he made off for Sitka in the *President*, with *Dido* sloop and *Brisk*, screw-corvette, in company.[66] Alas, the Northwest Coast yielded nothing in the way of Russian warships.[67] So finally, in mid-July, the allied squadron was obliged to recognize that there would be no action in the North Pacific and to scatter. Minor consolation was extracted from the Russians' inability to keep a naval force at sea, a situation likely to continue till the last day of the war if British ships kept watch at the strategic coastal, Californian, and Asian points.[68] Douglas reported the arrival of *Brisk* and *Dido* at Esquimalt to the company committee and governor in London, on 19 July 1855;

> Her Majesty's Propellor *Brisk* arrived here on the 19th Inst., having left Rear Admiral Bruce two days previously with the rest of the squadron off Sitka. . . . Her Majesty's Ship *Dido*, Captain Moorshead, also direct from Sitka, arrived here a few days after the *Brisk*, and both ships are now at anchor in Esquimalt Harbour and are abundantly supplied with vegetables and fresh provisions.
>
> The squadron called at Petropaulski in the first part of the season, and to their great regret found the place entirely abandoned, ships, troops and inhabitants having all fled. . . . The batteries and Government buildings were destroyed and the greater part of the Town was burnt "by accident".[69]

The visit was an anticlimax and, as such, reflected Bruce's whole campaign in the Pacific since 1 June when, in the steamer *Barracouta*, he had crossed Avacha Bay and seen the eerily deserted Petropavlovsk. One sick engineer from the *Brisk*, a scurvy case, went into Douglas's hospital which had been built to hold a hundred wounded men.[70] Of Bruce himself there was no sign; nor did the admiral, who was already on his way to San Francisco where surveillance of the (actually non-existent) Russians was regarded as essential, plan a visit to the colony in 1855.[71]

Dido and *Brisk* brought little news about the war to Fort Victoria that had not percolated to it earlier. From all of this, however, it by no means follows that the war in the Pacific, or indeed in Europe, lacked importance for the colony.

THE SIGNIFICANCE OF THE CRIMEAN WAR FOR THE PACIFIC COLONY

On one level, the very building of the three "Crimea huts," the function, size, and name of which were calculated to perpetuate the memory of warfare in a colony that had so long, and needlessly, supposed itself in danger from the Russians, was symbolic of the war's local significance. The huts were seen as pledges of continuing collaboration, and not merely sporadic contact, between colony and Navy. They reminded local residents and Navy men alike that the Americans were not the only possible antagonists on the Pacific slope; nor was it long before the Admiralty was again despatching warships to the North Pacific area, as Douglas had almost hoped would happen, with the Russians and their patently expansionist East Asian policy in mind.[72] As Russia's grip on "Tartary" grew stronger in the later 1850's and was finally considered permanent even by servants of the Admiralty Board,[73] the population of Victoria had even better reason to reflect upon the purpose of the large but empty huts on Duntze Head.

Hardly surprisingly, as he had written of a temporary structure to the governor in February 1855, Bruce was concerned to learn that £940 were owing to the colony by August, and that far from being makeshift, the "Crimea huts" had kitchens, operating room, and even surgeon's quarters. He reminded Douglas that he had spoken of a building to be borrowed or adapted as a hospital, which in itself might have suggested more economy. That done, however, Bruce accepted the *faits accomplis* and, moreover, showed his own belief that it was vital that a British naval base be formed at Fort Victoria-Esquimalt and his readiness to recommend the purchase of the structures on condition that a store and a supply depot be built in the immediate vicinity for long-term naval use.[74] Douglas had no stomach for a repetition of the wrangle that his chartering of *Otter* had occasioned and was anxious that the matter of the naval hospital be closed. He therefore urged the Colonial Office to begin pressing the Admiralty for the sum outstanding.[75] As he expected, the Lords Commissioners dragged their feet over the question: not till 1857 did the Admiralty meet the cost of putting up the three Esquimalt huts, purchase the seven-acre site on which they stood as well as certain other plots, reserve first-option rights to others, and pay interest and upkeep charges on its property. For Douglas and for his councillors, who had the Fraser River gold strike and the prospect of American invasion *inter alia* to vex them by the latter part of 1857, it was all extremely tiresome.[76] As certain officers observed with disapproval, it seemed that the Admiralty had determined *not* to found the shore establishment so obviously needed in the northeastern Pacific at the place with the most obvious advantages. It was a sorry story of delay, of "drifting into an arrangement" whereby Duntze Head, "a most unsuitable" position that might almost have been chosen "to encourage and invite" a shelling, was the centre of a British depot almost accidentally.[77]

It would be wrong to think, however, that the presence of an embryonic base or depot was itself the major legacy of the Crimean War to the young colony. The depot had been founded, after all, as a response both to the actions of the recent past and to the possible aggressions of the future; and the essence of response is attitude. Throughout the 1840's, the United States had rightly been perceived as Britain's major foreign rival and therefore the most probable aggressor, on the Northwest Coast. Company servants had viewed Russia as a distant power, and the feebleness of Russian North America had been not only more apparent than the strength of Russian arms in Bessarabia or other far-off parts, but also an inhibiting or checking element in local Russophobia. Americans, because more threatening, had stirred up deeper feelings. As a consequence of the Crimean War, in general and in its North Pacific setting, this perception of the Russian factor changed. Still, in the early 1860's, British subjects on the Northwest Coast regarded the Americans as their most likely adversary in the future — though indeed many preferred not to consider such a possibility at all. But Russia too was borne in mind, and even more so in the 1870's and early 1880's when reports of rising tension between Russia and Great Britain sent repeated shocks and tremors round the rim of the Pacific, from Esquimalt to New Zealand and Australia.[78]

Earlier Vancouver Island and British Columbia lacked both a caucus of ex-Army officers and men who had themselves fought Russians and a regularly Russophobic press, which was able and willing to embroider on anti-Russian pieces received from London or elsewhere and to manufacture copy of an anti-Russian sort with local interest. There were, of course, military settlers whose personal distrust of, and distaste for, Russia were profound, albeit tempered by a saving scorn: the first free settler and farmer on Vancouver Island, Captain W.C. Grant of the Scots Greys, was one. But these were very few in number, widely scattered, and exerted little influence on the colonial or company officialdom of the mid-century. The war itself did well enough what neither journalists nor veterans were on the spot to do by way of heightening colonial perception of the Russian threat. For all its modest population and its youth, British Vancouver Island showed its patriotic mettle in 1854–55 — when asked, for instance, to contribute to the Patriotic Fund set up in London to support widows and children of the new "Crimean heroes." [79] Within four months, in mid-September 1855, it had collected £60, a handsome sum per capita.[80] And shortly afterwards the effort was repeated for the Nightingale Fund with even more enthusiasm. If the settlers and company employees had themselves not seen a Russian warship on the coast, they had at least seen men whom Russian guns had wounded, and the hospital was standing to remind them of the fact.[81]

Never again did British colonists in the Pacific look on Russia and her ever-spreading influence with anything but deep mistrust. It was an attitude conducive to alarm and even panic when relations between Russia and Great Britain became badly strained, but to an ostrich-like attempt to pay no heed to Russian military strength or foreign policy at other times. The British on the Northwest Coast did their best not to reflect on Russian military-colonial expansion in Amuria and Sakhalin; and many successfully ignored it, throughout the 1860's, with the aid of local gold strikes and menace represented now by Fenians in San Francisco, now by Oregonians on San Juan Island. If expansion by a foreign power *had* inevitably to be faced, then the United States offered a growing threat that Russia could not equal.[82] Thus dismissed in normal times, the Russian factor in the North Pacific area stood by, ready to pounce in times of Anglo-Russian crisis, and to terrify especially those colonists who had been trying hardest to ignore it. In short, the Russian factor was transformed into an embryonic bogey by the colonists themselves.[83]

In reinforcing patriotic sentiment, implanting suspicion and dislike of all that Russia represented, yet encouraging an effort to dismiss the Russian presence in the East, the first and only war fought between Russia and Britain (or France) in the Pacific, strengthened attitudes that were maintained throughout the 1860's and 1870's by a majority of British subjects on the Northwest Coast. So too did Bruce's sailing south to San Francisco with his squadron and deciding not to call in at Esquimalt in July or August 1855.[84] Not for the first time, a reported understanding between Russia and the Anglophobic government of the United States cast shadows on the British Foreign Office which, in turn, affected naval operations and a cabinet's perception of the nice balance of power between Russia, the United States, and Britain in the North Pacific basin.

Plate 1. A late view of Novo-Arkhangel'sk (Sitka), after Russian interest in the area waned but before the sale of Alaska to the United States.

Plate 2. An early watercolour of Fort Victoria, established by the Hudson's Bay Company in 1843.

Plate 3. Rear-Admiral Sir Henry Bruce, Commander-in-Chief, Pacific, during the Crimean crisis. He wrote Douglas in February 1855 instructing him to provide a building "that may service as a temporary hospital."

4

5

Plate 4.   The Crimea "huts," erected
in 1855, from a later photograph. Far
from temporary, they helped advance
the notion that Esquimalt should
become the Royal Navy's base and
depot in the Northeastern Pacific.

Plate 5.   Rear-Admiral A. F. de
Horsey, Commander-in-Chief, Pacific,
at the time when Rear-Admiral K.
Pauzino's flagship, *Baian*, and seven
other vessels rendezvoused in San
Francisco bay in 1876. Alarmed, de
Horsey sent the *Opal* to Esquimalt at
once.

Plate 6.   H.M.S. *Shah*, de Horsey's flagship, in Esquimalt harbour.

Admiralty Coal sheds.   Cofferdam for Dry dock building.

Esquimalt

7

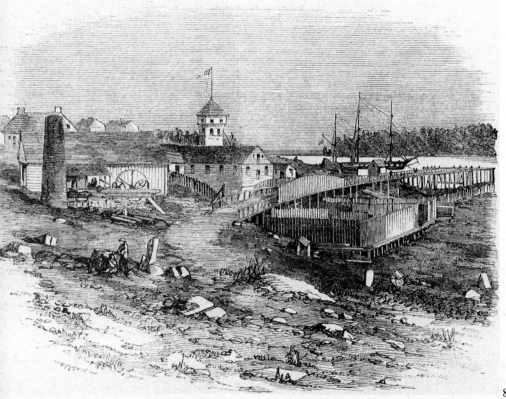

8

h June 22 1878.   Dockyard   Fisgard lighthouse

Plate 7. Panorama of Esquimalt village and naval establishment as seen from the north in 1878, by Captain F.D.G. Beddoes of H.M.S. *Shah*. From left to right are Signal Hill; the village; the naval jetty; coal sheds and repair facilities near and on Thetis Island (the height of land in the middle of the picture); the naval storehouses and old hospital buildings on Duntze Head; the Fisgard lighthouse at the harbour entrance.

Plate 8. The Coaling Station at Nanaimo, where there were large first rate seams.

Plate 9. *Afrika*, one of three American iron steamers purchased by the Russians in 1878. Its crew were given a hospitable reception when they visited Esquimalt in August 1881. Despite the many alarums, only two other Russian naval ships visited Esquimalt in these years, *Kalevala*, in 1862, and *Kreiser*, in 1878.

9

LT. COL. DE LA CHEROIS T. IRWIN.
INSPECTOR OF ARTILLERY.

Plate 10.   Lt.-Col. C. T. Irwin, joint inspector of artillery, examined the fortifications at Esquimalt in the summer of 1878 and continued the work at Macaulay's Point. In September Mackenzie's government in Ottawa ordered that the work should be halted.

Plate 11.   After a sweeping inspection tour and a critical report by Colonel F. Robertson-Ross in 1872, six new companies of regional militia were established by the mid-1870's. In the photograph of the Fifth Regiment, Canadian Garrison Artillery, 29 July 1878, their uniforms had not yet arrived.

Plate 12.   Here the Artillery is shown on the occasion of a military levee at Work Point Barracks on Macauley Point.

11

12

13

14

Plate 13.   The Victoria Volunteer Rifles whose ranks were depleted when fifty men moved into the new, and therefore fashionable, artillery.

Plate 14.   Rear-Admiral de Horsey's H.M.S. *Shah*, with H.M.S. *Opal*, H.M.S. *Fantome*. H.M.S. *Daring*, and H.M.S. *Rocket* in the mid-1870's.

4

U.S.-Russian Understanding and a New Balance of Powers

AMERICAN EXPANSIONISM AND PRO-RUSSIAN SENTIMENT: 1853-54

Thus far, the Pacific operations and American significance of the Crimean War have been viewed from the perspective of the British Northwest Coast itself. The localized colonial response to, and local assessment of, events in the Pacific since the early part of 1854 are given depth by a consideration of the overall political and military significance of the proximity of Russia's, the United States', and Britain's outposts on the Northwest Coast of North America. This overall, or intercontinental, survey may most usefully — and properly — be made with special reference to the peculiarly taut Anglo-American relationship of the mid-century. For as the Stikine River incident had gained in menace and political significance when viewed from London, so the cat-and-mouse campaign of the Pacific fleet in 1854–55 and, more especially, insistent rumours that a Russian privateer was preparing for a raid on British shipping or the British Northwest Coast from California, were somewhat differently seen in Fort Victoria and Britain.

While the Crimean War continued, Douglas and others were naturally far more troubled by the possible arrival of Russians in their midst than by American belligerence, on San Juan Island for example, under cover of that war. They well recognized that the Americans offered a far more potent menace in the long run; but the Russians were the present problem.[1] The authorities in London, by contrast, gave extremely little thought to Russia in the East or the Pacific, or indeed to Fort Victoria itself. Not even visions of a Russian-occupied Vancouver Island, it would seem, caused any loss of sleep among the war office or cabinet officials of the day. "Practically speaking," noted Colonel Manby (WO) in

August 1854, "the Empire at large" had "no such interest in the support" of his "outlying settlement" as Douglas supposed.[2] What even Manby and the British cabinet was forced to see, nevertheless, was that regardless of the war's local significance for such an unimportant "settlement," the very fact of the Pacific operation which had brought so many French and British warships to Hawaii and, in due course, San Francisco, reinforced pro-Russian sentiment in the United States. An Anglo-Russian conflict by extension seemed, in London, to have raised the future menace not so much of Russian forces in the East and the Pacific, as American. For it could hardly be denied that the Americans and Russians might collaborate in future against Britain and specifically against the British Northwest Coast and even realize the privateering project of which rumours had produced alarm at Fort Victoria. The Royal Navy would be hard pressed to respond to a co-ordinated, double threat in the Pacific Ocean, where its squadron was traditionally small, even too small.[3]

Most British statesmen of the period were fundamentally inimical to the United States and disappointed by American successes, first in Oregon, then in the recent war with Mexico.[4] In Oregon, as the British government well recognized by 1848–49, Britain had lost a valuable chance of re-establishing the old Anglo-American balance of power on the continent. The Mexican defeat had lowered spirits in the British Foreign Office. Local British representatives in the United States resented the aggressive foreign policy espoused by Polk, Pierce, and the Democratic Party and attempted, in official correspondence with their govern-ment, to magnify the danger that it posed to British interests and the insufferable nature of American self-confidence. To their regret and chagrin, London did not choose to back them up.[5]

The "loss" of Mexico was one matter, however: it was quite another to allow Americans to challenge British naval dominance through acquisitions of strate-gically important island bases and communication lines; for in a future war, it would be sea-power alone that compensated for the vulnerability of British North America in general, and of Vancouver Island in particular. President Pierce lent encouragement to talk of martial moves by the United States in the Pacific, as in Caribbean waters,[6] and, inevitably, viewed the European conflict that absorbed the energies of France and Britain with considerable satisfaction. No less naturally, Englishmen at home and in the New World were resentful of his attitude, the more especially when the impression grew that the United States were lending strong support to Russia, their antagonist. In truth, the sympathies of the United States did lie with Russia as so often in the past, and for the same historic reason: the United States and Russia were alike hopeful of humbling Britannia's pride, in one way or another.[7]

Britain and France declared war against Russia on 28 March 1854. For six or seven weeks by then, however, they had been cementing common policies towards the Russians and, if necessary, the Americans. And on 25 February, Clarendon had plainly told the House of Lords that the alliance, if concluded as expected, would have far more than the Holy Places question and the Near East in view: for on the plane of foreign policy, there was no quarter of the globe "in either hemisphere" with regard to which Britain and France were not "entirely in accord."[8] Pressed on this speech by James Buchanan, U.S. minister in London, Clarendon spoke vaguely of the open navigation of the Amazon and Paraguay Rivers and "of countries bordering upon them."[9] But Buchanan could not well misread public opinion as echoed in the daily press. Clarendon's warning had provoked approving editorials and letters to *The Times*, urging that once the Russians had been dealt with, the United States' turn should come. It was increasingly important, many sensible and influential Englishmen asserted, to contain the great republic and to prick its pride. One of its agents, Captain Perry, U.S.N., was reported to be rattling the gates of isolationist Japan and making sketches of the River Amur's shores.[10] It was time to make a stand, over a concrete issue yet to be decided on, as soon as Nicholas I permitted.[11]

Not surprisingly, American public opinion remained unfavourable to the allied cause in the Crimea. Russia, no less naturally, tried to realize its capital of goodwill by persuading the United States authorities to lend not only moral aid but also military support, in the Pacific for example where a blow might well be dealt to British interests as it could not be dealt in Europe.

STOECKL AND PRIVATEERING PROJECTS: 1854

Even by the late summer of 1853, several months before the start of hostilities with France and Britain, Russian government officials had been pondering the Russian Navy's options in the European war that seemed inevitable. As so often in the past, the Russian government was troubled by the possibility of an attack along the Baltic coast, if not on Kronstadt or St. Petersburg. The Black Sea coast was also vulnerable to an allied raid. The Russian naval staff, mindful of these facts and of the Russian Navy's weakness in the face of joint aggression by the British and French, gave no thought to any naval operation in the East or the Pacific. And, as seen, the Russian ministry of foreign affairs was content to recommend the quarantining of the North Pacific settlements. Like France and Britain, Russia was already planning for a European, not a worldwide, confrontation.[12]

Nonetheless, the Russian ministry of foreign affairs did give thought to the advantages that might be drawn from the traditional hostility and competition between Britons and Americans, and in October 1853 it was decided that the Russian minister in Washington, A. A. Bodisko, should discreetly try to ascertain if the United States would push its anglophobia beyond the limits of a strict neutrality in such a war as was expected, and allow its citizens to help the Russian cause. Specifically, would U.S. citizens be able to accept Russian commissions or fit out ships to prey on British merchantmen, in the Pacific for example? War in Europe would presumably reduce the Royal Navy's strength there.[13]

Bodisko and the secretary of legation then in Washington, K. Catacazy, broached the subject with U.S. Foreign Secretary Marcy. Necessarily, they couched their questions in the loosest terms, and Marcy had no need to give explicit answers. But he understood their thrust and gave his fellow Anglophobes to understand that the United States would certainly *be* neutral in the coming war. Bodisko so reported to St. Petersburg, late in December, at the same time suggesting that the value of American assistance in a struggle with the British would be large enough to justify commercial favours. If Americans replaced the British in the Russian market, or in one or other branch of trade or commerce, that was not important from the economic point of view, but might be useful diplomatically.[14] Nesselrode approved of the approach, but Bodisko's sudden death in January 1854 decreased the likelihood of its succeeding, in the shorter term at least: he was replaced as Russian minister in Washington by a considerably less experienced and subtle diplomat named Edouard de Stoeckl.[15]

Bolstered by the widespread indignation with which Clarendon's assertive speech before the Lords had been received in Washington, as by the warmth with which his own reports to Nesselrode of January were acknowledged by St. Petersburg, Stoeckl grew confident that the United States and Britain would attack each other — with a little help from Russia. Russia's game should be to lower tariffs for Americans, dangling more substantial economic benefits before their mercenary Congress, and to reach an understanding on the privateering question. Even talk of privateering was an effective weapon. It could send up the insurance rates for international shipping, shake up stable trading patterns, cause alarm in distant colonies, even deflect a naval squadron from the place where it was actually needed.[16] Like his predecessor, Stoeckl was particularly taken by the thought of Yankee raiders operating on the far side of the globe from the anticipated region of the conflict, on behalf of Russia. He too spoke to Marcy and drew comfort and encouragement from his remarks. If *he* were Russia, Secretary Marcy was reported to St. Petersburg as saying, he would fit out ships and send them off to sink or capture British merchantmen.[17] In the Pacific Ocean, there should certainly be prizes; and a single privateer or a single incident would send a ripple of alarm through many outposts.

It was now, however, that Great Britain took a stand on the connected questions of blockade and contraband that took the wind from Stoeckl's sails by satisfying the United States. During the war, the neutral's flag was to protect all goods afloat save contraband, and neutral cargoes taken from an enemy would be restored to the owner.[18] Weeks went by. Still the Americans would not commit themselves to any policy that sanctioned privateering under the Russian flag. Stoeckl did not give up the struggle. The United States would not come openly into the fray. It was apparent that a way had to be found of taking maximal advantage of the anti-British feelings of Americans without breaking their laws: individual Americans would go to trouble and expense to strike a blow against the British. In New York, in California, in Oregon, offers were being made to raid Vancouver Island or to prey on British commerce in the North Pacific, once the necessary letters of marque had been received. The very least that could be done to help these men, suggested Stoeckl in mid-March, was to invite them to Novo-Arkhangel'sk where their vessels could be armed and papers issued. Russian seamen might be placed aboard their vessels, thereby reinforcing the appearance of legality.

Stoeckl awaited the response to these suggestions with impatience. When it came, in early June, it dashed his spirits. Such expedients as he proposed, wrote Nesselrode, would hardly meet even the outward form of law. The naturalization of Americans in Russian North America would almost certainly be disregarded by the enemy. In all events, to turn the vulnerable settlement of Novo-Arkhangel'sk (for which arrangements had been made) into a base for privateers would be virtually to invite disaster for the Russian-American Company. Irregularities committed by Americans who were, or wished to be, in Russian service, might in some cases be overlooked; but the excellent relations subsisting between Russia and the United States should not be put at risk. Stoeckl put as good a face as possible on this development, for Marcy's benefit as for his own. His self-control and Russia's patience were rewarded in November 1854 when news that Clarendon and Newcastle proposed to introduce a new Foreign Enlistment Bill in Parliament reached Washington.[19] England was to brush the very nettle that the Russians had decided not to grasp. The question was: how to convert that happy circumstance into a Yankee-sponsored filibuster or attack on British settlements or shipping? Stoeckl gave the problem more attention in the dying days of 1854, as Anglo-American relations soured further.

RUSSIA AND THE SOURING OF ANGLO-AMERICAN RELATIONS: 1855–56

British fighting manpower was stretched to breaking point by the Crimean War. The notion of a flow of volunteers or recruits from the United States was a delightful one to British military authorities; and by December 1854 Newcastle's followers had seen the new enlistment bill through all three readings and the Royal Assent was duly given, on the 23rd.[20] As early as November, Clarendon had written to his minister in Washington, John Crampton, asking him to contact British consuls with a view to arranging enlistment programmes for the British forces at a yet uncertain future date.[21] Such as it was, the British effort to enlist in the United States was made from March to August 1855, when it was halted on instructions from the cabinet. It was a military and diplomatic failure and, predictably, the Russian embassy in Washington made much of it.[22] What is especially deserving of attention, however, is the readiness with which British officials, in London, the United States, and British North America frankly attributed that failure to the work of Russian agents, simultaneously focusing on the Pacific Coast and privateering rumours of the recent, and not so recent, past.[23] Possible Russo-American collaboration in attacks on British shipping or perhaps even Vancouver Island and the failure of the ill-conceived enlistment drive were seen by piqued British officials as connected consequences of an ominous entente which was directed against Britain's national interest in North America particularly. That they chose to view the pointless and embarrassing imbroglio of the enlistment effort in that light and to associate it vaguely with alleged American attempts to stir up troubles for Britain both in Panama and — far more dangerous — in Ireland did not of course mean they believed all they asserted. They, and the British government itself, were worried by a number of incidents over the past several months in which the anti-British feelings of Americans had had full play, and they reacted sharply now. It was vexing, in the words of Crampton, that an anti-British sympathy with Russia was "the popular cry" in Philadelphia, New York, and Boston, and that leading east coast daily papers had so heartily espoused the Russian cause.[24] And it offended British honour when the president of the United States, supposedly a neutral power in the circumstances of an Anglo-Russian war, came to "an understanding with Russia to annoy and thwart" Great Britain and to strengthen the impression abroad that Anglo-American relations were so bad that war was possible.[25] The Earl of Clarendon himself abhorred the prospect of a war with the Americans and did his utmost to preserve a friendly attitude towards Buchanan. Even he, nevertheless, could speak of Yankee privateers being fitted out for Russia in defence of a decision to send naval reinforcements to the North Atlantic and the Caribbean Sea "to the address of the United States" in 1855,[26] and could reiterate suspicions that had earlier been voiced by Aberdeen to the effect that Russian agents in America were tampering persistently with Anglo-American relations.

That Clarendon should even mention privateers to Buchanan, on 8 and 15 November 1855 if not before,[27] was a Russian diplomatic success. No Yankee vessel had in fact been fitted out to raid for Russia. No American had actually flown the Russian flag in the Pacific Ocean. Nonetheless, the British government and British outposts round the whole Pacific rim had long been feeling the effects of such alarms and rumours. As a method of lowering colonial morale, it was effective and extremely inexpensive. *How* effective grows apparent as one learns that Russia was in fact unable to realize her capital of Anglophobic sentiment in California and Oregon even in 1855, when the foreign enlistment controversy was on Pierce's and Marcy's mind for days on end.[28]

Stoeckl had not mentioned privateering officially to Marcy for at least five months when in the early days of 1855 he called on him, intending to extract acceptance of the premise that, if Britain were permitted to enlist in the United States, then Russia too, who had been scrupulously law-abiding where the privateering issue was concerned, should have some access to American resources for her war effort. Since Russia had no need of extra men, why should she not create a little privateering force in the American Pacific state of California? Senator Gwin, so he reported to St. Petersburg, had only recently arrived in Washington from California and spoke in glowing terms of San Francisco as a possible privateering base. Not only was that harbour full of new and speedy clippers, crews for which were readily available, especially for any raid against the British; it was also full of patriotic merchants, one at least of whom, named Sanders, was prepared to see his steamers armed and fighting for the tsar in the Pacific. It was good, but not enough, that British colonists and statesmen should alike learn of the noble Sanders's impulse and be worried. Better certainly to send the necessary Russian officers and funds to San Francisco and to give Vancouver Island something real to be worrying about. As twice before, in 1854, Stoeckl was forced for wait for months for a reply to an urgent question. As before, he was dejected by the answer when it came. Nothing should be ventured that could compromise Russo-American entente, the very fact of which, even if nothing concrete came of it, was useful and would probably become far more so. Only in "the harbours of Siberia" might Russia arm a vessel registered in the United States, adhering loosely to the letter both of Russian and of foreign law.[29]

Not surprisingly, Crampton in turn made much of Stoeckl's *tête-à-têtes* with Marcy, and in private conversations as in formal correspondence with his minister, he dwelt on the anti-British bias of the east coast press and on the likelihood of links between the Russian embassy and well-known Yankee Anglophobes like U.S. District Attorney McKeon of New York. ("That *he* is in continual communication with the Russian Legation, I know, and that money . . . comes from that source is indubitable.")[30] Neither Clarendon nor Palmerston, it seems, wholly believed Crampton's assertions that Americans and Russians were collaborating actively, in San Francisco and in east coast shipyards, on an anti-British effort. Nor in any case did such suspicions form the core of anti-American feeling in Great Britain in the latter part of 1855. As Kenneth Bourne has put it, "the British were offended and alarmed . . . by a whole parcel of incidents. There were the various filibuster expeditions . . . the recruiting affair, the suspicious investigation of British positions in the West Indies . . . and not least there were the rumours of Russian privateers."[31] As official British consciousness of Russo-American entente largely contributed to the continuing anti-Americanism of the time, however, so inevitably did it tinge responses to perceived threats of American expansionism, in the northeastern Pacific Ocean as in Caribbean waters and, especially, Central America.

Thanks to the privateering and recruiting issues particularly, a showdown between Washington and London looked distinctly possible by mid-September 1855.[32] On Britain's side, military preparations started with suggestions that at least two fresh battalions be sent to Lower Canada immediately and that the naval force at Halifax be much increased.[33] In the event, it was on naval reinforcements that the cabinet saw fit to concentrate, with the activities of Yankee agents in the Caribbean Sea in mind. More warships would proceed to Halifax, Bermuda, and Jamaica. "I mean," said Admiral Wood, the First Sea Lord, to Fanshawe, Commander-in-Chief on the Atlantic Station,. "to make a *parade* of it, the object being to show the world, and the people of the United States principally, that we have a spare force after all."[34] If there was to be a clash with the United States, however, there was little point in building up a force in the Atlantic and neglecting the Pacific. With its base in San Francisco Bay, the U.S. Navy was a menace to Vancouver Island, with or without active assistance from the Russians. It was obviously possible, for all that Commodore Charles Frederick and other naval officers might say about the non-existent Russian privateers vainly hunted in the closing weeks of 1854,[35] that Russian ships might enter Juan de Fuca Strait at some time in the future and deliberately undermine the British interest, on San Juan Island for example. As for Russian privateers, they could hardly be excluded from the reckoning in any future war in the Pacific that affected Russian interests. With all these points in mind, Admiral Wood instructed Bruce, as Commander-in-Chief in the Pacific, to inspect Vancouver Island with a view to establishing a base there that would allow the Royal Navy and the residents together to protect it and the British Northwest Coast from the Americans, the Russians, or a future combination of the two of the variety that Crampton was describing.[36]

Nagging consciousness in London of the possibility of a more active Russo-American entente in the Pacific Ocean somewhat hastened the development of the Esquimalt naval base and depot. Both, no doubt, would have evolved without that concern. In itself, the need to deal with American assertiveness, on San Juan Island for example, would have prompted Bruce to argue that Esquimalt should become a larger and efficiently protected depot, as he did on 11 September 1855 and subsequently.[37] Even had there been no Russian presence in America itself, the factors that eventually led the Admiralty to transfer the Pacific Station Headquarters to Esquimalt from Valparaiso in 1862 would have been operative: the decline of British interests in Panama and neighbouring Taboga Island as a likely base and depot, the expansion of American and British shipping interests in northeastern Pacific waters in the later 1850's, the increasing difficulty of maintaining Britain's dignity, and a considerable depot, on a waterfront and moored ship or two in Chile.[38] Still, what has always been neglected by historians, yet merits notice, is the part played by contemporary British consciousness of Russo-American entente in the decision to abandon Valparaiso and Chile for Vancouver Island.

Admiral Sir Charles Wood had been vexed by rumours of assistance and support given to Russia by the government of the United States, as by the citizens of California and Oregon, since early summer 1854. In January 1856 he had discussed with Clarendon the importance of establishing an adequate new base in the Pacific, where vessels sent to check the grand pretensions of the Russians,

Americans, or both, could rest, refit, and victual in safety.[39] In the longer term, a tiny enclave in a South American republic would not do. Within two weeks, he was instructing Bruce to visit and report on likely bases on Vancouver Island, in particular, Esquimalt.

Wood's initiative, which Clarendon and Palmerston supported, was enthusiastically received by Douglas and by Sir Edmund Head, the new Governor-General, on whom rested the burden of defending British North America from an incursion from the south. In Head's view, the defensive positions of Vancouver Island and of British Columbia were wretched; nor could Canada West in its entirety be viewed as secure.[40] If the Navy would assist him, well and good. Bruce duly visited the Island and approved Esquimalt as the best site for a base. He drew the government's attention to the fact that, cramped though Britain's access to Victoria already was by sea, it could be further squeezed in future by the two expanding powers of the North Pacific basin, the United States and Russia. A strong base at Esquimalt would deter at least the Russians from imperialist ventures on the coast.[41]

Other influential officers supported Wood in the belief that Russia-in-America, if not perhaps the stronger and more threatening United States, would be restrained by such a base. As some conceded, the Esquimalt harbour entrance might be shelled as a more sheltered cove could not. The point was strongly made by Rear-Admiral R. Baynes, whose own orders directed his attention to the relative proximity of Petropavlovsk-in-Kamchatka and Vancouver Island.[42] On the other hand, the place had "coal, wood and supplies . . . in a good climate,"[43] and the cost of more delay might prove considerable. The United States and Russia held advantages over Great Britain in the northeastern Pacific since both had well-established naval bases on the North Pacific rim. The sooner Britain had her base, observed Vice-Admiral W. F. Martin, First Sea Lord, in February 1859, the sooner Admiralty servants could "commence arrangements indispensible for operations in the Pacific, in the event of a war with the United States or Russia."[44] Barely ten years elapsed before the admiral's successors were, indeed, regarding Russia as a probable antagonist in the Pacific.[45]

RUSSIA IN THE "BRITISH COLONIST"

Founded at Victoria in 1858, the *British Colonist* expressed the attitudes and feelings of the patriotic settler while simultaneously speaking for the company and Legislative Council against all comers where the development of local trade and commerce was concerned. Its editor, the versatile and politically astute Amor de Cosmos, had no private axe to grind on the matter of Russia, but he saw no reason for refusing to reflect Russophobia in the columns of his newspaper. The *British Colonist* accordingly offered its readers a variety of anti-Russian items every month. Most mirrored colonists' unhappiness about the warmth of the United States' relationship with Russia. Not a few were taken from *The Times* of London, or reprinted from American or British periodicals in extract or *in toto*.[46]

As is evident from correspondence columns in the newspaper itself, the notion of a Russo-American entente directed openly or secretly against the local British interest hung like a mist over the educated and imaginative section of the colony by 1858–59. To what extent it troubled some who breathed it in, may be inferred from their obtuse or, rather, positively negative refusal to admit even the fact that the United States and Russia *could* combine forces against them on the Northwest Coast. Would the United States, ran one attractive argument, allow the Russians to commit aggression on the continent of North America and so tighten their grip on part of it? If she were sensible, wrote one man hopefully, America would never "look with envy" on Vancouver Island, or on British Columbia:

> For not only will they always afford a ready market for her produce; they form a barrier from the encroachments of Russia. And this latter reason, as well as the consideration of the ties of common brotherhood, will prompt them in our hour of need, if that should arrive, to come over and help us.[47]

In itself, the local nervousness of Russo-American entente would have kept anti-Russian sentiment alive among the ordinary settlers and Hudson's Bay Company servants; but the British press was ever ready to intensify that feeling. 1859 serves well as an illustrative year, since relations between London and St. Petersburg were then correct (the "Sardinian Affair," which Napoleon III was fanning, was disturbing both), while on the Northwest Coast all other news was overshadowed by the San Juan Island crisis and the Fraser River gold-strikes. There was less reason in 1859 than either earlier or later for British colonists to be distracted from their colonizing by phillipics against Russian guile or barbarity. In fact, they were reminded periodically throughout the year by the *British Colonist* as well as by imported British newspapers that Russia was a dangerous and semi-Asiatic power. Serfdom was not merely tolerated there: it was fundamental to the Russian state and to the welfare of the parasitic nobleman. ("A powerful party of nobles are opposed to the emancipation of the serfs, and are trying to diminish the power of the Emperor": 12 February.)[48] Certainly, however, said the *British Colonist*, reduction of the tsar's enormous powers would be good for all his European neighbours. As it was, even the arch-conservatives of Austria-Hungary felt threatened, and with reason. "Hungary is full of agents from the Russian Government, who are encouraging rebellion and are very bold": 8 July.[49] There was assuredly no reason to suppose that Russian agents, spies, or troops would be in short supply in future, clumsy and obtuse though they might be. ("According to tables prepared by the Central Committee of St. Petersburg . . . the population of Russia is seventy-one and a half millions. In all Russia, there are 8,227 schools

with 450,000 scholars, or seven tenths of 1% of the population": 21 September.)[50]
Hand in hand with wide illiteracy, as the *British Colonist* further reported sadly,
went corruption of the sort that had so hampered Russia's war effort in 1854–56.[51]
To de Cosmos and his readership, it seemed appropriate that such a vast and
backward nation, with its tendency towards extremes on every level, should be
struck alternately by winter ice and summer fires.[52] Britain, and the British
colonies, should look for nothing good in it.

THE RUSSIAN CORVETTE "KALEVALA" AT ESQUIMALT: 1862

To be provocatively hostile in print towards the Russian Crown and state was
one matter, however; to be hostile to Russian individuals and ships in the Pacific
was another. Necessarily, official contacts were maintained between Victoria and
Novo-Arkhangel'sk; nor did the reasonable, courteous behaviour of the latest
Russian governor, the Finnish-born K. Furuhjelm, discourage company officials
from a policy of watchful friendliness.[53] That friendliness paid dividends when, in
the late summer of 1862 and in the context of excitement fired by a gold-strike in
the Stikine Territory, neither Russian nor British officials on the coast proved
certain of the terms of access to it as agreed in the convention of 28 February 1825.
To avert misunderstandings with the Russians, and to clarify the British right to
navigate the Stikine River to a British hinterland, the Commander-in-Chief on the
Pacific Station, Rear-Admiral Sir Thomas Maitland, sent the *Devastation* sloop,
under Commander J. W. Pike, to talk the matter over with the governor. Furuhjelm
received Pike kindly, and the two men told each other what they knew about the
situation in the gold-field, co-ordinated their policing and provisioning arrangements for the territory, and effectively prevented every likelihood of Anglo-
Russian confrontation on the coast.[54] Within twelve months of their discussions,
most of the Stikine Territory was incorporated peacefully into the colony of British
Columbia.

Watchful friendliness likewise prevailed when, in mid-September 1862, a
Russian warship, *Kalevala*, paid a visit to Esquimalt on her way to San Francisco
Bay from Sitka. *Kalevala* formed a part of Rear-Admiral A. Popov's five-ship
"Eastern Squadron," then on exercises in the North Pacific. From his winter base
at Hakodate in Japan, Popov had called at Petropavlovsk-in-Kamchatka in *Abrek* in
early August. At Petropavlovsk, with his victuals, despatches, and the necessary
coal aboard, he had decided to transfer his flag to *Kalevala* and to call on
Furuhjelm at Novo-Arkhangel'sk, sending *Abrek* straight down to San Francisco
Bay. In California, a Russian ship could count on a hospitable reception. Popov
and his company spent four days at Novo-Arkhangel'sk and léft it willingly: its
constant rain and mists depressed most who were unaccustomed to the climate.
Four more days brought *Kalevala* to the British base and settlement, which Popov

had already judged it useful to examine. It was, after all, unlikely that a growing British colony replete with coal and naval base would not affect his own successors' scope of possible activity, and even tactics, in the East and the Pacific.[55]

Kalevala passed by Duntze Head, and so entered Esquimalt Harbour unexpectedly at approximately 2 P.M. on 16 September. What alarm she may have caused, if any, is unknown. Admiral Maitland's flagship, *Bacchante* screw-frigate, and *Mutine* sloop both being present, the alarm must surely have subsided almost instantly. At all events, news of the Russian warship's presence reached Victoria that afternoon and was reported calmly by the *British Colonist* next morning. What particularly interested the reporter and most readers of the newspaper, to judge by items published on 17 and 19 September, was the Russian company. Admiral Maitland, who was Popov's host as senior official present in the colony, took a professional interest in the corvette and her crew. The local press had this to say about the visitors or, as it called them, "Porpuff's Men":

> A number of the sailors attached to the Russian corvette *Kalevala* were turned loose yesterday. . . . They are a fine, robust looking lot of men, not very tidy in their dress or personal habits, but would no doubt prove good fighters if called on to test their capabilities in that line.[56]

Like the condescending tone, to which the mangling of Russian proper names ("3rd Lieutenant Poeleanski . . . 1st Master Garacernoff") gives a nineteenth-century and British resonance, uncomfortable realization that such vessels could be used against the colony itself, as a result of European "complications," set a pattern for future Russian visits. So too did the influential colonists' and senior officials' readiness to entertain the Russian officers, (though not the 170 rough-looking men) in the politely English manner. ("A select soirée . . . will be given at the Music Hall tomorrow night. . . . The Russian naval officers . . . will figure conspicuously.")[57] Better not to dwell on the significance of Russian naval movements, the development of Russia's Asian bases, or the presence in the area of several "neat looking" Russian ships. The visit passed off well enough. Popov had planned to stay three days, but stayed a week (16–24 September). When he left, it was with ample fresh supplies, a rested crew, and a full journal on the basis of which he shortly afterwards sent a report of his activities of early autumn 1862 to his superiors. That document, the relevant "Vancouver Island passages" of which follow in extract, seemed sufficiently important and engaging to the editor of *Morskoi sbornik (Naval Collection)*, an official periodical supported by the government but with a large general readership, to merit publication. It appeared in the first issue for 1863:

> The residence of the governor on Vancouver [Island] is at Victoria, a former settlement of the Hudson's Bay Company; as the bay on which that settlement

stands offers no more than ten feet of water at low tide, however, and as the tides there are irregular and insignificant, the English Government . . . is now constructing a military port in Esquimalt Bay, some three miles to the west. This is a peerless spot — a completely sheltered roadstead with a very even bottom at 6 or 8 *sazhen* [fathoms]. The steep and winding shores, destined by nature herself to provide quaysides and docks, are clear evidence of the celebrated Hudson's Bay Company's shortsightedness in selecting a site for the future Victoria. At the present, Esquimalt Harbour reminds one of de-Castries Bay in the number of buildings erected round it; but all similarity stops there. A splendid road with several bridges, each 50 or 100 *sazhen* [fathoms] across, already joins Esquimalt Bay with Victoria and the interior of the island; and a stone beacon, throwing a red light, stands at the bay's entrance on Fisgard Island and welcomes one in even at night. . . . There is no doubt that this place will enjoy the same brilliant fortune as San Francisco. . . . Victoria itself has more than 5,000 residents now, and almost all the conveniences of the best European towns; and on top of that, it is pretty well the cheapest spot in the Pacific Ocean.

During our sojourn on Vancouver [Island], the colonial Governor was away. Admiral Maitland, officer commanding on the English Pacific station, was due to the proceed the very day we met him to the southern hemisphere. However, he delayed twenty-four hours in order to invite us to dine the following day. . . .

It was on Vancouver Island that we learned from the newspapers of the attempt on the life of His Imperial Highness [Grand-Duke Constantine], the General-Admiral. The very next day, we held a thanksgiving service on board the corvette for His Highness's escape from peril. The English corvette *Mutine*, which remained in the roads with us after the admiral's departure in *Bacchante* frigate, perceiving our activity, decked herself in flags suitable for the occasion and fired a 21-gun salute. Her own commander, indeed, visited us during the ceremony and so witnessed the grateful Russian sailor's unfeigned and deep attachment to His Highness.[58]

An innocuous enough report indeed, to which no colonist or company employee could have taken exception, had he read it. But of course, no local colonist or servant of the Legislative Council or employee of the Company did read it; and the same was true of other Russian articles and books of the same period which dealt with Britain's prospects and achievements on the Northwest Coast of North America. Their tone was either neutral or approving, but the language barrier placed them beyond the reach of ordinary colonists, as from the great mass of the British nation.

As it happened, 1863–64 marked a considerable upswing, of which Britons were unconscious, in the Russian public's interest in British and American activity in the remote Pacific regions of America. As a result of Popov's celebrated "1863 fleet visit" to a watchful San Francisco,[59] several pieces dealing with Vancouver Island in some detail were printed in *Morskoi sbornik*, in the 1860's. One was Colonel Geimbruk's "The City of Nanaimo, Vancouver Island, and its Coal," a learned essay packed with relevant statistics on the output, quality, and price-patterns of that commodity. Another was a version of Charles Forbes's long official essay, which had actually been approved and printed by the legislature in Victoria, "Vancouver Island: Its Sources of Wealth and its Productive Strengths as a Colony."[60] Even of this, however, people in Victoria knew nothing. Ever willing to believe the worst of Russia, ever troubled by the prospect of a fully-fledged Russo-American alliance in the North Pacific region, they saw Popov and his men only through prisms of suspicion and of national parti-pris. Popov had unintentionally rendered the Victorians a service by his visit: they, at least, had *seen* the menace that had troubled Douglas in 1854–55. Had other colonists, in Queensland and New Zealand for example, been as fortunate, their "Russian bogeys" would perhaps have been less terrible over the coming twenty years.[61]

THE PURCHASE OF ALASKA AND THE BRITISH NORTHWEST COAST: 1866–67

Even seasoned Russophobes then on the Northwest Coast conceded that the 1863 Polish rebellion or revolution, so persistently and passionately covered by the British and the local press alike,[62] had little bearing on the future of the region in comparison with the result of the American Civil War. Northern victory, as one authority remarks, "destroyed any remaining possibility of a restoration of the balance of power in North America. Thereafter, Canadian-American relations and British policy with respect to the New World were posited upon the assumption that the United States had the preponderance of power on the continent."[63] For men whose capital and hopes had been invested in the twin Pacific colonies, it was the first and least expected of a series of political and economic earth-tremors. They hardly managed to acknowledge or react to the new balance of power, and the correspondingly increased importance to themselves of California,[64] before the cabinet in London was attempting to reduce the modest garrisons of British North America still further, while promoting a confederation of the British colonies in a belated effort, not to solve the problem of Canadian defence, but to evade it in the name of Home Defence for the United Kingdom and a safer Little England.[65] This, too, shocked some colonists, unsettled many, and provided food for thought to all on the Pacific Coast.

Feeling vulnerable, even expendable, as a result of policy decisions over which they had no influence, British Columbians and more especially Vancouver Is-landers grew more alive than ever to the danger of a working military alliance between Russia and the giant to the south. How unpredictably even American and

Russian friendliness could manifest itself became apparent when in 1864 work started on the Collins Overland Telegraph — a line that was to pass across Siberia, Alaska, and the British Northwest Coast, so linking Europe and America as the Atlantic line of 1857, which had failed after less than three months' use, was to have done.[66] British Columbia appreciated the advantages of being brought into a telegraphic network that was soon to span the globe. The single line laid from Seattle to New Westminster in 1865 changed life not only for the merchants of the colony, but also for the governor, the technologically alert Frederick Seymour.[67] To be glad that the United States and Russia were co-operating on a project with enormous military potential was of course another matter. What if either the United States or Russia cut the intercontinental line and thereby isolated the Pacific colonies in wartime? Any lever that the Russians or Americans could pull, argued the *British Colonist* belatedly in 1865–66, should be deplored. As for Russo-American collaboration on the North Pacific rim, it was a fact of local life which, "though baptised in champagne" by the Americans themselves, could only be regarded with "a feeling of uneasiness" by British subjects on the coast.[68]

It was an attitude with which Buchanan, British ambassador in Russia, fully sympathized; and more than once he warned the latest foreign secretary, Stanley, of the threat that Russia's politic goodwill towards the equally expansionist United States posed to the two Pacific colonies especially, but also to the British national interest in the Pacific and America in general.[69] What troubled the ambassador, though not Lord Stanley, was a more alarming prospect than the laying or the cutting off of telegraphic lines. It was the acquisition of Alaska by the government of the United States and a resultant "sandwiching" of British territory, possibly to be followed by its ultimate digestion and absorption by the U.S. body politic.[70]

Predictably, some settlers and company officials on the coast chose to regard the sale and purchase of Alaska, news of which caused deep unease, as an attack upon themselves launched not by Russia or indeed by the United States alone, but by the two in close alliance.[71] To what extent the Russian government *was* conscious of delivering a shrewd blow against Britain by agreeing to divest itself for cash of indefensible possessions that the British would have purchased if they could has been considered by a number of writers and will not concern us here.[72] Russian sources were inaccessible to the affected colonists, linguistically and even physically. By contrast, the Americans' reaction to the purchase of Alaska, if perhaps not the intentions of the House of Representatives or Congress in the matter, could be gauged by any reader of the leading U.S. periodicals and newspapers of early April 1867. British colonists had cause to be disturbed by the essential leitmotiv of what they read. Manifest Destiny had sent the Russians from America, the New World. The last remaining European power on the continent, Great Britain, had been weakened. British Columbia was now "in the uncomfortable position of a hostile Cockney with a watchful Yankee on each side of him."[73] "Full-blooded Americans" well understood that the United States would in the end "absorb not only Russian America, but all British possessions" on the continent, however large or small.[74] "Politically considered," as the *New York Herald* put it, "this cession of Russian America . . . indicates the extent to which Russia is ready to carry out her 'entente cordiale' with the United States."[75]

Vancouver Island residents did not disguise their feelings of discomfort and resentment. To the British cabinet, the *British Colonist* suggested with a touch of melodrama, but with cause, it was a matter of indifference whether or not Vancouver Island or the neighbouring British Columbia could keep the Yankee tide at bay. They had been left to sink or swim. As for the Fenians, that "brotherhood" of militantly Anglophobe Irish-Americans now well entrenched in San Francisco, it was not long since they had threatened to raid or even occupy a portion of the British Northwest Coast; and they might very well have carried out their plans but for the presence of three British warships when it had mattered: the *Alert, Forward*, and *Sparrowhawk*.[76] Rumours spread and were believed. Here is part of a suggestively entitled piece, "The Rumoured Proposition to Cede this Colony to the United States," which appeared in the *British Colonist* on 25 April 1867:

Since the cession of the Russian Possessions to our neighbours, the command that the Americans have obtained over the greater portion of the British Pacific Coast is almost overwhelming. . . . In 1825, the blundering of British statesmen over the Northwest Boundary gave a coastline of 350 miles to the more wide-awake Russian, who only the other day used the concession granted forty-two years ago to pay us off for interfering in his little game in the Crimea. But it is not alone the encroachments of our neighbours that have created a widespread feeling of alarm and discontent here. It is the extraordinary indifference and apathy with which our demands are treated by the Home Government.

What was the point of "an expensive civil list"? It did not foster the development of trade and commerce. Was Esquimalt Harbour to be used, or not? Would the Americans consider selling Maine to a consortium of foreigners? Of course not; and in consequence there were no rumours in that country of the sort that were unsettling the British Northwest Coast. Perhaps, some said sarcastically, it would be better if the colonists whose lands could be "devoured at a single bite" at any time made application to the government of the United States and sought admission to the Union.[77] ("*Is* Annexation the Only Panacea?")[78] Such a pitch of indignation was not easily sustained, either in North America or in the Australasian colonies where it was similarly shrill by the late 1860's, thanks to long years of penny-pinching on imperial defence by the authorities in London;[79] and in May it did, in fact, begin to moderate among irate British Columbians who now more fully understood that, pushed too far, those same authorities might call their bluff and let them "sink," that is, make terms with Washington.

"THE ENTIRE ABSENCE OF ANY MILITARY FORCE IN THE PROVINCE": 1866–76

An uncomfortable awareness that land and coast defences were alike being neglected on the British Northwest Coast lay at the heart of local feelings of resentment towards London in the later 1860's. Such neglect meant that the colonies were far more vulnerable to a raid by outside forces than they need have been. Only sustained improvement in the state of those defences and a consonant improvement of morale in the colonial militia, who would certainly be called on to defend British Columbia in the event of an emergency, it followed, could have smoothed away such feelings by the early 1870's. Thanks in the first place to the "bring-the-troops-home" outlook of successive British cabinets, who wished to concentrate the Army and Navy on the English Channel and so ward off any remote chance of invasion by Napoleon III, and in the second place to an unwillingness at all levels of government — imperial, Canadian, provincial — to accept the task of properly equipping and emboldening British Columbia so that American attack would be improbable and doomed to certain failure if attempted, no such overall improvement came about. The British Northwest Coast was thus, almost inevitably, vulnerable to the alarums of the 1870's and early 1880's.

Paradoxically, it had been largely the *desire* for increased security and longer term protection from its neighbour that resulted in the union of British Columbia and the more populous Vancouver Island, and which barely four years afterwards induced British Columbia to enter the Dominion of Canada, albeit with misgivings.[80] In the circumstances, one might reasonably have supposed that by the middle 1870's such British vessels as were anchored at Esquimalt would at least enjoy the shelter of a well-manned heavy battery or two and that the overall responsibility for the protection of New Westminster and other growing centres would be passing from the Admiralty's hands. In fact, the whole province's safety still rested, loosely and unsatisfactorily, on the Royal Navy's presence on the coast. The results were accumulatively serious for the defences of the province, and pointed to the need for a more sensible and comprehensive treatment of the problem of imperial defence. Because the French had been developing their naval base at Cherbourg and building partly iron ships, it seemed, and more especially because the British government and public now discounted naval power as an adequate defensive shield for the British Isles, expenditure on garrisons and military works in distant regions of the Empire, for instance at Esquimalt, was to fall; and no account was to be taken of the special situation on the coast.[81] (In fact, the danger posed to widely scattered areas of British North America by Fenians in 1866–67 did result in temporarily increased imperial troop levels; but the general withdrawal of the legions then continued at a brisker rate.)[82] Would the security of Britain be appreciably strengthened by the presence of the few trained men who might have held British Columbia for Britain in an international crisis? Were the economic and strategic values of the province to the Empire not known? The Fenians cast a shadow on Victoria because Britain failed to respond with confidence to the dilemma posed by Washington's new military and economic challenge on the Northwest Coast.[83]

Such arguments and observations, which were made by British officers and colonists alike by the late 1860's, cut no ice in London. And indeed it was with undisguised relief that Gladstone's government withdrew all British troops from the Dominion of Canada save those required to maintain small garrisons at the "imperial," and therefore vital, naval bases: Halifax and Esquimalt.[84] Having said as much, however, and accepting Brian Tunstall's comment that "the failure to co-ordinate strategic thought with technical achievement" did no credit to the "publicists" and "statesmen" of the age, or to the War Office and Admiralty Board,[85] some portion of the blame for the condition of defences in the new Pacific province nevertheless lay with Ottawa. The federal authorities had after all assumed financial and political responsibility for the militia in *all* provinces that made up the Dominion. The British North America Act itself, on which their powers rested, had in 1867 made allowance for the gradual establishment of standardized militia in those provinces; and there was no doubt that the Pacific province stood in need of a considerably larger, more dependable, and better armed militia force than that which had sprung up during the Fenian invasion scare of 1866–67, all too soon to fade away. In the words of R. H. Roy, that little force, whose ardent spirit was "applauded but unmatched" by the authorities, had soon "subsided into apathy. . . . By 1871, the militia. . . . was but a shadow of its former state. Armed with outmoded muzzle-loading rifles," it was weak in training, leadership, equipment, and morale. Lucky the foreign landing party that encountered such a force in North America, and in the age of Elswick-Armstrong guns and Snider-Enfield rifles.

For the agent of the Crown in a remote, weakly defended British outpost, there was always the temptation to exaggerate external threats in an attempt to gain, or keep at hand, imperial resources to be used to deal with internal problems. J. W. Trutch, lieutenant-governor of British Columbia, showed some restraint in this respect. Unlike so many of his counterparts, in Australasia for example, he was genuinely faced by foreign-instigated threats and so did not cry wolf.[86] Even the realistic Trutch, as various despatches of the Fenian-beclouded early 1870's show, however, saw no reason why allusions to such threats should not be general enough to cover Russia at a pinch. Captain R. P. Cator, R.N., observed with recent Fenian disturbances in mind, "the entire absence of any military force" within the province made recurrences of "such alarums" likely. If an enemy *did* make a hit-and-run attack, say, on Victoria, there was no hope of timely aid arriving from the east, always assuming that the town had not been occupied or burned.[87]

Trutch's urgings brought results, eventually: nine months later, Colonel F. Robertson-Ross, adjutant-general of the Canadian Militia and an officer respected by the minister responsible for federal defences, George E. Cartier, reached British Columbia from Kingston. Six new companies of regional militia were established in the province indirectly or directly as a consequence of his unprecedented, sweeping tour of inspection and report.[88] Rifles and other basic infantry equipment went from England to Victoria where, finally, a drill-shed was erected.

Well and good, but what of heavy ordnance to guard Esquimalt and Victoria, if not the other population centres of the province, in the absence of all Royal Navy guns? What of entrenched modern artillery,[89] to keep American or Russian raiders off? Here, as Major-General E. Selby Smyth and Colonel G. F. Blair reported independently to Ottawa (1875), the situation was not merely bad, but becoming dangerous given the constant technological advances of the age — effects of which were to be seen in naval gunnery.[90] It was ridiculous that, on the one hand, there was nothing but a scattering of obsolescent 68– and 32–pound cannon to deter a foreign warship from attacking the provincial capital,[91] while on the other hand 7″ 40-pounders and their shells remained in mothballs at Esquimalt. On Macaulay's Point at least, midway between Esquimalt and Victoria, a battery was desperately needed.[92]

Selby Smyth's and Blair's warnings were dismissed by Ottawa, where all defence expenditure was now restricted to the minimum that House and press would countenance. Indeed, the federal militia budget was repeatedly reduced, in the mid-1870's, as seemed appropriate to a majority of Liberals and of Conservatives alike in view of much improved Canadian-American relations and the major agricultural depression of the period.[93] Moreover, east-west railway construction was already being spoken of, and genuinely treated as, a larger and more proper contribution to Canadian defensive capability and, by extension, the security of British North America as a component of a global empire, than either the creation of an adequate, well-trained militia or the strengthening of strategic positions. In remote British Columbia, the economic, the political, and even the military value of a railway connecting East and West were plain enough to thinking men. Few, on the other hand, could see a (yet unrealized) transcontinental link as any answer to a present military need; nor was there comfort to be drawn, on the Pacific, from such tendencies in Central Canada to look on railway construction and, indeed, new westward settlement itself, as contributions to defence. As will be seen, Macdonald's "National Policy," by which these attitudes were consciously developed through the early 1880's, were to leave British Columbia as poorly protected against Russian (or American) aggression as expediency — and a periodic outcry in Victoria — permitted. In the shorter term, the stage was set for crises and alarums in a province whose militia lacked not only uniforms and guns but even target ammunition and whose largest town was patently exposed to close-range shelling by a Russian ship at sea.

5

"The War-Clouds Lowering"

Sir — As far as the prosperity of this country is concerned, I imagine that a Continental war will not do us any great amount of injury, beyond the oblivion into which the colony will be thrown. . . . *Our* prosperity depends in a very great measure on the prosperity of America.[1]

Thus, in a letter to the *British Colonist* of 1859, had one intelligent, far-sighted settler expressed his feelings with regard to the "Sardinian Affair," the remote and complex European problem of the day. He spoke for many on the British North-west Coast for whom the rapidly developing commercial link with California was an essential fact of life in North America.[2] Identical sentiments were voiced in 1870–71, the European problem then being the Franco-Prussian War and its aftermath, by correspondents of the *British Colonist*, ever a useful sounding-board for majority colonial opinion on an international matter, and by members of the Legislature in Victoria.[3] Vancouver Island and the British Northwest Coast were in America, and that was all there was to it. *The Times* was right to comment, on 18 December 1869, that California offered the closest "civilized community" to both.[4]

Even while doggedly insisting on the hard facts of geography, however, most Victorians and mainlanders were deeply conscious of the moral, social, naval, economic, and religious ties, as well as the political main-hawser, that connected them to England.[5] As iconoclasm is itself a demonstration of the target's own vitality, so might the settlers' insistence on their newly gained American identity and threats to jilt the British Crown for the United States, in 1867 and again in

1869–70, be viewed as an unconscious affirmation of a special Britishness. This cloudy subject is frequently pursued by students of the growth of "the Canadian identity."[6] Suffice it to observe here that senior officials administering British Columbia in 1866–70 were in the main of British birth;[7] that they and members of the local press looked to the confidently Tory land of Palmerston for guidance in imperial and world affairs; that, as patriots and children of the Russophobic England of the 1840's and the 1850's,[8] they had naturally brought distaste for, and suspicion of, the Russians to the province;[9] and that, not surprisingly, the Russophobic British press was influential in a district of the Empire where London-oriented news was always welcome. Understandably, the colonists were even readier to welcome European news, whether of British provenance or not, and to discuss it publicly, if it related to Pacific matters or their own regional future. The development of intercontinental telegraphs during the 1860's and the consequently greater impact and immediacy of reports of major happenings in Europe only sharpened an already growing appetite. Even a crisis in a far-off principality of which few colonists knew anything whatever gained significance when Russia and Great Britain were potentially involved in it and when the news was fresh enough for heat and passion to be felt at New Westminster.

One such crisis was the rising of the Christian Slavs of Bosnia-Herzegovina and Bulgaria against the Turks in May and June 1876. By mid-July, a Serbian and Montenegran army was advancing on the Ottoman positions to its east. Within a month, the Russian government was sounding out Great Britain on the prospects of co-operative action by the powers to contain the Balkan conflict and avert a major European struggle. By November, a belated, useless conference at Istanbul was ending and the Russians, affronted by the secret aid that Britain had been offering the Porte, were preparing for another in their long series of wars against the Turks. British neutrality was sought, refused, negotiated for. If it is piquant, in historical perspective, to observe with what attention the involved Herzegovinan and Bulgarian strategic situations were considered by the *British Colonist* and by the *Mainland Guardian*, recently founded at New Westminster, and analysed by persons who could hardly have been less affected by them, it is no less interesting to observe how, from the outset of the Russo-Turkish crisis, both adopted a position on the prospect of a European struggle in which Russia and Great Britain might be enemies to which in general they would be faithful for a decade. Briefly, their view was that the crisis in the Balkans was a terrible and bloody one, such as no Englishman could view with equanimity ("Battle of Bayonets: Terrible Combat at Saitschary," cried the *Mainland Guardian* on 2 December), but that even so a far worse European struggle was not only likely, but would also very probably confirm and strengthen Britain in her paramount position in the world — to the general vexation of the European Powers and the fury of the tsar. The *Mainland Guardian*, indeed, gave the impression that this wider struggle would begin — not before time in view of Turkish bestiality and Russian jealousy of Britain's might and wealth — as a *result* of the diplomacy so lately shown at Istanbul:

> We may look forward to a very pretty diplomatic contest over the next two months, which will probably end — as diplomatic contests of this lively kind invariably do — in war.[10]

The detached and easy manner was maintained in other editorials and articles over the next four weeks, for instance, in "Moslems Gathering for War!" and "The Czar at Review" (30 December 1876). Not till the Eastern Question seemed directly and dramatically to bear on the welfare and security of British Columbians themselves — when an eight-ship Russian force arrived at San Francisco — did that tone begin to falter, and the European war itself to edge grain prices and the Cariboo election from the columns of their press.[11]

WATCHING OUT AND WEIGHING ODDS IN THE PACIFIC: JANUARY — MAY 1877

For the neglected Russian Navy of the early 1860's, ever conscious of French and British naval strength and so of threats posed to it even in the Baltic, the essential problem had long been naval obsolescence. The appearance of such European ironclads as *Warrior* and *Gloire* (1859–60) had impressed upon the Russian naval staff how useless wooden ships would be in any future action fought at sea. And so, belatedly, the Russians had begun to sheath their wooden fighting ships with iron and to build new iron vessels. Technologically, they lagged behind their rivals, Britain, France, and Bismarck's Germany:

> The problem was not so much that the Russian Navy was numerically inferior to both the British and the French, as that England and France had built ocean-going ironclads during the 'sixties that were capable of lengthy voyages and were armed with heavy guns. . . . In fact, the Russian Navy could not take on a hostile fleet in open seas. The naval ministry reached the conclusion that the only way for Russia to maintain her prestige as a naval power was to build new, iron, ocean-going frigates. Of the models submitted, the best was judged to be that of A. A. Popov, which he named the *Krieser*. The very name carried the meaning: ocean-cruising.[12]

The Grand-Duke Constantine, General-Admiral of Russia and the tsar's brother, lent his energy and personal prestige to an intensive ship-construction pro-gramme, carried out in Russian Baltic yards like Bird's, Semiannikov's, Macpher-son's, and Poletika's.[13] And from the outset, as much emphasis was placed on long-range, lighter vessels of the kind that A. A. Popov had envisaged on manoeuvres on the far side of the globe, as on heavy, first-rate cruisers, some with 12″ plate.[14] Eight of these second-class, all-iron, speedy "clippers," that in due course spread alarm through British colonies in the Pacific as had earlier been planned,[15] were launched from Galley Harbour or New Admiralty Yard, St. Petersburg, by 1880:

> *Kreiser, Dzhigit, Razboinik, Strelok, Naezdnik, Vestnik, Plastun'* and *Oprichnik* . . . were of 1,334 tons displacement and armed with between one and six 6″ guns and with seven to ten quick-firing 37mm and 47mm cannon. . . . From these vessels, the naval ministry created four cruiser squadrons, one to be actually stationed in the Far East.[16]

Could Russia's naval capability in the Pacific and the East be seen as dangerously large as a result of these developments and of the growth of naval bases in Amuria and even, for the incidental benefit of Russia, in Japan?[17] Certainly not, given the growing strength of Britain in the China Seas and her potential at Esquimalt. Quite apart from the extremely modest size of the revolving Far East Squadron kept by Russia (two small clippers and a solitary corvette, with little wooden sailing vessels in attendance while in Russian coastal waters), lack of Russian-owned facilities for bunkering and general refitting to the east of Japan placed a restraint on any Russian Commander-in-Chief's strategic freedom. As for Russia's heavy use of Hakodate in the 1870's, it was a sign that even Nikolaevsk on the Amur River did not altogether answer to her need for a dependable warm-water harbour, or at least an ice-free harbour, unaffected by the vagaries of currents or provisionment, in Asia.[18] By the same token, the fact that Russian warships often called at San Francisco in the same experimental, probing decade, suggests they needed to do so and hints at St. Petersburg's dependence on American goodwill (and useful jealousy of Britain) for whatever progress Russia might make with her "ocean-cruising" programme in the North Pacific basin.[19]

Even so, the presence of a Russian naval squadron in the North Pacific did imply the constant danger of its unexpectedly being enlarged. Puny though its units might remain during the 1870's, it was an embryonic fleet; and exercises calling for the joint participation of vessels sent from Kronstadt for a two- or three-year tour in the East and of the craft in the Siberian flotilla periodically created eight- or even ten-ship Russian forces.

One such exercise, involving signalling and target practice, cat-and-mouse manoeuvres off Hokkaido and Sakhalin, and a rendezvous in San Francisco Bay, occurred in mid-December 1876. The first of Rear-Admiral K. Pauzino's vessels to arrive at San Francisco, on 27 December, was his flagship, *Baian*. A screw-corvette of 1,998 tons, she was armed with four 6″ and other, less impressive, muzzle-loading guns, but lacked all iron plate. Among the seven other vessels that rejoined her by 20 January, two at least were second-class corvettes armed with torpedoes, *Vestnik* and *Abrek*. Three, on the other hand, were ageing little craft with modest armament and much the worse for wear after their voyage from Japan by arcing routes: *Tungus, Iaponets*, and *Ermak*, of the Siberian flotilla. As for the *Gornostai*, the seventh vessel, she was positively old: parts of her hull were rotting badly and her rigging was in need of prompt attention. All in all, it was a squadron as deficient in essential sailing qualities as it was short in firepower. Its commander showed good sense when, on 20 January, he completed his arrangements with the Mare Island Navy Yard authorities for his entire squadron to be checked or refitted. On the 21st, his ships entered the well-equipped, capacious yard, and there they stayed till early May.[21]

As was predictable, given the strained state of relations between Russia and Britain as the former braced for war over the Bosnian, Bulgarian, and other Balkan Christians, the reports of Pauzino's squadron that reached Vancouver Island to the north, and Rear-Admiral A. F. de Horsey, Commander-in-Chief in the Pacific, then off Chile, were misleading.[22] Pauzino's true objective in delaying on the west coast, it was argued, was (of course) to be in place to make a raid on British shipping in the area, or on the British Northwest Coast, should news arrive at San Francisco — slightly earlier than at Victoria — that Russia and Great Britain were at war as a result of Balkan complications. It was certainly unlikely that Esquimalt or Victoria, or any other population centre on the coast, could keep a well-trained Russian raiding force at bay.[23] Nor was there hope of prompt assistance from de Horsey: as so often in the past, the larger part of his Pacific squadron was attending to its duties off the shores of South America.[24] Rear-Admiral de Horsey made no bones about expressing *his* concern over the presence of so large a Russian force in California, given the brittle international situation. He, however, was responding not to local lamentations but to messages received at Valparaiso direct from San Francisco. As he put it on 17 March to the Secretary of the Admiralty:

> My continued detention on the southern part of this station, in consequence of the non-arrival of the *Shah*, has been to me and remains a matter of some anxiety, viewing the considerable Russian squadron collected at San Francisco. I have directed the *Opal* to proceed . . . to San Francisco and thence to Esquimalt, making the passage as far as San Francisco with dispatch.[25]

Opal (Captain F. C. Robinson), a recently commissioned screw-corvette of 14 guns, duly made haste to San Francisco Bay with orders to shadow and report on Pauzino's lurking vessels. Her activities were in their turn reported to Victoria, where they did something to control local anxieties.

It was just as well that concerned British Columbians could see that Rear-Admiral de Horsey had at least acknowledged that the Russian squadron was a threat to be kept under surveillance day by day. Within a fortnight their anxieties and his were multiplied by two pieces of news. One was that Russia had in fact begun hostilities against the Turks, despite Great Britain's line that her neutrality depended strictly upon Russia's neither launching an attack on Istanbul itself nor making territorial advances at the Turks' expense. The other was that even if an Anglo-Russian war were to break out within the next few days, de Horsey could not bring his whole force north to aid the colony: a crisis had developed in Peru, where British subjects had been placed under arrest and where a rebel iron turret ship, *Huascar*, mounting two 300-pounder guns, was trying to extort protection money from the international merchant shipping of the area. The *Shah* alone could fight her, if it came to that. Victoria sent fresh representations to the government in Ottawa, no longer seeking, but demanding as a right, some more reliable and permanent means of defence against a seaborne enemy.[26]

In San Francisco Bay, meanwhile, Captain Robinson and his lieutenants had been gathering intelligence about the Russian ships at Mare Island. What they saw, heard, or deduced was reassuring. Five of Pauzino's vessels were of 700 tons or less and somewhat undergunned (though over-manned), while the *Baian*, the Russian flagship, was an older wooden craft. These reassurances, much qualified by the observers' ignorance of Pauzino's destination and objective once repairs were completed, were sent off to de Horsey and by him both to the Commander-in-Chief of the China Seas and to the Admiralty. Captain Robinson and *Opal*, it appears, were specifically entrusted with the task of bringing comfort to Esquimalt and the people of Victoria. Here are extracts from Robinson's general report to Rear-Admiral de Horsey of 10 May, entitled "Russian Ships of War: *Opal* at San Francisco":

> The flagship, the *Bayan*, is a wooden corvette more than 20 years old, ship-rigged. . . . The *Vasdnick* and *Abrek* . . . appear serviceable and effective vessels for their size. The *Gornoskai* is a clipper of smaller class. . . undergoing extensive repairs and reported to be decayed in her hull . . . *Japonetz* is out of repair as to her engines. . . . I have been informed that the *Bayan*, *Vasdnick*, and *Abrek* are fitted out with torpedoes resembling the "fish," fired through a bow tube under water and exploding on contact. I have been able to confirm their carrying torpedoes, but of what kind I cannot yet ascertain as a certainty. . . . P.S. On the 12th Inst., I received intimations that the Russian C.-in-C. has received telegraphic instructions from the East to put to sea at once. . . . The *Vostock* sailed today and it is reported that the squadron will sail on the 17th, under sealed orders.[27]

The Russians did, in fact, leave on 17 May — as they were bound to do, if San Francisco was to stay a neutral port during the Russo-Turkish War;[28] and Captain Robinson made haste to reach Esquimalt, to forestall them there in the grim eventuality that Pauzino's orders were to raid it or some other British settlement. In the event, no Russian warship touched the British Northwest Coast for nine more months. *Opal* was welcomed at Esquimalt, with great pleasure and relief nonetheless, as half-a-dozen nervous items in the *British Colonist* in early May such as the one below show:

> The Russian war vessels now at San Francisco might batter down Victoria, shell the dockyard, and seize or destroy the great collieries on the east of the Island. Property to the value of many millions of dollars lies absolutely at the mercy of an invader! The local Government have time and again drawn attention to our defenceless situation; we are not aware that any steps have been taken to materially strengthen the Naval Forces on this Station.[29]

Opal's broadside more than equalled that of *Abrek* and *Baian* together. In itself, the presence at Esquimalt of another well-trained company of 232 "brave Tars" boosted the colonists' morale. Together with the *Daring*, 4-gun sloop, and *Rocket*, gun vessel, which were on station at Vancouver Island, *Opal* proved "material" enough an increase in the regional defence force to prevent any collapse of that morale when, in July, the news arrived of Russian military triumph in the Caucasus and progress on the Danube. But as news of Pauzino's strength, and weakness, had been slow to reach Victoria, so had the Robinson report from San Francisco of 10 May been slow to reach the government in London.[30] As a result, the imperial authorities were not in a position to encourage and calm British Columbia when they might usefully have done so. The colonial fears aroused by the knowledge that de Horsey lacked the means to keep the coast safe from attacks by Russian cruisers in an Anglo-Russian war were thus extended by echoes in London, as a consequence of the logistics and communications problems that traditionally plagued the overstretched Pacific squadron — long-term problems that had weakened Rear-Admiral de Horsey's hand by scattering his vessels, a priori.[31] To their credit, the Colonial and Admiralty secretaries of the day seized on the crisis that the Pauzino squadron had produced, and on Victoria's excusable alarm, to bring Esquimalt once again to the attention of the semi-permanent Defence Committee of the Colonial Office.[32] So too, predictably, did a concerned Royal United Service Instituion, whose objective it had been since its establishment to see that cabinets discharged their full responsibilities in matters of defence.[33]

Such was the Institution's consciousness of the deplorable vulnerability of British (if perhaps not of Canadian or local, west coast), interests, given the recently reported Russian moves in the Pacific and the situation in the Near East, that in the early part of May it asked the specialist in naval and imperial defensive strategy, John Colomb, R.M.A., to give a lecture on that subject. Many of the participants in the debate that followed Colomb's talk on the 25th, including high-ranking and influential officers or former naval officers, expressed a passionate regret that in the face of Russian menace, whether real or imaginary, Esquimalt and British Columbia should be so wretchedly defended. One such officer was Captain Bedford Pim, R.N., M.P. Another was Sir Henry Codrington, Admiral of the Fleet. The ardent Pim had this to say about the crisis on the British Northwest Coast:

A small man-of-war in the Straits of Juan de Fuca could lay in ashes Victoria and Nanaimo without possibly losing a man, and when this meeting reflects that at Vancouver's Island we have every atom of stores for our squadron in the North Pacific . . . and that all our coal is drawn from that source and that our ships are unfit to keep the sea under sail . . . I think this meeting will very clearly understand the critical position in which we are placed, at this moment, in the North Pacific. . . . At this moment, lying in San Francisco Harbour, there are eleven Russian ships. . . . To my certain knowledge they are in the most splendid order. They have about 2,000 men on board, and a larger number of guns than we have in the very weak squadron we have, distributed from Chili right up to Esquimalt. . . . Are those ships stationed in San Francisco for the purpose of attacking Turkish men-of-war, or merchant ships?

Supposing Russia was to declare war against us, in six hours from the time war was declared, the commanding officer of those eleven ships in San Francisco would have the declaration in his hands; in four days very moderate steaming, at eight knots an hour, he would be in Vancouver's Island; but how long would it take before *our* ships were informed that war had broken out? I will undertake to say not six hours, but six weeks.[34]

Pim, who had served on the Pacific Station and had published a book about the British national interest in North Pacific waters,[35] spoke *à thèse* and saw no reason for avoiding either slight exaggeration or the local colour of historical romances; but he faithfully reflected the opinion and mood of the majority of Captain Colomb's listeners. So too did Sir Henry Codrington in his expression of concern over the latest Russian threat and in his urging that Esquimalt be protected as became a most important British base and *point d'appui*:

In the event of sudden hostilities, it is utterly impossible that anything we could send [to Esquimalt] would have any material influence on a war that has just suddenly been declared by telegrams to us. We are at present in the situation, it appears to me, of being simply swept out of the Pacific; and we must remember that, supposing . . . an enemy has got possession of Vancouver's Island, our only base of operations, he has shut us out of it entirely.

As often in the past, senior Royal Navy officers whose own service experience or breadth of vision made it possible for them to recognize the value of Esquimalt to the Crown and to the colonists around it[36] would have built up its defences and enlarged the little squadron that it sheltered, and which sheltered *it*, and would have done so straightaway — if they had only the support of those political authorities to whom, for service reasons, they declined to make their case.[37] The question was: could those authorities themselves, or for that matter the authorities in Ottawa, continue to neglect Esquimalt in the face of Pauzino and of mounting agitation on the coast, in naval circles, and in London? Even large and rapid steps taken to strengthen Britain's naval and political position on the coast, as Captain Colomb emphasized, would come too late to help "the military forlorn hope of our empire," the "loyal band" of volunteers and militiamen who even then were helping *Opal* and her seamen to protect British Columbia from eight, if not eleven, Russian wolves.[38]

THE WAR-CLOUD LOWERING: PROVINCIAL ATTITUDES
(MAY 1877 — FEBRUARY 1878)

By early May 1877, both the *Mainland Guardian* and the *British Colonist* were running regular and lengthy editorials-cum-feature articles entitled, actually or approximately, "England and the Eastern Question." They increasingly reflected an awareness of the extent to which political events in Europe, and Russia's fortunes in her war against the Porte, would determine whether British Columbia was to continue to be liable to Russian-linked alarums and excursions, quite regardless of whatever tardy steps the British government might take to reinforce the Royal Navy in the North Pacific area. Initially the concentration of the Pauzino force in California had led the colonists to focus on the local and immediate significance of any Anglo-Russian conflict. After four months they began to take a broader view of the European crisis and political manoeuvring, without relapsing into condescending attitudes however or completely overlooking the immediate, provincial meaning and potential of the European war. This tendency was much encouraged by the news of Russian military successes in the Caucasus, achieved, it seemed, despite the Russian Army's sorry weapons and equipment and its venal and disorganized general staff.[39] Russian successes, after all, placed pressure on the "doves" around the "hawkish" Beaconsfield, made British intervention in the conflict less improbable, and alarmed those who were already thinking there would be a demonstration of Russian naval strength on the British Northwest Coast. Typical of the provincial editorials of early summer, with their willingness to see the latest Russian thrust against the Porte in a time-frame of two centuries at least, and in an almost global context,[40] was the *Mainland Guardian's* of 2 May. The *Opal*, it should be remembered, had yet to reach Vancouver Island from the south:

We must touch upon the extraordinary manner in which Russia has been able to impose upon the world, since the days of Peter the Great. Commencing with an insignificant duchy, a barbarian population, and little or no influence in European councils, he and his successors, by dint of the most horrible cruelties, have been enabled to create one of the most powerful empires that the world ever saw.

But had Great Britain been asleep whilst Muscovy had grown, insidiously, to her present size? Unable to accept the thought, and "shocked" by Russian diplomats' "unblushing diplomatic lies," the *Mainland Guardian* inclined to view Confederation in a novel light:

England has not been asleep. The confederation of her [North American] colonies, securing combination in case of attack, was simply one of the safeguards adopted by her in the course of preparation for the grand struggle which is slowly, but surely, approaching.

To the *British Colonist*, it seemed less probable that England had been readying for a titanic struggle with the Russians for a decade; but of Russia's might, expansionist ambition, and potential for destruction there could be no doubt. Thanks to her in particular, but also to the French and Germans, the whole of Europe was a nervous military camp; and there were economic costs as well as psychological and allied pressures to be borne by one and all because of it. Some European governments (according to a leading French economist, M. Girardin) were facing bankruptcy, yet were continuing to purchase weapons. Russia spent no more than $238 per annum on her private soldiers, but recently the defence or military budget had been running at $100 million annually.[41] Her expenditures, ambitions, and aggressions were colossal, as indeed were her reported losses in such actions as that fought against a formidable Turkish army at Batum. "Great Battle Near Batoum: The Russians Mowed Down Like Grass." proclaimed the openly pro-Turkish *British Colonist* on 17 May. Four thousand Russians had been killed or wounded on a single day! Was there not something to be said for the vitality and Russophobic vigour of Islam?[42] Certainly only a terrible mortality rate could reduce the fighting manpower of Russia in a militarily important way: just as at Batum, so at Plevna in September, Russian dead were quickly buried — and replaced by a minute percentage of the huge reserve. It was enough to bring not only Turkish generals, but also partisan British Columbians, close to despair on occasions:

For every Russian who may fall at Plevna, *two* stand ready to take his place and . . . the loss or waste of munitions is instantly replaced. In fact, a stream of men and munitions pour constantly over the pontoon bridges to reinforce the attacking forces.[43]

And again: "It does not follow that, because success has not crowned their efforts during the first six months of the war, the Russians will not achieve success hereafter." [44]

The *Shah's* and *Amethyst's* encounter with the pirate ironclad *Huascar* off the little port of Ilo in Peru, in May and June,[45] had given the British west coast press an opportunity, gratefully taken, both to sermonize (on the temptation that defencelessness must offer to the strong, on the disgraceful rate of economic progress in the province, on imperial indifference and so forth), and at the same time to keep only half an eye on Russo-Turkish confrontation. The halt of Russia's southward march at Plevna in October and November was another such chance. "Clouds," it was enough to comment warily, were still "gathering thickly" on a menacing "political horizon"; any "spark" would set "the European powder-keg ablaze."[46] Until that time, nevertheless, British Columbians might tend more energetically to their immediate concerns. It was a respite from anxiety, a lull before the storm which broke out when, on 14 December, the Russian victory at Plevna freed 130,000 troops for the advance on Adrianople.[47]

Intermittently during these months, note was taken of the conflict. In the spring and early summer, the provincial press occasionally reflected on how the European struggle might immediately bear on the province and, indeed, on one or other part of it, in future weeks. Predictably given its interest in the New Westminster (Vancouver) area, the *Mainland Guardian* viewed matters differently from the *British Colonist*, which emphasized the concerns of the Island-based provincial legislature, when it did so. To emphasize the point and show the rivalry between Esquimalt and the other would-be site of an imperial defensive complex, to include a naval base, dry-dock, and arsenal, as well as army barracks, here is an extract from the *Mainland Guardian's* lead article for 18 July, entitled "Burrard Inlet, the Sebastapol of British Columbia":

> Of late we have noticed a great many allusions to the unprotected state of British Columbia in the Victoria newspapers, and many sage suggestions for the protection of the present capital and the arsenal at Esquimalt. It has even been stated that McCauley's Point, at the entrance to Victoria harbour, has been chosen for some kind of fortification. . . . We have no objection to a fort being erected. . . . Have we not the Seymour Battery on the Fraser? The question is how the arsenal at Esquimalt would fare. . . . Our impression is that the Imperial Government would hesitate before expending money in the vain attempt to guard an untenable position. How different it would be in the case of Burrard Inlet. The harbour seems to have been formed by nature as the site of an impregnable fortress. . . . where an arsenal could be established

free from all danger of attack from within or without. Where dry docks are almost ready for the gates, and of any dimensions. Where supplies of every description can be had at the shortest notice. . . . Although the landowners and partisans of Esquimalt may plume themselves on their really snug little harbour, and the presence just now of the naval stores, gunboats, etc., they must not run away with the idea that the Imperial authorities are likely to accept their estimate of its value.

Of such skirmishing between Victoria-Esquimalt and New Westminster, suffice to note that, by and large, New Westminster was the aggressor; that it lasted till the early 1900's, leaving little mark if any on the governments in Ottawa and London but considerable scars on the antagonists; and, finally, that neither party scrupled to make use of any (real or imaginary) Russian threat, during the later 1870's or afterwards, as ammunition in their partisan campaigns either to gain or to retain the custody of Britain's single naval base and depot on the Northwest Coast.[48] Self-interest itself, as well as loyalty to Queen and Empire, ensured that it died away when, as in January 1878, a real menace could be seen to cast its shadow on the whole coast. A swift winter advance, begun at Plevna, had in six weeks brought the Russians to within a short distance of Constantinople. Would British warships, which alone (in the provincial view) could ward off the climactic Russian conquest of that city, which would undermine the whole balance of power in the East Mediterranean, if not of Europe, be sent on into the Sea of Marmora? If so, would Russia view that move as an aggression that demanded a response, in the Pacific Ocean possibly?[49] Well might the Legislative Council and the *Mainland Guardian* ask themselves, "Will England Intervene?" and ponder darkly on "The Horrors of the War."[50]

THE WAR-CLOUD LOWERING: OFFICIAL ATTITUDES IN OTTAWA AND LONDON (1876–77)

Such were local attitudes towards the Russo-Turkish War and the related Anglo-Russian crisis, insofar as these directly bore, or seemed to bear, upon British Columbia. It may be useful, at this juncture, to survey contemporaneous official attitudes in London and Ottawa towards the military predicament of the remote Pacific province. Were the British or Canadian authorities affected by the loud representations made by Victoria since May 1877, when the double-headed eagle of Russia had indeed seemed to be hovering just over its horizon? Had the Pauzino-centred tremors on the coast induced either the British or the Canadian government to reinforce Esquimalt swiftly and considerably, as requested, that same month, by the extraordinary defence committee of a tense Legislative Council?[51] Merely to consider the extent to which the Liberals of Alexander Mackenzie had permitted the Canadian Militia to decline in 1873–76, despite Mackenzie's own experience as a militia officer during the Fenian alarums, is to recognize how probable it was that they would try to close their ears to the subsequent warnings of General Selby Smyth, G.O.C., Canadian Militia, and Albert Richards, the lieutenant-governor of British Columbia, that the Dominion's Pacific ports were practically defenceless and its batteries all undermanned.[52] In Ottawa, it was traditional to keep defence expenditure not merely to the minimum held safe by experts, but below it. Nor indeed was there much difference between Conservative and Liberal suspicions of the military and readiness to treat Canadian Militia estimates as overgenerous, however much they were reduced.[53] Mackenzie had campaigned against such "waste," and like Sir John A. Macdonald and the Tories he was well aware that Canadians in general drew comfort from the Treaty of Washington, which removed causes for continued friction between Britain and their mighty neighbour, and inclined to think the lack of an immediate external menace to themselves sufficient reason for neglecting the defences of the country.[54] Since Canadians did not even think the increasing military and naval strength of the United States was a reason for revising their opinion of the Dominion's militia and defences, they were hardly likely to view Russia's capabilities and possible aggressions of the future as a reason for doing so. Mackenzie's Liberals themselves, at all events, were deeply anti-military, and willing to forget about the Russians and the Fenians alike. Such progress as *was* made in regard to the Dominion's defences in the 1870's, moreover — for example, the appointment of the able Selby Smyth, a British officer, as G.O.C. of the Militia and the founding of a military college to train officers — did nothing in the short term to improve the situation in remote British Columbia. Like that of Colonel G. F. Blair, R.A., also made in 1875, Selby Smyth's report on the state of its defence received more lip-service than actual attention from the government; and, in the main, those of his numerous recommendations that were acted on 1876–77 had no bearing on Esquimalt — or on any other likely Russian target in the province.[55] As was proper, Selby Smyth himself and the lieutenant-governor took full advantage of the nervousness occasioned in Victoria early in 1877 by the Russian squadron then at San Francisco to observe that, notwithstanding those reports of two years earlier, and others of the 1860's, there were still no adequate land batteries of heavy, rifled ordnance to keep an enemy from shelling Esquimalt or Victoria. In view of the uncertain international situation, would the government not purchase from the Admiralty Board at least the 40-pounder muzzle-loading pieces that were lying idle at Esquimalt Yard, awaiting shipment back to England, and give orders for their mounting on an earthwork battery, say, at Macaulay Point, which local men could raise? And as the Deputy Adjutant-General, Lt.-Col. Houghton, had been asked to work for the formation of two new militia companies by mainlanders, who were concerned about the weakness of the province's defences in the light of recent European news and Russian movements nearer home, would the

Honourable A. G. Jones, as minister responsible for the militia and defence, induce the cabinet to countenance a small upward adjustment of the military budget for the fiscal year 1877?[56] To these and other, less particular, requests for speedy aid to an allegedly beleaguered (and unquestionably ill-defended) province, Ottawa's reply was negative. No Russians would be raiding the interior of British Columbia or of Vancouver Island: they were therefore not a factor in defence planning for most localities. As for the coastal towns which Russian guns could reach from open water, they depended for security on British naval might and, more specifically, upon the Royal Navy's presence at Esquimalt. That, in turn, had been discussed by the Canadian and British governments at frequent intervals since the Confederation of the colonies; and Ottawa had plainly undertaken to exert its influence on London to maintain Esquimalt as a naval base when British Columbia had joined Confederation in 1871.[57] It had been doing so, regardless of ephemeral or passing foreign threats; but it did not propose to alter the arrangement, which was understood in London and in Ottawa, that Britain would retain responsibility for sea communications and defences and for British naval bases and facilities, while the Dominion assumed responsibility for land defence.[58] Victoria, Nanaimo, and New Westminster, the hypothetical chief objects of a seaborne enemy's attentions, had militia companies. The government was not obliged to purchase ordnance that would be used against a naval enemy.

Such, in broad outline, was the Liberal position on the question of the west coast and the Russian scare of 1877. In its frankness and its narrowness alike, it angered those with land and family or other interests in a potential target area and made apparent, yet again, how gladly Ottawa would turn its back on its defence responsibility towards Vancouver Island if it could.[59] The major pretext was, as ever, that the Royal Navy presence at Esquimalt was an adequate deterrent against any seaborne raid, the major motive — false economy. That this was so, neither the Commander-in-Chief, Pacific, Rear-Admiral de Horsey, nor the angry Legislative Council doubted when, in early autumn, Ottawa declined even to reassess its stance on the Esquimalt dry-dock problem.[60] The necessity of such a dock there had been evident to naval officers in the Pacific and in London, to the trading interest, and to the Legislative Council since the 1860's. Mare Island floating dock, the only dock in the Pacific north of Chile to which British ships had access, was unable to take vessels drawing more than 21 feet 6 inches of water, and besides, it was in American, and therefore possibly unfriendly, territory.[61] Work on a dry-dock had been started at Esquimalt in 1864, but it had quickly proved prohibitively costly. Guaranteed and reasonable loans for the completion of a dry-dock had, indeed, been sought and offered when the province had in due course joined Confederation. Even so, the sluggish rate of progress and continually escalating cost to the provincial tax-payer had caused two councils to resign. Nor was the project nearing completion in 1877 when, with Russia and the threat of war in mind, de Horsey vigorously noted that the dock was, inter alia, a "mercantile necessity" and indispensible "for the prosperity of this portion of the Empire."[62] It was unfortunate that the completion of strategically so vital a facility should be the burden of a poor province and that Ottawa should take no interest in it, despite the recent apprehensions caused by Pauzino's squadron.[63] Then, if ever, might Mackenzie and his cabinet have stepped into the breach to the benefit of the provincial government, west coast population, and Dominion. They did not do so. If the Russian bogey was to frighten the dominion authorities, then it would need to make more noise.

Partly no doubt because of Rear-Admiral de Horsey's urgent comments of the past six months about Esquimalt's poor defences and the way in which his own modest resources had been stretched by Russians, Fenians, Peruvians, and others,[64] but more generally as the result of an acceptance by the Tories of new principles of both imperial defence and naval strategy for peacetime, the imperial authorities paid rather more attention than Mackenzie to the shadows thrown by Russia on Esquimalt and Victoria in 1877. Since official British attitudes and policy towards Esquimalt and the Northwest Coast itself, with or without threatening Russians, was increasingly reflecting these new principles,[65] it is important to describe the early work of Captain J. C. Colomb, their originator and most tireless defender,[66] insofar as it relates to the Pacific province.

Colomb's booklet, *The Protection of Our Commerce and Distribution of Our Naval Forces Considered* (1867), was a comprehensive statement of the problems of imperial defence in times of coal-fired and screw-propellored ironclads, immense new European armies, and dramatically improved communications. It discussed general principles of naval and imperial defence and strategy and, focusing on ends rather than means, ignored both localized and single-service problems. In particular, it paid no heed to technical debate of the variety that had absorbed most naval strategists and writers since the launching of *La Gloire* and *Warrior*, the first steam-driven, armoured, all or partly iron fighting ships, in 1860. By avoiding the specific and particular, in terms of place, duty, and service, Colomb freed himself not only to express the Royal Navy's (all too often overlooked) strategic claims just when the shibboleths of "Home defence" and "Fortress England" were beginning to be questioned in the press, but also to enunciate ideas that encouraged full co-operation between land and naval force of the Crown.[67]

Seeking some essential element on which to found his argument, as he reflected on the use of personnel and transport by his own Royal Marine Artillery, he found it in the growth of commerce. Commerce, he suggested, is the chain of empire; to snap the chain would be to conquer "Fortress England," without so much as landing troops. Militarily, however, the security of England's paramount position as a trading nation, which was intimately linked with her security *in se*, depended on three things: the adequate protection of the homeland, the security of the imperial possessions and Dominion, and maintenance of safe communications between homeland and colonial and foreign trade centres. That England should be strongly fortified was good; but it was always to be kept in mind that, deprived of her supplies and sustenence by any power that could interrupt her sea communications, England could be beaten. By the same token, no isolated portion of the Empire or naval base or fort could be reliant for security on land forces alone. If their sea communications were attacked and cut, they could be starved into submission by blockade. As to the parts of Britain's worldwide trading network, or the areas of maritime and trading concentration, that were most deserving of attention, it was not for any private individual to name them. Commonsense, he said, dictated that the English Channel was essential to the nation.

Had Colomb's thought gone only thus far, it would certainly have militated against any build-up of the Navy in the North Pacific and, indeed, against imperial involvement with the fortunes of Esquimalt. In the first place, the value of direct exports from British Columbia to England was so slight compared with that of exports from a range of other regions of the globe that it could not have justified the use of many costly ships for its protection. In the second place, it would have left the fortifying and protection of Esquimalt more than ever a Canadian responsibility, if not a local one. But there were other, vital parts of Colomb's practical strategic thought that led him, by the early 1870's, to view Esquimalt as a place of great importance to the Empire. The new coal-fired Royal Navy, Colomb realized, depended for effective operation on the proper distribution and protection of its coal supplies: for, obviously, large warships whose bunkers were empty or depleted would be little use in a distant crisis. Furthermore, the ocean wear and tear to which all iron hulls were liable made the provision of appropriately sited, well-equipped, and guarded dry-docks, more important for the steam and iron fleet than they had ever been when wooden ships had been the norm. For both these reasons, Britain should regard Esquimalt as strategically significant and worth retaining. And because the Navy could itself not guard the place, unless its freedom and attack potential were severely to be circumscribed as in the past, Esquimalt's protection should devolve on shore-based units of artillery and infantry. British Columbia and Canada were, after all, deriving benefit from the existence of the base and should secure it with men and funds so that the Navy was at liberty to keep all enemies at bay in wartime and in other times to watch over the sea communication and supply lines. The Canadian authorities were unimpressed by this analysis of the defence position on their own west coast. In London, on the other hand, it gained supporters whom the passing of time brought to positions of political and military influence by the later 1870's.[68]

The question was, however, whether these would manage or indeed choose to impress upon the government the great strategic value of Esquimalt in comparison with other British bases overseas that likewise merited attention — for example, Singapore, Jamaica, and Mauritius — given British Columbia's commercial unimportance and the relatively modest trade being conducted between Britain and Vancouver Island. For the genuine "Blue Water" advocate of the mid-1870's, Esquimalt was a problem. On the one hand, it was Britain's only North Pacific base and depot and would probably be needed in a war with Russia. (In a war with the United States, it could be either an essential asset or a liability, depending on the state of its defences and the Royal Navy's strength and distribution.)[69] On the other hand, there was no vocal City lobby to support the argument that Britain's North Pacific trade needed increased naval protection — at the expense of the Atlantic, Australasian, China, and Near Eastern trades, by implication. In the circumstances, it was perhaps not surprising that the government delayed decisions about distant, and potentially extremely costly, bases, till the semi-permanent Defence Committee of the Colonial Office, with assistance from the Admiralty Board, had heard the arguments for and against specific measures and defence priorities and had submitted a report.[70]

Delay itself strengthened the hand of Colomb's men both in the House and in the London press. Fortifications experts, led by Colonel W. F. D. Jervois, R.E., who had had some experience of Canada,[71] supported Colomb's argument that only overall naval supremacy could properly protect the lines of commerce of the Empire, but he stressed the sad condition of the Royal Navy's fourteen coaling stations overseas. Esquimalt, wrote Jervois in an indignant "Memorandum . . . With Reference to the Defenceless Condition of Our Coaling-Stations and Naval Establishments Abroad" of 7 January 1875, was virtually unprotected.[72] Was the government intending to invite a Russian raid? At this juncture Admiralty, War Office, and Colonial Office arguments in favour of particular priorities for large-scale fortifying of imperial positions overseas were brought together. The resultant "Memorandum on the Relative Importance of Coaling Stations," drafted by C. H. Nugent of the Colonial Office, placed Esquimalt eighth in importance among twelve such British bases overseas. Nugent stressed the obvious: that Britain needed one strong base at least for the Pacific Station, and Esquimalt filled that role.[73] Nevertheless, the economic argument against it had been felt. 1876–77 brought no interim increase in funds for Admiralty use there, nor would any increase in the following, less stringent, fiscal year have been large, had mounting Anglo-Russian tension and reports of Russian movements off the Northwest Coast not caused the cabinet to view Esquimalt in another light. Belatedly, it grew apparent that the arguments and urgings of Jervois's and Colomb's men over the past several years had not only reached the cabinet, but also given it a mind to answer Russia at Esquimalt by enlarging the imperial commitment to a part of a self-governing Dominion. Even in 1877, Russian menace — real or imaginary — was pointing up those dangerous divisions of defence responsibility and rule between the British and Canadian authorities, which had existed on the "British" Northwest Coast for many years.[74] Whereas Ottawa elected to ignore these however, in the shadow of a crisis that involved Russia and Britain, the imperial authorities did not.

J.C.R. COLOMB AND ESQUIMALT ON THE EVE OF CRISIS (1877)

Captain Colomb summarized his argument for an explicit and immediate enlargement of imperial commitment to Esquimalt and, indeed, Vancouver Island in a paper read by formal invitation to the Royal United Service Institution on 25 May 1877. The paper, entitled "Russian Development and Our Naval and Military Position in the North Pacific,"[75] was on one plane an immediate reaction to the recent and disturbing news of Russian naval movements in the North Pacific Ocean, sent from Valparaiso by Rear-Admiral de Horsey and Victoria by Albert Richards, the lieutenant-governor of British Columbia; and it was certainly so viewed by Major-General T. Collinson, R.E., an eminent fortifications officer of Colonel Jervois's school, who took the chair. On another plane however, Colomb's lecture was his effort to enunciate his principles of integrated, commerce-based, imperial defensive strategy within a North Pacific context and with reference specifically to Russian naval menace and Esquimalt. As he prudently admitted to his listeners, among whom sat the leading specialist on Russian ventures in Amuria, E. Ravenstein, and half a dozen Navy men with wide experience of the Pacific, it was not an area to which — until the past few weeks — he had devoted time and thought. Nevertheless, he meant to add general comments to a survey of the growth of Russian strength on the Pacific shores of Asia and Siberia since 1638 and the foundation of Okhotsk. It was to Colomb's observations on the present and, especially, the likely future of the British national interest in North Pacific waters, about 5,000 words, to which predictably the audience responded in a question-time so long and full of interest that the proceedings were adjourned until 29 May. Discussion of his argument that Britain should at once commit additional resources of materiel and personnel to British Columbia and the Pacific, then continued for some time.[76]

Colomb lamented that a "British territory," full of "gaslit cities, mines, and huge commercial interests" (he had decided at the outset that he would indeed regard them as "enormous"),[77] should be virtually lacking in the means of self-defence. Given the coal stores of Vancouver Island, and the Russians' well-known lack of such supplies on the Pacific rim, the situation was provocative. The Russians had evinced an interest in the Nanaimo seams. Loss of Vancouver Island, with its coal and food supplies, would undermine even the China Squadron's usefulness in time of war:

In 1875, the output [of Nanaimo mines] was over 110,000 tons. There were three companies at work, with plants including eighteen engines. . . . Now, the established garrison of, not Nanaimo, nor yet of Vancouver's Island, but the whole territory known as British Columbia, consists of 200 local militia, composed of two companies of infantry and half a battery of artillery. . . . If ever attack should come, it will be the military forlorn hope of our empire of the sea in the North-East Pacific Ocean. No stores, no reinforcements, and no succour can reach that loyal band.[78]

Two further factors weakened the position of the province and the naval base alike in any future war with Russia: lack of local manpower and maritime resources and the want of telegraphic lines passing exclusively through British territory:

> From St. Petersburgh to Vladivostok there is a continuous wire, and the latter place and Nikolayevsk are similarly connected. . . . But a message sent from London or Ottawa can only reach [Vancouver Island] through the United States. . . . Both the American line to Mare Island and the Russian line to Vladivostok are safe from all interference. The same cannot be said of telegraphic communication with Hong Kong.
> In the event of war with Russia or America, both could in a few minutes put forces in motion, at or close to their respective seaboards. The Russian peace system of cruising is usually by squadrons, while our mode of protecting commerce or peace cruising is on no fixed system.[79]

The dependence of Esquimalt and Victoria on foreign-operated telegraphs, Colomb observed, might have induced the British government to play a far more active part in the construction of the overdue Canadian Pacific Railway — had it appreciated fully its imperial importance and not "shoved it aside . . . as a Colonial speculation."[80] As the situation was, lack of direct and safe communication lines even with Ottawa compounded that dependence, and increased British Columbia's vulnerability to seaborne raids. So too did the misguided principle of "Home defence," now thoroughly discredited but still impinging on the lives of colonists in the Pacific:

> The sources of Russian maritime strength are in the true sense of the word, localized. Not only is it possible for her to sustain a fleet, but it is possible for her to create a swarm of small steamers, and to arm them independently of the resources of her European dockyards. . . . Our fleets are dependent on home dockyards for succour and reinforcements, there is no local power of support, no local means of expansion. . . . We have spent millions on extending the dockyard accommodation and resources of home yards — as the *sole basis* of operations which must cover the world. Had one half the money . . . been expended on the creation of a real dockyard in the other hemisphere, our naval position would be incomparably stronger now than it is. . . . I do not know a more unique practical example of the true value of the theory of "home defence," indiscriminately applied, than the fact that it is expected 200 Englishmen [sic], 15,000 miles away from help, can . . . defy any expedition-

ary force Russia might be able to dispatch either from Vladivostok, Nicolayevsk, or Petropaulovski.[81]

In general, his audience — both actually present and elsewhere in London and the Empire — accepted Colomb's thesis that Esquimalt and Vancouver Island should be reinforced without delay. Among his backers on the Institution floor were influential naval officers, including Admiral Sir Henry Codrington, Admiral of the Fleet.[82] Reservations or objections of three kinds were indeed raised to Colomb's plans: that they would lead to an increased defence expenditure that British taxpayers would bitterly resent;[83] that new imperial activity so close to the United States' frontier might itself impose a strain on Anglo-American relations at a time when Britain looked for no new problems overseas;[84] and that activity of the variety and on the scale that the speaker had envisaged would no doubt produce political effects in Ottawa, always assuming the Canadian authorities had given Britain leave to undertake it in the first place. ("The Queen reigns over them, but the Parliament . . . and responsible Ministers of this country have no authority whatever over them.")[85] Nevertheless, General Collinson felt justified in noting, in his summary of two evening discussions, that the "general opinion" was in support of Captain Colomb's view:

> There is very good reason for a national inquiry to be made by the Imperial Government, in connection with the Colonial Governments concerned, as to the best places for naval and military centres. . . . Even at the present time, the naval power of Russia in the Pacific, as compared with our own, is sufficient to cause alarm to our colonies.[86]

Could such a body as the Institution's council properly "impress its opinions on the Government," assuming that its members all endorsed the sense of Colomb's presentation? Admiral Sir Henry Codrington supposed so.[87] He was right: pressure was duly brought to bear on the Colonial Defence Committee, which in mid-December and with prospects of an Anglo-Russian war firmly in mind, turned its attention to Esquimalt and the armament available to it.[88] Within a month, Adrianople was in Russian hands and Suleiman defeated. War seemed imminent, as Hornby's fleet steamed on towards the Bosphorus. The work of the committee went ahead. Whether its findings or the pressure of events would force the government in Ottawa to face up to the Russian threat, as it had many times refused to do, Sir Henry Codrington and the Canadian electorate itself had yet to see.

6

1878

RUSSIAN SHIPS "UNCOMFORTABLY NEAR VICTORIA"

By early February 1878, the press, legislative assembly, and more vocal residents of British Columbia believed that war was imminent, and that their lives and future would directly be affected by it. News now reached Victoria from London, even from the Balkans, only two or three days old, so that the Russians' rapid march on Istanbul and British naval preparations in the East Mediterranean had an immediacy on the Northwest Coast that they would not have had a decade earlier.[1] The *Mainland Guardian* expressed the popular anxiety in its particularly sombre leader of 9 February, "War in the East," which vented a violently anti-Russian animus:

> By last advices, the progress of the Russians had been stopped, but not before they had reached a point about twenty-four hours' march from Constantinople. . . . When we think of the horrors perpetrated by these Muscovite savages in the name of the Christian religion, we are no longer surprised at the progress of free thought in the present day. The fact of 150,000 Russians and Roumanians now lying under the soil of Bulgaria, or lying rotting by the wayside, is but a drop in this bucket of blood. . . . A terrible price will no doubt have to be paid by England.

Thousands of Muslim refugees from "Russian bayonets" were dying of starvation, cold, or both, while Russian infantry and cossacks raped their wives, sisters, and daughters, then employed "horrible cruelties." Such scenes almost sufficed to drive the thought of the Canadian Pacific Railway from west coast heads (only belatedly and briefly did the leader-writer note that, in the atmosphere of crisis,

London would most probably give generous assistance for its prompt completion).
They were certainly more gripping than the west coast news, with the exception of
one item also published in another paper on the same day under "Naval News."

> The Russian corvette "Crayser" has arrived at San Francisco, making the
> voyage from Callao under sail. She carries 18 officers, 160 men, and is a
> vessel . . . with compound engines of 250 horsepower. Her captain expects
> several other vessels of the Russian Squadron [in the North Pacific] to
> rendezvous shortly in San Francisco harbour.[2]

The position, left unspoken by the *British Colonist* because it was so patent,
almost duplicated that of the preceding spring. Again, a Russian squadron was
assembling in California for purposes unknown; again, British Columbians who
had no way of gaining solid information[3] on the subject short of travelling to San
Francisco were assuming that it wished to be conveniently close to them and yet in
neutral waters in the secret expectation of instructions to be sent the moment
Russia and Britain were at war over Turkey. Insofar as the position *was* distinct
from that of the preceding year, it was graver for the province; first, because war
was now more likely; second, because *Kreiser*, with her modern 6" guns and rapid-
firing 47mm cannon, was a faster and more formidable vessel than even *Baian* had
been.[4] It was a fact that Rear-Admiral de Horsey now had *Shah* on station, though
regrettably she was in Chile, thirty days away; but this was balanced by the
likelihood that other iron clippers, and not aged wooden vessels, would be
gathering, as the Seattle press unkindly emphasized, close to British Columbia
and far from South America. The *British Colonist* seized on the point:

> The Seattle *Dispatch* thinks the Russian war vessels now at or near San
> Francisco will be uncomfortably near Victoria in case of war between England
> and Russia. Admiral de Horsey is at Concepcio, Chile . . . but there is a large
> British fleet at China, from which a few ships might be spared for the
> protection of this part.[5]

Tension grew over the next few days as news arrived first that a Russian corps
was at Istanbul itself, then that most sectors of the British press were clamouring
for war. Belatedly, the undefended coal mines at Nanaimo were visited by
members of the legislature and the captain of *Opal*, F. C. Robinson, and urgently
discussed. A new appeal for assistance with the coast and land defences went to
Ottawa.[6] Then on the sixteenth, the futility of such appeals and discussions being
obvious to the legislative assembly, and the silence of the San Francisco telegraph
oppressive, the assembly met with naval and militia officers then in Victoria and
undertook to raise a local corps of volunteer artillery. Captain Robinson agreed to
place the necessary guns at the immediate disposal of the province and to supervise

their mounting at selected points to cover the approaches to the harbours. An artillery instructor was at once detailed from *Opal* to the embryonic corps. The *British Colonist* rose readily to the occasion with a burst of patriotic prose: "H.M.S. *Opal* and *Rocket* will be got ready for active service. . . . We need not point out to citizens of every nationality the importance of volunteering in defence of their hearths and homes." [7] Within twenty-four hours, volunteers were enlisting under Colonel Houghton's eye and being drilled. Time seemed short. An air of urgency induced both the citizens at large and the authorities to take yet further steps to meet the international crisis. While the former made contingency arrangements for a Russian raid or went to Albert Head, where earthworks were expected to be built within a week, the latter sent the steamer *Sir James Douglas* to Burrard Inlet on the mainland for the latest telegrams. As if nature sympathized with human stress, a gale had "prostrated" land-lines on the Island and, it seemed, broken the Strait of Georgia cable. The news gathered on the mainland brought no comfort. "War," observed the *Mainland Guardian,* "is considered to be almost certain."[8] Rear-Admiral de Horsey and his squadron were, belatedly, proceeding north towards Esquimalt.

THE CORVETTE *KREISER* AT ESQUIMALT (FEBRUARY 1878)

Late in the afternoon of Monday, 18 February 1878 — some forty-eight hours after the decision had been taken to establish an auxiliary corps of volunteer artillery for the Victoria-Esquimalt region, and before one extra gun had been put in place along the coast — the Race Rocks telegraph above Esquimalt signaled the approach of a foreign warship. Shortly afterwards, the Russian iron clipper or corvette[9] *Kreiser*, of 1,334 tons displacement, altered course and made directly for Esquimalt Harbour.[10] Tremors of alarm ran through the settlement. The senior naval officer on duty, Captain F. C. Robinson, and members of the legislature were alerted. It was still quite light when *Kreiser* steamed past Fisgard Island then, unhesitating, stopped and anchored by the Royal Navy Yard, that is, just north of Duntze Head out of the wind.

The name of San Francisco's recent visitor was recognized as soon as it was legible, through telescopes on Duntze Head. Esquimalt therefore knew what guns she carried only shortly after her captain, whom the San Francisco press had called Nasimoff, could have opened fire, with a ranging shot on Duntze Head perhaps, if his intentions were belligerent. The fact that he did not, together with the readiness of one or two 68-pounders on the Head and other guns elsewhere to reply if necessary, brought relief to those who watched *Kreiser*'s deliberate approach. Nevertheless, tension remained acute. Perhaps the Russian had ignored merchant shipping off the province, which would certainly have been a softer target than Esquimalt, though a capture or a sinking could have taken place at sea without the province knowing of it yet. But it was also possible that he had had advance notice that war would erupt between St. Petersburg and London on a certain date, the eighteenth or nineteenth possibly, and meant to take maximum advantage of his secret information. In that case, fate would have assisted him by sending storms to interrupt communication with the mainland.[11]

All in all, the naval and civilian authorities were not disposed to think that *Kreiser* had immediately hostile objects. Such, at least, was their belief once the uneasy period of her approach was over. But again the Russian ship, whose arrival was itself so unexpected and improbable in view of Anglo-Russian tensions that had lately changed the texture of daily life, disconcerted them by failing to acknowledge the Esquimalt Dockyard ensign, as was necessary in the circumstances, by dipping her flag. The dockyard waited in vain. Finally, a launch went out, and Captain Nasimov stated his business. One version of what he said, or was reported to have said, appeared in the *British Colonist* next morning:

> The Russian Sloop of War "Craysser," Captain C. N. Nasimoff, arrived in Esquimalt yesterday. . . . She had left San Francisco on the 11th inst. On the 17th inst., about dark, Mr. Wilson, a midshipman, was thrown overboard. . . . Shortly after starting again, the jib-boom was carried away beside a quantity of canvas. The Captain then thought it necessary to put into some port for repairs and consequently steamed for Esquimalt.[12]

Captain Nazimov's explanation of his presence was received by the authorities politely, by the populace with open scepticism, as is clear from the *Mainland Guardian*'s Victoria report or "letter" of the twenty-first:

> On Monday evening, when everyone was talking peace or war and discussing the probabilities of a Russian man-of-war coming this far or not, into the harbour of Esquimalt unexpectedly steamed a Russian corvette. . . . She gave all sorts of excuses for coming here, but it is generally thought she only popped in to see what preparations we are making in the event of war.

In the absence of Nazimov's sailing orders and particular (secret) instructions, both at Kronstadt and (perhaps) at San Francisco,[13] it remains impossible to exonerate him completely from the charge of entering Esquimalt Harbour first and foremost to examine the defences and to gather other information useful in a future raid. It would have been surprising had he not had standing orders to that general effect, for naval officers have always had surveillance duties and have everywhere gathered data on the ships and port-defences of their past and possible antagonists. Nevertheless, given the circumstantial evidence, it is unlikely that the understandable suspicion of the colonists that an examination of defences and of warlike preparations was the *Kreiser*'s aim was justified. There had, in fact, been gales on the sixteenth and the seventeenth of February, and the *Kreiser*'s jib-boom, mid-shipman, and canvas were apparently put out of action at the same time as the Strait of Georgia cable and the land-line to Esquimalt. If the Russians had in fact been less than one day's steaming from Esquimalt when the storm had struck them, as Nazimov said and as the circumstances indicated, then Esquimalt was indeed the closest harbour with repair facilities and naval workmen.

How unfortunate the timing of his visit to that harbour was, in all events, became apparent to Nazimov quickly. Captain Robinson, and other British officers most likely, brought him up to date with European military and diplomatic news.[14] Nazimov slept on this. Next morning, conscious of his own exposed position, he made steam and headed out to sea, leaving behind "several mourning tradesmen" and provisions ordered barely twelve hours earlier.[15] An incident at San Francisco five days previously, which had ended with a merchant, Jacob Goldsoll, filing suit against him and his officers for sixteen hundred dollars on a signed but broken contract and a meeting with the Russian consul and the dry deputy sheriff of the city's nineteenth district,[16] reinforced his resolution to be gone while there was nothing to prevent him.

Retrospectively, the people of Esquimalt and Victoria might well remark that *Kreiser* would have been "a nice prize . . . for our men-of-war, had war been declared while she was here."[17] At the time, however, they had felt less blithe about her presence on their coast. That being so, they had done their best to minimize the menace that she posed by representing her, in public, as a little ship, "not very formidable," suitable for coastal survey work but not for unsupported action. The defences were inadequate and could be judged as such by agents of the Russian fleet like Nazimov. To belittle his importance was a natural reaction, to be echoed by the conduct of the government in Ottawa when, far too late, *it* learned of *Kreiser*'s fleeting visit to Esquimalt on her way to the "Okotesh Sea" and "Russia in the East."[18]

THE "CIMBRIA" AND PRIVATEERING ALARMS (APRIL 1878)

Kreiser had left the Baltic weeks before the fall of Plevna and the swift Russian advance on Adrianople had induced the Queen to urge her ministers to think of war.[19] Her presence on the Northwest Coast therefore was not directly linked to an expected Anglo-Russian conflict, though assuredly it spoke of international crisis in a general way. Early in April, however, news of naval steps taken by Russia in February, in immediate response to the alarming situation in the East Mediterranean, at the same time as the *Kreiser* had been causing consternation in the province, reached Victoria.[20] For the six weeks after *Kreiser*'s departure, the volunteer gunners had been drilling by the waterfront and undergoing training on the *Opal*'s deck. There was no sign of the earthworks promised for Macaulay Point and other coastal sites on which new batteries were to be placed; nor, even now, was Rear-Admiral de Horsey's squadron present in the province as a unit.[21] It was fortunate, in short, that what arrived in early spring was only news of *Cimbria*, a German steamer under charter to the Russian government,[22] and not the ship herself.

Even in January, members of the Russian naval staff had been completing their contingency arrangements for a British naval strike along the Russian Baltic coast.[23] Russia knew that if she secured a total victory against the Porte, Great Britain might feel bound to make a move against her. News of Suleiman's defeat increased the tension in Russian naval circles. Both strategically and psychologically, some step had to be taken. J. von Kronenfels, a German naval officer who knew and made a study of the growing Russian Navy of the 1870's, thus summarizes the events that followed:

The war with Turkey and the tense situation in Europe . . . compelled the Russian Government to move to protect Russian interests in the face of England's aggressive policy. To this end, and given the example of the year 1863, it was above all necessary to send a number of cruisers out to sea. Since however only a few Russian warships were abroad in the winter of 1877–78, and since no Russian ship could leave the Baltic [by February] because of the weather conditions, the Naval Ministry resolved to send a special mission of naval crews to America, there to acquire cruisers, fit them out for war service, and take them out to sea. This mission set out from Kronstadt at the close of March 1878.[24]

New Englanders were greatly surprised when *Cimbria* reached Maine carrying sixty-six young midshipmen and officers and 606 ordinary seamen — a sufficient number, it was afterwards conceded by the English-speaking leader of the mission, Captain-Lieutenant Semechkin, to man three locally constructed privateers. Captain Semechkin and his people hastened to New York and so to Washington, where, with help from lawyers known for their pro-Russian sympathies and embassy employees, they not only dealt with less obliging sectors of the east coast press and even congressmen, but also started talks with representatives of two large east coast shipyards, William Cramp and Sons of Philadelphia and Roach and Son of Chester. What was wanted, these were told, was the provision and immediate internal alteration of three iron steamers that were suitable for reconfiguration as small cruisers. The potential prey, everyone understood, was British merchant shipping off the shores of North America itself.[25]

News of the arrival of so sinister and ponderous a mission in America, while the United States and Britain were at peace, alarmed Alexander Mackenzie's government in Ottawa as neither Pauzino's squadron nor the *Kreiser* had. Of the Dominion's commercially or militarily important seaboard towns and ports, only

Halifax had adequate defences. Ever ready to avail himself of any opportunity to urge that the dominion defences should be strengthened by the government, but also genuinely troubled by the implications of Semechkin's mission, Selby Smyth, the G.O.C., Militia, sent warning memoranda to the garrison and naval base at Halifax and to the minister responsible for the Canadian defences, A. G. Jones. His first concern was for Atlantic ports and shipping; but Vancouver Island too was in his thoughts. *Kreiser* was still in North Pacific waters, and whatever privateers Russia bought from the United States' efficient east coast shipyards could, of course, make their appearance off Victoria within a little while:

> I have so frequently brought to notice the totally unprotected state of the harbour of Victoria and the entrance to Esquimalt in Vancouver Island, as well as the immensely important coal mines of Nanaimo, that I need only once more, very earnestly, urge that guns now lying in Esquimalt Dockyard . . . be handed over and mounted on Macaulay's Point to command the entrance to both harbours.[26]

Meanwhile, Canadian and east coast press reports on the Semechkin mission were beginning to be copied or extracted, on the west coast, for the benefit of other readers. Distance seemed to double the enormity of a deliberately anti-British move by the Americans and Russians, made moreover while the former were ostensibly at peace with England and not aggravating any Anglo-Russian problems that might possibly exist in southeast Europe.[27] It was all too reminiscent of the tacit understanding between Russia and the U.S. in the 1850's, which had similarly thrown a shadow on Victoria and local, west coast, shipping. Such concern about the probable results of the Semechkin mission as was felt in May by British Columbians grew deeper when they learned in early summer, first, that *Kreiser* and at least one other Russian ironclad were in the area,[28] and second, that the Russians had in fact purchased three iron steamers which were being overhauled and reconfigured, at considerable cost, as fast as human ingenuity could manage:

> The names of these vessels were *State of California, Columbus*, and *Saratoga*. After the purchase, all three were taken to the iron shipbuilding yard of Messrs. Cramp at Philadelphia, there converted into war-vessels, and renamed the *Europe*, the *Asia*, and the *Africa*; under these names they were completed, fitted, and equipped for service, armament alone excepted.[29]

Like their counterparts in Australasia, the authorities and educated settlers of British Columbia looked at the Russian acquisition of these relatively fast and modern vessels with suspicious disapproval.[30] They considered it a certainty that in an Anglo-Russian war they would be used as commerce-raiders and/or harbourshellers and that one or more would be loose in the Pacific, spreading ripples of alarm from Burrard Inlet to New Zealand if not actually harming either. They noted that all three were being fitted with significantly larger, fireproof coal-bunkers, as well as new barque-rigging, to enable them to undertake long voyages without refuelling, in the Pacific, for example, where the Russians were dependent upon foreign coaling stations.[31] Such provincial apprehensions were not groundless: raids of the varieties envisaged by the isolated colonists themselves had almost certainly been spoken of, if not precisely planned, by Russian officers attached to naval staff headquarters in the Pacific and in Kronstadt.[32] For that reason, and because she had besides a certain psychological significance for the Vancouver Islanders over the next several years as the flagship of a larger Russian squadron in the North Pacific basin, it is well to look again — through the contemporary eyes of Captain Kronenfels — at *Afrika*, ex-*Saratoga:*

> *Afrika*, the third ship, was built at Roach's yard, Chester, on the Delaware, and purchased for 1,407,000 Marks. . . . She is divided by watertight partitions into nine compartments, five of which hold coal. Her compound engine achieved 1,500r. during its trial, giving a speed of 13 knots. The bunkers hold 975 tons of coal; thus, given a fuel consumption of 28½ tons per 24 hours, this vessel can cover more than 10,000 miles under steam. And apart from the main engine, 16 ancillary motors are mounted on *Afrika* . . . who carries a complement of 28 officers and 241 men.[33]

She was, in short, a formidable cruiser of the second class. Strong in her ironwork, having been launched at Chester only in July 1877, fitted out with combination sail-steam rig and boasting an efficient engine, she was scarcely 38' in the beam, yet longer than the *Aziia* (at 273') and shallower in draught than the *Evropa* (drawing barely 16'). Her "main advantages," in the informed opinion of J. W. King, chief engineer in the U.S. Navy and an officer who knew her well, were "light draught of water, comparatively high speed, and considerable sail-area" [1,244 square metres].[34] A contemporary Melbourne colonist agreed. "The *Afrika*," he noted with her light wrought-iron armour at the waterline and known high speed in mind, "is what may be classed . . . one of those floating dodgers, well calculated to hit and retire in good order."[35]

Yet on leaving William Cramp's, she had no armament. Should she remain to have guns fitted, as had earlier been planned, or risk a North Atlantic passage? With the meeting of the Congress of Berlin, at which the issues raised by Russia's recent victory over the Porte were considered by the European Powers, that risk had lessened. The signing of the Treaty of Berlin, in mid-July 1878, removed it. *Afrika* set sail from America for Kronstadt, putting in at Copenhagen on the way. At Kronstadt, at a somewhat calmer pace, she was in due course armed with five 6" or 15 cm and assorted smaller guns. By June 1879 she was en route for the Pacific station (Admiral Avraamii Aslanbegov) and her subsequent appointment at Esquimalt.[36] Fourteen months had now elapsed since news of the Semechkin mission had alarmed British Columbia. That the provincial press was still resounding with its echoes[37] spoke as plainly of inadequate responses to the actual emergency of March to May 1878 as of its longer-term importance, not for Canada perhaps, but for the province.

RESPONSES TO A CRISIS (MARCH TO JUNE 1878)

Recognizing crisis when they saw it, in the shape of Anglo-Russian confrontation in the Bosphorus, both the provincial government and the lieutenant-governor of British Columbia had cabled Ottawa in February, urging that the weak defences of Esquimalt and Victoria be strengthened at once with the Royal Navy's help. Specifically, they wished to borrow naval guns from the Esquimalt store and have them mounted on the coast immediately at the province's expense.[38] As usual when he received requests for extra money on defence, Mackenzie thought the matter over for a week or two: news of the *Cimbria* had yet to break. The Earl of Dufferin, governor general and so recipient of Albert Richards' messages from British Columbia, which he had lately visited,[39] responded rapidly by contrast. The lieutenant-governor's suggestions with regard to the Esquimalt naval store and the importance of at least deterring Russian raiders from attacking by a good show of activity, were forwarded within two days to M. Hicks-Beach, the secretary of state for the colonies, with Dufferin's endorsement.[40] But a week before this warning-and-request arrived in London, Hicks-Beach had, in fact, already sent a secret circular to all the colonies exhorting them to take immediate precautions against possible, and even probable, attacks by Russian cruisers. Hicks-Beach knew that his prime minister did not intend to let the latest Turkish crisis drag the country into war with Russia, loud though press and backbenchers might bay for Russian blood. He thought it likely that the prospects for an Anglo-Russian clash, which had been dwindling as March drew on to April, would continue to diminish. He also knew, however, that political and even military advantage might be won by the imperial authority from the resurgent Russian bogey in the colonies. Mackenzie might be pressed to form a standing military force in Canada, for instance, formally connected — in some way to be determined — with the British Army.[42] There is thus a suspicion of some disingenuousness (though assuredly there were strategic elements to justify it on the basis of contemporary Admiralty warnings) in the secret circular where Hicks-Beach by no means *minimized* the danger of a Russian seaborne raid of the precise sort dreaded from Victoria to Auckland, and from Cape Town to Nanaimo:[43]

The danger against which it would be more immediately necessary to provide would be an unexpected attack by a small squadron or even a single unarmoured cruiser, with the object of destroying public or private property . . . rather than any serious attempt at the conquest or permanent occupation of any portion of the colony.[44]

Spurred on by news of *Cimbria*'s threatening mission, as well as by Dufferin's despatches with enclosures by Sir Edward Selby Smyth and A. N. Richards, among others, the Colonial Defence Committee hastened its assessment of the minimal defence needs of Vancouver Island. Weeks would pass, its members recognized, before their findings could be acted on. They therefore issued an extraordinary advance report on the defence needs of Esquimalt and Victoria in April.[45] Eighteen medium and heavy guns should be dispatched for their improved defence at once. Since these would take some time to reach the province from England, however, guns in Admiralty storage at Esquimalt should, as Dufferin and others had suggested, be loaned to the dominion authorities. The latter, in the view of the committee, might reconsider the refusal to contribute to the coast defence of the Dominion that had itself deepened the crisis and should understand that the imperial authorities would not accept financial loss as a result of any temporary loan of naval ordnance. If needed by Her Majesty's commissioned ships on the Pacific Station or elsewhere, this would instantly be yielded up by the Dominion. But meanwhile "the whole armament in store at Victoria and Esquimalt, whether belonging to the War Office or the Admiralty, "would be placed at its disposal for the purpose of defending those two "points" against attack by any Russian naval force.

Hicks-Beach's note to Dufferin explaining these provisions and accompanying the Colonial Defence Committee's secret and advanced report on the defences of Esquimalt and Victoria was signed on 11 May and went to Ottawa by cable.[47] It arrived one week too late to calm a passing, atypical attack of nervous apprehension on Mackenzie's part. The news of *Cimbria*'s arrival in Maine and of her passengers' intention was received in Ottawa some days before Mackenzie acted on it. When he did so, on 4 May, it was with painful consciousness of past inertia where the coast defences were concerned and of its possible political and even national repercussions if a single undefended ship or harbour were destroyed by a marauding Russian cruiser — in full view of Canadians. Discussion in his cabinet revealed a complete absence in Canada of modern rifled ordnance appropriate for coastal batteries, that is, with range and armour penetrating force to cope with ironclads. As for Canadian defence vessels, not one was in commission.[48] The Dominion accordingly requested London to dispatch "fast cruisers" and, indeed, to station them in the St. Lawrence till the Russian threat had passed.[49] Seven days later, and coincidentally within twelve hours of the sending of the Hicks-Beach secret circular to Dufferin encouraging additional defensive measures by the government in Ottawa, Mackenzie was again addressing London in a hopeful vein. This time, the old spectre of Russo-American entente was troubling him, and he feared that the outbreak of an Anglo-Russian war would encourage a Canadian adventure by Americans still watching for a chance to bring about "Manifest Destiny" by undermining and absorbing the Dominion. It was above all vital, he observed to Dufferin and London, that Canadians be told when war was imminent.[50]

The Admiralty sent no answer to Mackenzie's plea for cruisers to be stationed in Quebec. In May, however, came the news that it would lend the guns in storage at Esquimalt. This was something to be grateful for, but also something, as imperialists, west coast members of the House, and even Dufferin repeatedly remarked to him, that needed an appropriate dominion response, namely, a contribution to the setting up of formidable coastal batteries so that in future there need *be* no such alarums. Pressure mounted on the cabinet which, willing to delay defence expenditure even in times of international stress, listened for news of diplomatic progress at the Congress of Berlin. The good news came, but not before Mackenzie — duly bowing to political necessity and military commonsense at last, as he invariably did[51] — had promised to commit $150,000 to Vancouver Island's coast defences. The decision was announced to Dufferin, and so to London, with a flourish soon regretted:

> We will not ask the Imperial Government for anything, as we think Canada should have, and does have, pride enough to be above shirking her duty in providing for the defence of her own coasts. We are part of the Empire and will bear our share of its burdens . . . etc.[52]

Other, calmer times and more specific information about what the latest coast defence equipment cost made the assertions seem, if not impolitic, then too emphatic. Summer came to Ottawa and, with its welcome heat, a falling off of Russophobic fever. What should Canada expect to pay for heavy guns? In England, there were many engineering officers, some with experience of the Dominion, ready and anxious to advise. They did so through the channel of Sir Alexander Milne, a former First Sea Lord, now chairman of a government committee charged to look into the question of imperial defences in the light of recent Anglo-Russian crisis.[53] The Canadian authorities were shocked by the initial estimates. On the defence of Sydney and Saint John in Nova Scotia alone, they were advised to spend a quarter of a million dollars, plus the pay of men to work the guns indefinitely.[54] It would work out cheaper, Dufferin said they expostulated, to allow the Russians to destroy whatever took their fancy.[55] It would certainly be necessary to consider all expedients whereby such sums could be avoided. For example, could Victoria not use old smooth-bore guns rifled in Canada, as Selby Smyth had once or twice suggested? It was, after all, not certain that a Russian ironclad would be the enemy: the Russians still had wooden warships in the East and the Pacific. The suggestion was dismissed by the imperial authorities, embodied in Sir Alexander Milne, as parsimonious and even dangerous.[56] Then came another blow for the Mackenzie cabinet. The Admiralty sent its answer to the earlier request for anti-Russian cruisers to be locally employed off the St. Lawrence. It considered the arrangements in effect for the protection of Atlantic shipping more than adequate. If war should come, they would be changed. But the Dominion itself, in that event, would doubtless move to strengthen the protection of its own commercial shipping and its (arguably vulnerable) seaboard ports on the Atlantic and in British Columbia alike.[57] Mackenzie's boast that the Dominion would ask for nothing cap in hand and would defend its own west coast would have been costly to live up to had the instinct to retrench on such expenditure whenever feasible not been ingrained in the Canadian Liberals and Conservatives alike,[58] and had the Treaty of Berlin not let his government, and conscience, off the hook in mid-July 1878. By then however it was happily too late for any government in Ottawa to countermand the orders that had sent Lieutenant-Colonel C. T. Irwin, joint inspector of artillery, from Kingston to Victoria in May[59] or to undo what he had done by way of coast fortification since arriving there.

EARTHWORKS AND BATTERIES: LT.-COL. IRWIN AT ESQUIMALT (MAY-AUGUST 1878)

When he learned from Dufferin of the imperial decisions to release all guns in storage at Esquimalt, on 11 May, the G.O.C., Sir Edward Selby Smyth immediately ordered Irwin to proceed by train and steamer to Victoria and there to direct construction of a set of coastal batteries using whatever local manpower, civilian or other, was available.[60] The colonel was already in possession of the Blair plan for a proposed set of defensive batteries, on Fisgard Island, at Macaulay Point, and at the foot of Beacon Hill[61] and had been briefed by Selby Smyth himself. He had been waiting for the order to go west and travelled fast, by rail then by ship from San Francisco, when he got it. He was in Victoria by noon, 27 May, and that same day met Colonel C. F. Houghton, still provincial deputy adjutant-general, and Captain C. Dupont with whom, at 6 P.M., he found the energy to watch the first regular muster and enrolment of the local volunteer artillery ("militia battery"). Some thirty men enlisted, and he addressed them. As an augury, the evening was a happy one.[62]

Over the next several days, Lt.-Col. Irwin met not only Rear-Admiral de Horsey, Captain F. C. Robinson, R.N., of Opal, Captains A. L. Burrows, R.M.A., Flag Captain F. G. Bedford, and Lieutenant Lindsay, of the Shah, not one of whom declined to voice opinions on the best siting of batteries for the Esquimalt harbour area,[63] but also members of the local government and civic dignitaries. To his credit, he was courteous to them and showed some willingness to take informed opinion, notably that of Captain Robinson and Gunnery Lieutenant Lindsay, into cognizance. He seems, indeed, to have discussed the pros and cons of many sites for earthwork batteries with these and other officers, having surveyed the ground quite scrupulously for a week (1–8 June). In general, the military and naval views diverged only on sitings for the battery to guard the entrance to Victoria, and not Esquimalt harbour. That a battery should be erected at the latter's mouth, as Colonel Blair had suggested and as Irwin judged essential, and a second on Macaulay Point, as Selby Smyth and many naval officers had urged, there was complete agreement.[64] Nor did Irwin doubt the soundness of the Navy group's insistence that Macaulay Point be treated as the most important site.

Defensive works had actually started on Macaulay Point, under the auspices of the provincial government, before Irwin's arrival on the scene. They had been prematurely halted when the owners of the site on which the battery was ultimately to be placed, seeing a possible financial coup, had asked $2,000 for the crucial acre and a half. Impasse remained unbroken on 9 June 1878. Awaiting the authority from Ottawa to take possession of the needed site, Irwin decided to accommodate the people of Victoria, from whom he was to draw his labour force, by starting work at Beacon Hill.[65] For this project, the naval party lacked enthusiasm of the kind inspired in them by the plans for Fisgard Island and Macaulay Point. As Rear-Admiral de Horsey put it crisply, in July, no hostile ship of any size could enter Victoria harbour, which was shallow, and in any case the city could be taken from the rear by an enemy who had been landed, say, at Cadboro or Cormorant or any one of twenty other bays within a quick march of the place.[66] Nevertheless, Lt.-Col. Irwin had his labourers report at Beacon Hill by 7 A.M., and earthworks duly scarred its base, though not the preferable Holland Point from which a battery would have a greater arc of fire. Once again, there were financial complications.[67] Being local men, with vested interests in the Victoria locality as well as a respect for daily wages in a period of economic turbulence, the labourers worked hard. When, in July, they moved *en masse* onto Macaulay Point, a naval party from the *Opal* moved the allocated guns to Finlayson and Point Victoria, both by the base of Beacon Hill, and mounted them in pairs.[68] When in due course they moved west to Brother's Island in the entrance to Esquimalt Harbour, which had finally seemed preferable to the craggy Fisgard Island for familiar financial reasons, *Opal*'s men took three 7″ muzzle-loading pieces to Macaulay Point and placed them, *en barbette*, behind the newly finished breastworks. Finally, as August was about to end, an 8″ (nine-ton) gun and two 64-pounder muzzle-loading pieces were emplaced on Brother's Island. Like Macaulay Point's "three sisters," the Brothers Island 8″-gun was sheltered by a solid wooden shed. Guns, slides, and carriages were thus protected from the elements.[69]

That Irwin and his labourers had worked so well, and that civilians and seamen had co-operated fully on the batteries, albeit under threat of an attack by Russians or at least under the cloud of recent panics on the coast, was quickly shown to be most fortunate — by the reaction of the government in Ottawa, and not St. Petersburg. Even in July, Mackenzie's Liberals had been considering how best, and with the least risk of political embarrassment, to trim the cost of not "shirking" their "duty" to their countrymen and Queen, where external defences were concerned. By August, they were anxious to delay decisions bearing on the purchase of expensive guns for coast defence. The Russian spectre shrank, and, as it did so, Irwin's presence at Esquimalt seemed itself, from the perspective of Ontario, to be no trifling response to passing dangers. By September, Irwin's work was being scrutinized from Ottawa within the context of an imminent election, seemingly improved relations between Russia and Great Britain, and an urgent obligation to deliver on at least *some* formal promises to the Militia, to the voters of affected coastal ridings, and to the government in London to attend to the Dominion's defences. It was paradoxical: politically and militarily, expensive steps had to be taken, yet the Anglo-Russian crisis had receded. And Mackenzie, who had always been in sympathy with the Canadian Militia whose decline he supervised, now found himself obliged by hard political and military realities, and in his final weeks of power, to support it publicly by word and deed.[70] A question of defence priorities had to be faced. As Dufferin himself well knew, money was tight in Ottawa, and a commitment had been made — with some provisos — to the long-delayed completion of the dry-dock at Esquimalt.[71] That facility, it had been argued in the House, would bring increased security and economic gains to western Canada, yet was beyond the means of the provincial government. Again, the larger eastern ports were patently in need of coastal guns. Mackenzie and his ministers delayed until 27 September. They then agreed to purchase large-calibre ordnance for installation on the coasts of eastern Canada and ordered that the work proceeding at Esquimalt and Victoria, under the supervision of Lt.-Col. Irwin, should be halted at once. In the cabinet's opinion, commitment to the dry-dock at Esquimalt was response enough, taken together with the coast fortification that the colonel had directed all through summer, to the province's appeal for increased protection against seaborne enemies, Russian or otherwise.[72]

ESQUIMALT COAST DEFENCES: PROBLEMS OF COMMAND AND MAINTENANCE
(1879)

Irwin's works were temporary by their nature. Even so, their upkeep and the problems of maintaining four separate batteries and manning ten additional large guns indefinitely weighed on the provincial and dominion authorities alike. Irwin had stressed to Captain F. G. Bedford of the *Shah* that with the fifty volunteer gunners who had recently enrolled in the Victoria "militia battery," he could have only five guns working — and the men themselves would doubtless have a preference for Beacon Hill whence they could see their homes.[73] Nor had he failed to appreciate that the militia rifle company had been depleted even by the move of fifty men into the new, and therefore fashionable, volunteer artillery.[74] Just as funds were short for batteries, so were men. With Rear-Admiral de Horsey's backing, Houghton seized the problem by the horns and wrote an eloquent appeal to the government in Ottawa for an "extraordinary" unit of marine artillery, perhaps one hundred men, to work the guns at — and indeed to settle permanently in — Esquimalt.[75] It was evident that extra gunners would be needed if the batteries, so recently erected, were to operate as taxpayers had every right to think they would, and if the Russians of the future were in fact to be deterred. The appeal was received unsympathetically in Ottawa. Houghton was permitted to increase the volunteer artillery establishment already drilling in Victoria from fifty men to eighty-five, but he was told to expect no more concessions of the same expensive kind.[76]

Lieutenant-Colonel Houghton had good reasons to hope for a less dampening response. Since May Mackenzie had been readjusting his defence planning to cope with overseas threats (from the Muscovite barbarians) as well as with a possible American incursion overland in the interior, and should the Liberals lose power and Macdonald be returned to office, the Conservatives were hardly likely to reduce defence expenditure at once. Macdonald was known to support the notion of a modest standing military force for the Dominion.[77] That being so, it would have been surprising had the British Tories not responded to Mackenzie's actual defeat in mid-October, and Macdonald's return to power, by suggesting that Canadians share the cost of building permanent fortifications on their own Pacific shores. They did so, shortly after the election, simultaneously wondering aloud if the Dominion might not acquire cruisers of the sort that had so urgently been asked for, five months earlier, and even found a small naval reserve. Macdonald's answer disappointed many. He was ready to allow Mackenzie's military programme to proceed, but with less emphasis on coast defence and more on the repulsion of attacks across the border. Russian raiders seemed to him unlikely guests, and there were now large guns above Esquimalt and Victoria. His government would not, therefore, embark upon a costly programme of erecting permanent defence works like those in Halifax in British Columbia, with or without imperial assistance.[78]

Unexpectedly, since Tory governments were in power in both London and Ottawa and since the imperial authorities had resolved to send new guns to be emplaced on Brothers Island and Macaulay Point,[79] the various problems linked to the defence of the Victoria-Esquimalt region soon became too acute to be dismissed. In Victoria, Houghton now questioned the ability of volunteer gunners to maintain accurate fire on a moving, armoured ship. In London, the committee pondering imperial-colonial defences, chaired by Milne, was taking note of Horsey's memoranda to the Admiralty of the past several months, which touched directly on the question of command at and around Esquimalt Yard. Milne was himself an admiral, and he was acquainted with de Horsey and with the documents that had persuaded the Colonial Defence Committee, on 1 April, to support the Admiralty view that earthworks should at once be raised above Esquimalt and Victoria.[80] He sympathized with de Horsey's attitude that the confusion of authority and blurred divisions of command among civilians, militia men, and naval officers in the Pacific province, as indeed among imperial, dominion, and local government officials, were inherently dangerous and should be clarified before another international crisis broke. As matters stood, "Imperial resources" were inadequately guarded by a "trifling number" of Canadian militiamen. Esquimalt, which was, so to speak, the Halifax, Bermuda, and Jamaica of the North Pacific Ocean and beyond "possible reach" of reinforcement should be guarded, manned, and paid for by Great Britain. But the government of Canada should build effective permanent defences and should pay for their efficient long-term maintenance. It was the old annoyance: if the naval base were not defended by a land force, British warships must perforce remain "as mere floating batteries," unable to pursue a Russian raider, for example, or to ward her off at sea.[81] The government in Ottawa declined to take advantage of the 1865 Colonial Naval Defence Act and of other, recent offers of imperial assistance to create a small naval establishment for the defence of the Victoria-Esquimalt region.[82] It should therefore be willing to provide British Columbia with permanent defence works and the necessary units of professional artillery. Half-measures would be noted by Americans and Russians, who might then begin to plan how to "destroy the Dockyard and be masters of the [area], until again ejected by hard fighting."[83]

Milne and his colleague, General Sir Lintorn Simmons, the inspector general of fortifications, put some pressure on the British government starting in March 1879 to push Macdonald harder on the matter of improved defences for Esquimalt. Dufferin was told to raise the question. In reality, he had been raising it at intervals since the Canadian Conservatives' return to office.[84] But again Macdonald's answer disappointed. In the end, as a concession to imperial opinion and not, as he made plain to Dufferin, from a conviction that Esquimalt needed stronger batteries, he undertook to send an officer from Kingston to co-operate on an exhaustive military survey of Vancouver Island and the Lower Mainland with the British engineering officer whom, it appeared, the imperial authorities were sending. His selection was Lieutenant-Colonel T. B. Strange, R.A., the British officer — Lieutenant-Colonel J. W. Lovell, R.E. Macdonald emphasized that work on the defences at Esquimalt and Victoria was not to be continued for the present, or at all, unless an ultimate decision to do so was arrived at by his government on the basis of both officers' reports.[85]

Lovell and Strange made independent and extremely thorough surveys of the actual defences and probable defensive needs of British Columbia. Their main recommendations, as presented in their separate but linked reports (November and December 1879), were similar. The province, both declared, was indefensible against invasion from the south; but such an enemy as Russia *could* be kept at bay, at a considerable cost. For Victoria, Lovell proposed a battery of half a dozen 10"- guns on Beacon Hill, for Esquimalt — twelve new Armstrong (40-pounder) fieldguns, two armour-plated gunboats, and a system of electric mines. At least eleven hundred British troops should be on hand and five hundred militia men as extra infantry to make Vancouver Island quite secure. Eight more Armstrong guns should be emplaced over Nanaimo, and others on Points Atkinson and Grey to cover English Bay, Vancouver. Strange concurred that many guns and troops would certainly be needed to secure the province from seaborne raids such as the Russians might eventually launch, and he likewise stressed the absence of a telegraphic link around Vancouver Island's southern tip, to give some warning of a hostile ship's approach. He too commended new "torpedo" (electrically detonated mine) defences to the government in Ottawa, at least for the approaches to Esquimalt Harbour, and observed that use could well be made of ten or fifteen blockhouses — and a Canadian Pacific Railway, to channel in supplies and ammunition, troops and guns.

The two reports dropped silently, like stones, into the pond of the Macdonald government. Of the approximately three dozen joint recommendations by Lt.-Cols. Strange and Lovell, only one appears to have been acted on by 1883: that a battery be mounted at Nanaimo. Useful though the data so assiduously gathered might have proved, the double survey was, in fact, a case of misdirected energy. The blame lay squarely with Macdonald's government, which, with imperial relations in mind, had left both officers[86] with the impression that Esquimalt might indeed become another Halifax and that an enemy like Russia was indeed to be deterred by an expenditure of money, time, and sweat from ever damaging one building on Vancouver Island. From Lovell's work, as from an elephant, emerged a mouse-like note for the attention of Sir Alexander Milne's successor as the government-appointed student of imperial defensive needs, Carnarvon: "I would recommend that the batteries [at Esquimalt] should be left as they are, in charge of the Dominion Government."[87] The problems of command and maintenance of the defences of Esquimalt thus remained unsolved despite the crises and alarums of the previous twelve months. Macdonald would have shelved them entirely if the British government, now thoroughly alive to the whole question of imperial defence, had not deliberately jogged his arm.

SIR JOHN A. MACDONALD, THE CARNARVON COMMISSION, AND ESQUIMALT

The interdepartmental Milne Committee, struck in June 1878 and charged with an emergency review of the state of defence of British bases overseas and of "the more important ports," had been a speedy and direct response to near-collision between Russia and Great Britain by the Sea of Marmora. It had been struck at the suggestion of the Earl of Carnarvon, the colonial secretary, and, with Admiralty and War Office support, had done good work in hastening the building or improving of "important port" defences at Esquimalt, Cape Town, Singapore, and Mauritius among other places and in focusing public attention on the need — of which John Colomb had been speaking for a decade — to protect essential coal supplies and oceanic cables.[88] Government and press had been reminded, when the catalytic Anglo-Russian crisis had subsided and imperial-colonial defence matters might well have been neglected, that the Russian Navy could indeed present a threat to isolated British outposts and that many colonists and settlers were well aware of it.[89]

The Milne Committee was dissolved on 2 May 1879. By then however both its chairman and Sir Lintorn Simmons had convinced Hicks-Beach and Stafford Northcote among other members of the government that a more permanent advisory committee or commission was required to continue and expand its work. Specifically, a body was required to advise the government on the controlling and apportionment of all imperial defence costs in the future and on ways in which the central and colonial authorities might split them. The Canadian reluctance even to debate such questions, in regard to Esquimalt, had been noted.[90] Hicks-Beach duly sponsored the establishment, not of a powerful political committee, which could easily have kept in touch with both the cabinet and the colonial authorities, but of a Royal Commission for the Defence of British Possessions and Commerce Abroad, and asked Carnarvon, his predecessor as colonial secretary, to become its chairman.[91] That a high-level political committee might have operated faster and in some ways more effectively was evident to Hicks-Beach. A royal commission was preferred, it seems, for two main reasons: first, in deference to opposition in the Commons to the prospect of a Tory-hued imperialist junta, secondly, in recognition of the fact that British cabinets could not give orders to, for instance, the Dominion of Canada. No eminent colonial was named to the commission in the hope of rendering its ultimate recommendations and advice more palatable, to the government in Ottawa for instance;[92] nor would Hicks-Beach have the "pushing" Captain J. C. Colomb on it, knowledgeable though he doubtless was.[93] As though to diminish the political significance of the commission's work deliberately, its terms of reference were next revised. It was to deal neither with the home defences of Great Britain, nor with those of Malta, Halifax, Gibraltar, and Bermuda.

On the other hand, Carnarvon and his colleagues were indeed to look into the problem of protecting Esquimalt properly and sorting out the linked issues of finance and control there. They did so with a will, in the misguided supposition that Sir John Macdonald, the Empire-minded new prime minister of the Dominion, would also wish to see the resolution of the old Esquimalt problem — even if, as seemed most likely, the Dominion was asked to pay the costs of building and maintaining stronger coastal batteries. Macdonald was a personal acquaintance of Carnarvon and had worked with him on drafts of the British North America Act of

1867. As it happened, he was soon to visit London. It was understood that he would be requested, by Carnarvon, to appear as a witness before the commission and to give his views on the defence needs of Victoria-Esquimalt. Questions were accordingly prepared and, it seems, sent off to him so that his answers could be adequately weighed before delivery.[94]

Macdonald's testimony deeply disappointed those who had been hoping for a generous Canadian commitment to a set of permanent defence works round Esquimalt naval base. Obviously, Russian aggression had not been in his thoughts as it remained in those of some commission members, notably Sir Alexander Milne and Thomas Brassey, M.P.[95] New, permanent defence works on Vancouver Island, he observed, were quite superfluous for the protection of Canadian shipping and commerce and could only be contended to be vital for the Royal Navy's, that is, Britain's local purposes. Canada would concentrate on building up her land forces (although Americans could easily invade a part of the Dominion if they resolved to do so, and a war with the United States was best not thought of). The Empire at large would gain in strength from the Canadian Pacific Railway, which was itself a contribution to imperial, as well as Canadian, defences. War with a European power, Russia for example, would most likely not revolve round issues that directly interested the Dominion and would in any case expose its coasts only to temporary raids. It was financially impossible to prevent all such raids. British Columbia had an extensive littoral and many coastal settlements. In the event of any Anglo-Russian war in which the Empire was tested or in which large interests or principles were patently at stake, England might count on the affection of Canadians. Ten thousand men would aid her "on the spur of the moment" in a patriotic mood.[96] Until that time, his government would not be troubling about the tsar.

These uncompromising comments took a good deal of digesting. The commissioners had hardly started to appreciate how widely they themselves differed in private on the question of Esquimalt's future and how much they had been troubled by Macdonald's words, however, when the government was beaten at the polls and Gladstone, who was known to be unsympathetic to their work, came into office. Discussion of Esquimalt was postponed. Gladstone decided to allow Carnarvon and his colleagues to proceed. At this juncture the commission split over Esquimalt, the majority contending that, unless Macdonald's government would build appropriate defences and maintain a proper garrison in the Esquimalt Harbour area — in which case Britain should provide advice and guns — the Royal Navy base should be transferred to other parts. Too remote to be supplied in time of war and indefensible against American attack, Esquimalt was a liability. More pressure should be put on Ottawa so that the base could be retained or readapted and developed fully.[97] The minority position was, in brief, that to withdraw de Horsey's squadron was to make attack by the United States or by one of its allies rather likely. The only matter to be settled was whether Britain was to pay for permanent coastal defence works at Esquimalt wholly or in part. In all events, any proposal to remove the squadron from its present North Pacific base was *ultra vires* for the commission since it infringed on functions of executive departments of the state. The base ought not to be abandoned.[98]

Of the fate of the Carnarvon commission's three-volume report, suffice to note that it was never published in entirety or formally adopted by a British government; that Parliament declined to vote funds for a number of the projects that it strongly recommended, on the ground that even military experts thought the sums required far too large;[99] and that the government in Ottawa, conscious of Gladstone's "Little England" policy and of the possibility of doing nothing where Esquimalt and the west coast was concerned (always a popular approach in central Canada),[100] felt able to ignore its harping on the subjects of imaginary Russian raiders and inadequate defences. Whether they subscribed to the majority or to the Barkly-Milne minority report on the defences of Esquimalt, it is pertinent to comment, the commissioners had thought of Russia as the likeliest aggressor on the coasts of Canada, apart from the United States, and as a major long-term menace which Macdonald should acknowledge. That Macdonald could refer so calmly to the temporary risk of coastal raids to which Canadians might be exposed by future conflict between Russia and Great Britain illustrated the divergence of the Ottawa and London attitudes towards that danger and towards the growth of Russian naval strength since 1860. Seen from London, Russia was an intercontinental, even global, threat, whereas from Ottawa she was a distant state that could, conceivably, destroy some property on either fringe of Canada and cause alarm.

News of the signing of the Treaty of Berlin, which diffused the immediate and real Anglo-Russian crisis of the day, had been timely for Mackenzie's government. Even so, it is doubtful if war between the Russians and the British over Near Eastern matters would have led to the reversal of a policy of minimal commitment to defence which, like the great mass of Canadians without a vested interest on the Pacific (or Atlantic) Coast, both major parties found congenial. However that may be, the resolution of the crisis in the Near East confirmed the Liberals, and even the Canadian, unwillingness to meet defence responsibilities on the Pacific at a higher cost — some argued — than the likely cost of raids that Russian warships might attempt. In this respect, it marked a watershed in the official and acknowledged attitude towards the west coast, Russian raiders, and defence. Only a few short weeks beyond that watershed lay the Canadian electorate's acceptance of Macdonald's "National Policy." Consolidation of Canadian possession of the West, expanding trade and industry behind a tariff, and the grand, transcontinental railway, the CPR, were the Dominion's preferred responses to the challenges of national growth, cohesion, and defence. If revenues were to be spent on the Dominion's defences, it should be with the United States and the interior in mind, not Vancouver Island, which the military experts thought untenable in a war with the Americans and which would therefore remain vulnerable even if sufficient men and guns *were* put in place to make the island, and the whole west coast, semi-secure against Russian seaborne raids.

7

The Russian Menace and Colonial Defencelessness: the 1880's

At the time of the Crimean War, Russia had lacked sufficient strength in the Pacific necessary even to have planned a raid on Fort Victoria. Her only formidable warship then in North Pacific waters, the *Avrora*, 44 guns, had for months avoided action. These realities, together with the indefensibility of Novo-Arkhangel'sk against an Anglo-French attack, had predisposed the Russian Naval Ministry and Ministry of Foreign Affairs to approve the quarantining of Russian North America as both Russian and British trading interests suggested. Russian attempts to hire merchantmen or fast passenger steamers from Americans and send them out from San Francisco Bay as privateers likewise stemmed from *and reflected* an essential naval weakness. Even rumours that a Russian privateer had been fitted out to raid Vancouver Island or commecial shipping off the Northwest Coast, indeed, caused alarms there, so wretchedly was it protected against European (or United States) aggression; but at least Governor Douglas had seen the full strategic implication of the Russian Navy's absence from the northeastern Pacific and was rightly calculating that, with five hundred well-armed company servants at his back, he could attack and "conquer" Russian North America.[1] In retrospect, both Palmerston and Clarendon regretted that the governor had been prevented from securing it and so forestalling "the Bargain between Nicholas and the Yankees."[2] Russia's naval weakness in the North Pacific area, in short, was a strategically significant reality during, and after, the Crimean War, though it was sometimes underemphasized by settlers and others on the British Northwest Coast influenced by privateer-related nervousness and/or the spectre of a Russo-American alliance.

Thanks in large measure to Rear-Admiral A. Popov's energies and General N.

Murav'ev-Amurskii's spectacular political and military successes in Amuria and Sakhalin since the mid-1850's, Russia's maritime and naval presence in the East and the Pacific grew significantly in the 1860's. By the Treaty of Aigun (1858) alone, Russia obtained not only large new territories on the left bank of the Amur down to the Ussuri and on both its banks below the confluence of those rivers but also an extensive coastline. Shortly afterwards, she gained a north Pacific seaboard down to 43°N., replete with harbours far superior to those at Nikolaevsk and Shilkinskii Zavod. As British and American observers[4] of the period well recognized, Vladivostok and Nikolaevsk with their mineral- and food-rich, semi-settled hinterlands might well prove aces in an international card-game for political and even naval dominance of northwestern Pacific shores and waters. They were certainly well worth protecting with an extra ship or two and a few small modern craft were duly sent from Europe to form a permanent and stronger East Siberian flotilla.[5]

North American and British visitors to Russia's new "Maritime Province of the East" were, by and large, deeply impressed by its commercial and military potential. Not a few drew the attention of their countrymen and governments to Russia's growing power on the seaboard north of China and, indeed, within the ancient Chinese sphere of influence on the Ussuri. Their efforts sparked no more than casual and transitory interest even in London, and almost none in British Columbia, a province then preoccupied with its internal development and isolation and with little time or energy to spare for Russian progress on the far side of the North Pacific Ocean.

Very different was the colonial response to Rear-Admiral A. Popov's naval squadron, when it made its way around the northeastern Pacific in 1862–63, calling ultimately and climactically, at San Francisco. Popov's San Francisco visit and the more or less contemporary Russian naval visit to New York of 1863,[6] as was recognized in European Admiralty circles shortly afterwards, were a response to Russian fears lest Great Britain, feeling bound to take up Poland's cause after the quashing of the recent nationalistic insurrection, should blockade the Russian Baltic fleet and towns or even shell them. As the press and government of the Pacific colonies had paid no heed to those events across the ocean that suggested *future* Russian strength, however, so they misinterpreted the movements of a squadron, part of which had come from Kronstadt, as an indication of present naval strength and capability, not of dangerous inferiority at sea. The point is illustrated by collation of the article, "The Russian Sailors," in the *British Colonist*, Friday, 19 September 1862, with Popov's own remarks of January 1863 about the *Kalevala's* crossing to the Northwest Coast from Petropavlovsk-in-Kamchatka. "The vessel," wrote the *British Colonist*, "is Finnish built and a very neat looking craft." "On our way to Sitka," records Popov, "we lost much time because more of our royals and stunsails were under repair than could be raised." [7]

Other comparisons of Russian and contemporaneous colonial materials confirm a tendency among the British settlers on the Pacific to exaggerate the menace — to themselves and to the wider British interest — of any single Russian man-of-war at hand. Of his corvette, *Bogatyr'*, for example, Popov was as critical as his essential love of armoured screw-corvettes would let him be. To Melbourne residents in March 1863, the *Bogatyr'* was a symbol and an omen: "For several hours, she had the shipping at the anchorage at her mercy." [8] Melbourne, certainly, had better reason to be apprehensive of the growth of Russian naval strength in the Pacific than had British Columbia.[9] Nevertheless, British Columbians were not outdone by the Australians' suspicion of, and readiness to magnify, whatever evidence they saw of Russian naval enterprise in the Pacific, that was, not along its northeastern extremity.

In British Columbia, these tendencies to magnify a modest present show of Russian strength while overlooking progress in Siberia, Amuria, and even Japan, where Russian men-of-war were virtually based by the mid-1870's,[10] came to a head during the Pauzino crisis (March to May 1877). By that year, as Captain Bax, R.N., of *Dwarf* had stressed to *his* superiors, and as Canadians at large could read,[11] the East Siberian flotilla had eleven ships, twelve hundred sailors, and its own shipyard and foundry. As for the place recently marked on British Admiralty charts as Port May, but which the Russians had renamed Vladivostok or "Ruler-of-the-East," it was in Bax's words "a deep, safe harbour . . . well capable of defence, which from its position with regard to Japan, the Corea and China will be a most important station." [12] Unconcerned by, if not ignorant of, moves to reinforce the East Siberian flotilla in the later 1870's and of the fact that the flotilla was distinct from the Pacific squadron but could always be released from coastal duty to enlarge it suddenly if necessary, British Columbian civil authorities and settlers had eyes only for ocean-going forces of the kind they associated with naval power on traditional, and British, lines. Popov's and Pauzino's squadrons were such forces, weak and slow though they might truly be by the contemporary standards of the major naval powers.[13]

More than anything since the appointment of the Grand Duke Constantine as the Grand Admiral of Russia and the crisis of the early 1860's, which had led to Popov's San Francisco visit and intensified the shipbuilding activity in Russia's Baltic yards, the Anglo-Russian crisis of 1878 fostered the Russian Navy's overall modernization and expansion, in the Black and Baltic Seas especially but also in the East and the Pacific. For the first time, Russia formed a squadron for Pacific duties, sent it to Japan, and undertook not to allow its strength to fall below one screw-corvette, two smaller cruisers (of the second class), and two support craft when in Russian coastal waters. Both the small cruisers and the screw-corvette were to be modern ironclads, well armed.[14] Initially, this squadron was comprised of *Afrika, ex-Saratoga, Vestnik,* and *Plastun'*. All three mounted quick-firing 37mm cannon, 6″-guns of German (Krupp) or Russian manufacture, and assorted smaller guns. The *Afrika*, of 2,800 tons, also had Whitehead detonating mines aboard.[15] From time to time over the next three years, the squadron was augmented by the presence of two more modern cruisers of the *Kreiser* class, like *Vestnik* and *Plastun'*, that is, of thirteen hundred tons. Based in Japan, it flew the flag of Rear-Admiral A. Aslanbegov (1822–1900).[16]

The strength of Aslanbegov's squadron or the Russian Navy's capability in the Pacific in the early 1880's should not be exaggerated. Both are put into correct perspective by a glance at the contemporary strengths of the American and British navies in the North Pacific basin[17] and at Russia's naval programme for the Baltic, where by June 1877 there were stationed and prepared for action twenty-four modern or fairly modern ironclads.[18] Always, the major Russian effort was at Kronstadt. Nor, even in 1881–82, was it the view of Admiral S. S. Lesovskii and the Russian naval staff that first-class ironclads, like the 10,000-ton *Petr Velikii* or the *Novgorod*, were needed or would probably be needed in the East or the Pacific. That Japan possessed two heavy ironclads and twelve or fourteen armed screw-steamers and was building up a navy fast was undeniable. Nevertheless, argued Lesovskii in April 1882, "Japan . . . does not yet make it necessary that we, for our part, keep modern first-class ships on station in Pacific waters." [19] Accepted by the government, his attitude was echoed by statistics and reports in which, significantly, mentions of Amuria, Japan, and the United States abounded, but allusions to Esquimalt and the British Northwest Coast — as Russia viewed British Columbia until the 1920's — did not. Twenty-nine new cruisers of the first or second class, it was resolved in April 1882, would be constructed for the Baltic fleet, and ten for Black Sea service. The Siberian flotilla would receive eight iron gunboats, six torpedo-carriers, and extra transports. Ships would not be built specifically for the Pacific squadron, but would be dispatched as necessary to sustain the strength-level agreed upon in the late 1870's. By that arrangement, Russia could reduce the risk of having a significant proportion of her active fleet reduced to impotence by enemy activity or by the Baltic winter ice and simultaneously answer the demands of naval training and morale. A few cruisers could always be at sea; and those on station in Japan could likewise look for extra safety in mobility. So, in the early 1880's, was confirmed the policy, tried out experimentally and fitfully during the 1870's, by which small ironclads were sent around the globe, in ones and twos, to show the flag, train naval companies, lend weight to Russia's presence on the littorals of Asia, and relieve or strengthen her Pacific squadron.[20] Aslanbegov, Commander-in-Chief on the Pacific station in Lesovskii's absence, made the most of that new policy and of the welcome opportunities for long-range cruising that it offered. His career, which had started in the age of sail and had bloomed in the Crimean War, when he had captured Turkish brigs, stood at Sevastopol as the commander of a battered frigate *El' brus*, and been decorated for his service as a gunner on the Malakhov Redoubt, was almost over.[21] He was not disposed to slip into retirement without one final, sweeping tour of the kind not only possible, but also natural, given the latest "cruising" policy and the considerable force at his disposal by the late summer of 1881. By August three cruisers of the *Kreiser* class were under his orders and ready to move — *Evropa, Afrika* and *Aziia* of the American-built steamers, and for good measure, two modern frigates, *Kniaz' Pozharskii* and *Gertsog Edimburgskii.*[22] In range, tonnage, and firepower, Aslanbegov's was the most impressive Russian squadron ever to have crossed the North Pacific and the first that — under other circumstances — might have ventured to attack Vancouver Island with a certain confidence. With this in mind, it is worth surveying the progress being made on the provincial coast defences and in British Columbia's militia companies during these years and to assess what interest the Russian government itself now took in them.

"CATTLE RANGE OVER THE PARAPETS" (1879-82)

Even by June 1879, Lieutenant-Colonel Houghton's warning of the previous September that Victoria-Esquimalt lacked the population necessary to maintain a rifle company and a "militia battery" and that the former was in danger of absorption by the latter had been borne out by the roll-call. Plans were made to hasten an apparently inevitable process by converting the Victoria Rifles into gunners. Soon, Victoria had three small batteries of garrison artillery, in fact, its own brigade.[23] Nevertheless, Lieutenant-Colonel Irwin's doubts were also justified: it proved impossible to serve all the new batteries in the Victoria-Esquimalt area efficiently, by manning them all continuously and with companies of regulation strength. The problem troubled Houghton greatly till, in mid-October 1880, he was moved to Military District No. 10, with headquarters in Winnipeg,[24] and exasperated his deputy, Captain Dupont, thereafter. Dupont, who had done well as local battery commander in Victoria, was only acting deputy adjutant-general from 1880 to 1883. Modest though Houghton's influence had been in Ottawa, Dupont's was considerably less. Not surprisingly under these circumstances, numbers and morale of the provincial militia, which the Anglo-Russian crisis had not only halted but reversed, declined unabated. Only in Victoria itself did the artillery retain its earlier enthusiasm and, indeed, remain a militarily effective force throughout these years of neglect.[25] But, as de Horsey had observed, no Russian raiding craft was *likely* to a sweep past Holland Point into the shallow harbour. What if Aslanbegov shelled Esquimalt from the south at dusk or even tried to burn New Westminster? Macaulay Point battery's earthworks were beginning to collapse for want of lateral protection. Worse, its guns were not ready for instant use:

There are no fences around the batteries and cattle range over the parapets and tramp them down; mischievous persons take out and throw away the quoins and tampions and fill the guns with sticks and stones, hence everything movable is taken away and kept under key.[26]

As for the Seymour Battery based at New Westminster, its guns were almost dangerous to use. The drill hall, where the infantry and gunners met for exercises and instruction, was in bad need of repair and would certainly have leaked intolerably but for funds donated by the town. Battery field-days and annual inspections now depressed Captain Dupont and the reporters of the *Mainland Guardian* equally. After a visit from Dupont, "The corps," noted the paper in November 1882, "were put through infantry and some gun drill, but owing to the *disabled* state of the guns it was impossible to work them." [27] Carriages were rotting, muzzles were rusty, and the local population was extremely critical. Small wonder that the G.O.C., Sir Edward Selby Smyth, shrugged off the Milne Committee's criticisms of his "home bored" and reconditioned smooth-bores and continued his experiments with the resource-saving expedient in Montreal (at the Gilbert arms plant) and in Kingston.[28] Clearly, Ottawa did not intend to channel extra funds to the Eleventh Military District and Dupont.

But what of progress with Esquimalt's graving-dock since October 1877, when the provincial government and Rear-Admiral de Horsey had united in reporting to Mackenzie and the Admiralty Board that such a dock was "of paramount importance" to the province and the regional strategic interest of Britain?[29] To summarize a chapter of (avoidable) miscalculations and resultant setbacks, the provincial government had undertaken something that it lacked the funds and expertise to finish in the stipulated time.[30] The dock was to be built by contract. The document was carelessly drawn up. Victoria was to receive regular subsidies from the dominion and British governments to lighten the financial burden of the project. But payments did not come with any regularity, and they were provided on conditions that changed from time to time. By 1881, the estimated building costs had trebled: vast amounts of masonry and concrete were required, since the Admiralty wanted the dock to be large enough to handle vessels of the *Nelson* class, of 7,320 tons. About the same tonnage of concrete was eventually poured into the basin. But by then, the public outcry and the findings of a special executive committee struck to look into the matter had resulted in the fall of Premier George Walkem's government. In April 1882, work on the dock stopped altogether during a twelve-week period of angry recriminations.[31] It was in this winter (1881–82) that Aslanbegov's squadron reached its full strength and began its North American and South Pacific tour.

Since at least 1876, the Russian government had been receiving such official publications as Canadian and Australasian annual militia and defence reports.[32] It was a function of the Russian naval staff especially to gather and collate all published and, indeed, unpublished works available on foreign naval strategy, resources, ships, and bases;[33] and, accordingly, its Scientific Board's librarian, as well as the research division of the Naval Minister, received a wide range of colonial, for example, Canadian, and British service-oriented periodicals and almanacs. These included blue books and gazettes, both unofficial and official, and the journals or proceedings of significant societies and institutes. Among the many British publications was the *Army and Navy Gazette*, in which, early in 1880, there appeared extracts from the last *Report on the State of the Militia of the Dominion of Canada . . . 1879*. The passages in question had been written by the G.O.C. and touched directly on the problem of defending Canada's Atlantic and Pacific ports and shipping lines against attack by Russian cruisers. Not surprisingly, so little time having elapsed since the Semechkin mission and the allocation of three modern cruisers of the second class, *Strelok, Plastun'*, and *Vestnik*, to Pacific duties, Russians took an interest in Selby Smyth's remarks. They were translated and reprinted, as an item headed "The Defence of Canada," in issue no. 7 of the Russian naval periodical *Morskoi sbornik* for 1880, and an extract follows:

In his report on the state of the Canadian militia for 1879, Lieutenant-General Sir Selby Smyth writes the following, *inter alia*: "Canada is short not only of arms for coast defence, but also of guns for coastal batteries. Not long ago, one foreign government adopted a peculiar system of armament with the object of conducting offensive operations against large merchant fleets; and this system demands very serious attention on the part of England and her colonies, Canada especially. . . . The system consists in the purchasing of many fast ocean-going steamers, which are then armed for warlike purposes. The object of these steamers in the event of a war, as everyone knows, is to burn and destroy the mercantile fleets of the richest State in the world. . . . However, there can be no doubt that these cruisers would soon be destroyed by the ocean-going steamers of England, Canada, and Australia, if the latter were similarly armed and fitted out for the purpose; and the British Admiralty has already in fact begun discussions with the Canadian Government on the subject of preparing large steamers to receive artillery, much as was done in the experiment with the steamer *Hecla*. So it remains for us only to concern ourselves about the rifled guns with which the steamers would need to be armed. At the moment, there are only fifteen such guns in Canada; but it is satisfying to know that we are in a position to manufacture them here. . . . The factory of Messrs. Gilbert proposes to turn out, by 1 May next, six 9″ (14-ton) rifled pieces, complete with sights, for $4,000 each; six 7″ (8½-ton) rifled guns for $3,000 apiece; two 90-pounder 5-ton guns, converted from 68-pounders, for $650 each; etc. . . ." According to Sir Selby Smyth, the Government of Canada has placed an order with Messrs. Gilbert of Montreal for two 7″ (8½-ton) guns and ten 64-pounder rifled pieces, all converted 32-

pounders. A start has thus been made in arming Canada with her own guns.[34] (author's translation)

The tenor of the piece was neutral, verging upon friendly. Even so, it was of interest to Russian naval officers — both those who would have remembered other articles in *Morskoi sbornik* that discussed the coal wealth of Vancouver Island[35] and others who were soon to visit it like Aslanbegov — that the coastal batteries of the Dominion were, for the moment, seriously understrength and that its government was satisfied with cheap, re-rifled guns. In Russia, where the military budget was traditionally large, other priorities obtained.[36]

A. B. ASLANBEGOV AND THE ANGLO-RUSSIAN NAVAL NEXUS

At the Imperial Naval Cadet Corps and throughout his early service years, Aslanbegov had been raised in the progressive and, though patriotic, also anglophile traditions of the celebrated circumnavigators of the early nineteenth century: I. F. Kruzenshtern, F. Bellingshausen, M. P. Lazarev, P. S. Nakhimov.[37] For a century at least, by the time he joined the corps, English and Scottish naval officers had played a fundamental role in the development of Russia's Baltic fleet.[38] Dozens of Russians had been trained, as volunteers, in the Royal Navy. I. F. Kruzenshtern, director of the corps in Aslanbegov's day, was one of these, and, as an officer who had in his youth met veterans of Captain Cook's last voyage,[39] he was regarded as a living link between *Discovery* and Kronstadt by his own cadets. Inevitably a youth like Aslanbegov, with his literary bent and exotic origin (the Muslim House of Aslan-Bey), grew extremely conscious of this ancient Anglo-Russian naval nexus which had gained in strength, if anything, in the Napoleonic age. To make it more so, his association with the ageing Kruzenshtern was followed by close contact with Nakhimov, in the early 1850's.[40] As a young lieutenant in 1822–24, Admiral Nakhimov had sailed with M. P. Lazarev, so incidentally calling at Hobart Town, Tasmania, where they were handsomely received by the colonial authorities.[41] Aslanbegov comforted Nakhimov as he died of a head wound on the Malakhov Redoubt, Sevastopol, in 1854. His dealings first with Kruzenshtern, then with Nakhimov, which were incidentally conducive to his ultimate professional success, also gave a pre-Crimean War days colour to his whole career. Aslanbegov was not uncomfortable on iron vessels: rather, his earlier experience had fixed his attitudes towards the naval life. His literary skill and choice of subjects, for example, a biography of A. S. Greig, son of the Greig whose victory at Chesme Bay over the Turks (1770) and Scottish modesty had smoothed his path to flag-rank at St. Petersburg and gained him the respect of Catherine the Great;[42] his tender care for ordinary seamen; his respect for, and his warmth towards, those British naval officers whom he encountered on his travels in the 1870's and 1880's; his acceptance and encouragement of technological advance, in navigational technique especially: all placed him firmly in an Anglo-Russian maritime tradition that was fading fast by 1850, and by 1880 was a fragment of the past.[43] Orders apart, his outlook predisposed him to report on British progress in Australia, where Russians had been civilly received since 1807,[44] in New Zealand, known to Russians through the *Voyages* of Cook and Captain Bellingshausen's narrative of 1831,[45] and — more important from the standpoint of the young maritime province — on the British Northwest Coast. He did so in a series of despatches, some of which were essay-like in form and style and immediately placed in *Morskoi sbornik* as he certainly intended that they should be.[46] One of these, sent to St. Petersburg from San Francisco on 24 August 1881, gave an account of his first "British-colonial" courtesy visit of the tour, at Esquimalt-cum-Victoria.[47] He had no need to visit either. He could well have made for San Francisco Bay directly in the *Afrika*, having already named it as his rendezvous with the commanders of *Plastun'* and *Vestnik*. *Afrika* herself was not in need of the repair facilities of the Esquimalt naval yard.[48] He called because he wished to do so, in a spirit of essentially unwarlike, though pragmatic, curiosity.[49]

THE VISIT OF THE RUSSIAN CRUISER "AFRIKA" (AUGUST 1881)

Afrika anchored in Constance Cove, Esquimalt, at approximately 8 P.M. on Wednesday, 13 August 1881, after an uneventful passage from the former Russian post of Unalaska. By agreement with the "Port Captain," "the usual salutes and visits" were postponed until the morning. The provincial government and the lieutenant-governor, Cornwall, were notified by naval courier of Aslanbegov's presence which, however, caused no panic in Victoria. Relations between Russia and Great Britain were correct in 1881 despite the former's efforts to regain lost influence in the umbrageous new Bulgaria and British apprehensions of some military consequence of the *Dreikaiserbund* just reaffirmed between St. Petersburg, Vienna, and Berlin. The *Afrika* expected, and was given, an hospitable reception at Esquimalt.

Aslanbegov's first impression of the place, to judge by his report, was highly favourable. It was safe and spacious — so spacious, indeed, as to produce a new impression: one of under-use, almost of emptiness. Two British warships stood in Constance Cove with *Afrika*, the ten-year-old ram-bowed corvette *Thetis* and *Rocket*, whose service as the "local" gun vessel went back to 1868. No other naval craft were to be seen, nor were there merchantmen arriving or departing. Rear-Admiral Sir Frederick Stirling, Commander-in-Chief on the Pacific Station, and the best part of his squadron, were at Callao in Peru. They had been gone several weeks and they were not expected back until October. Nor was *Thetis* planning any sudden movement, since her topsail was under repair and her spars being examined by the foreman of the Admiralty Yard. It was, in sum, a tranquil scene. If there was little visible human activity even about the coal wharf or on Duntze Head, the Russians realized by midday on 14 August, there was no *in*visible activity. The *Afrika* could coal at any time, for $9 a ton, using her own people as labourers and boatmen. Similarly, canvas could be mended in the yard ashore, with minimal assistance from the local workforce. Aslanbegov put his men to work and, with a group of officers, called on the lieutenant-governor. His favourable first impression was confirmed by his reception, by the new road to Victoria through handsome stands of timber, and most of all by the abundance and cheapness of provisions, ("excellent meat at 7½ cents per English pound weight, bread for 4½ cents, vegetables for 1¼, and abundance of various sorts of fish"). With the commander and officers of *Thetis* and *Rocket*, he discussed the prospects of the province, taking notes on what he heard and saw. Much of the talk, it seems, was of the incomplete dry-dock, at which he looked attentively, and of the C.P.R.:

> The Vancouver Island station may justly be called an excellent one. . . . But hitherto, this port has been of very modest political and financial significance. Now, with the building of the dock and, especially, the completion of a railway, it is acquiring first-rate mercantile significance and may stand on an equal footing, among the English colonies, with Singapore and Hong Kong. It is impossible not to be envious and to say that, unfortunately, Vladivostok, Castries, Dui and Korsakov fell to our lot — places with a severe climate . . . constant mists, all manner of shortcomings including an absence of steamer and mail communications. It would have been good to have just one spot like Vancouver.[51]

Aslanbegov made a point of learning what he could from the obliging British officers and settlers about Vancouver Island coal. During his visit or a little time before it, the coaler *Bercar* reached Esquimalt from Nanaimo. The local gold and timber industries also arrested his attention, and he noted down statistics. Gold-mining, he learned, had once driven the Island population up to 30,000. Now, in 1881, it stood at 6,000. His feeling that the place was short of men was thus confirmed, as it was also when, escorted by the "Port Captain" and certain of the *Afrika*'s own officers, he inspected the Admiralty Yard. In Russia's Asian ports, there was no want of manpower, but all types of equipment and machinery were constantly in short supply and/or outmoded. Here, the situation was reversed:

> I carefully examined the Admiralty Yard on Vancouver [Island], which is situated on the cape opposite the entry beacon. It contains, in miniature, every possible sort of workshop; but warships in need of repairs send their own people to them; and in the sail-room I came on sailors from *Thetis* who were mending their mainsail. . . .

As to stores in the naval magazines, the Admiralty Yard is so well supplied that it can furnish all the requirements, not only of the Particular Service and Pacific squadrons, even with regard to guns, but of squadrons twice as large. On the shore lay three 9″ guns and ten 7″ guns, all muzzle-loaders; and the Port Captain said that they have in reserve one gun and one mount of the appropriate type for each vessel sent to the station. . . . Apart from the fleet depot itself, there are also rifles, guns and gun-carriages, revolvers, broadswords, and shells in considerable quantity, together with an entrenching tool for the land command. The powder and bombs ready for use are kept on the little island in the inlet facing the Yard. On the adjacent hill stands a mast up which the flag is raised. By it stand four little cannon and the only armed sentinel in the entire port. In Victoria there is a small battery which, in the absence of all ships-of-war, can reply to salutes. There are no soldiers on Vancouver Island, though a colonel known as an inspector is attached to its administration. They say that when soldiers are needed, they will be sent.

Aslanbegov did not disapprove of such arrangements, at least for a foreign "colony," as he considered British Columbia to be. But he evidently thought them curious. It was as if Esquimalt had been well equipped but still awaited the arrival of the necessary personnel. Small though it was, with beds for only forty men, the naval hospital (the old "Crimea huts") seemed spacious and expectant. Like the store-rooms and the workshops, it was neatly organized and competently run — for the benefit of men far off in South America or the Pacific Islands. In itself, the spectacle of 9″ guns lying ashore, unmounted and apparently unwanted, was impressive to the visitor; but it was also odd.

Less odd, in view of recent Anglo-Russian tensions, was the local and dominion authorities' attempt to build a dry-dock large enough for ships of 7,000 tons. Yet here, too, Aslanbegov was impressed by the *futurity* of the design, important though it obviously was to the whole province. Work proceeded slowly, less for want of funds than for want of gangs of labourers:

> The dock will be 400′ long, 90′ wide, and when flooded will hold 26½′ of water. The cost was estimated at 500,000 dollars, but it is now supposed that it will really cost not less than a million. . . . It was proposed to complete the dock within three years; but even the construction engineer in charge of the project doubts if it is possible to finish it in less than five years from now.

Certainly, there was no hint of nervousness in Aslanbegov's hosts' admissions that the port was sometimes empty, that the Island had no troops, that such a dock was far from ready. On the other hand, the *Afrika* herself drew larger crowds of curious colonials each day, including several reporters from the mainland:

The reception given us by Governor Cornwall and the residents of Vancouver Island was most cordial. The newspaper reporters praised the cruiser daily: in their opinion, a better ship had never been seen at Vancouver Island, and they indicated her speed as 15 knots. And visitors came out to us every day. Finally, on Sunday 16 August, there emerged from Victoria Bay a steamer that 400 or 500 of the public had hired in order to be able to inspect a Russian cruiser. The steamer went round us several times. The public waved hats and hand-kerchiefs with sympathy, and, by way of response to their manifestation [of friendliness], we played music all the time.[52]

How was such confidence, together with such obvious unreadiness to cope with any foreign enemy, to be explained? Firstly, no doubt, in terms of overall British superiority at sea, a certainty that any enemy who did land troops or shell the port would soon be brought to task by British ships. But there was something else at work in this "most cordial" reception that Victoria accorded Aslanbegov, in the visit to the Admiralty Dockyard, in the hat-waving and friendly contacts on the *Afrika* and *Thetis*: the impossibility of not appearing confident as well as cordial. That certain local residents felt deep misgivings at the sight of an efficient Russian cruiser, notwithstanding all the music on her deck and in the public gardens of Victoria, is evident from newspaper reports in which her armament is thoroughly described and mention made of the inadequate provincial coast defences.[53] That not all the British and Canadian officials who received or were received by Aslanbegov and his officers felt unadulterated cordiality towards them and the state they represented is apparent from remarks made publicly twenty months later by the former deputy adjutant-general of the Canadian Militia, J. W. Laurie. Laurie, a candidate for Selby Smyth's post as G.O.C. in 1884, a long-term resident of Canada (where he had actually farmed for twenty years and made politically important friends while on the active list),[54] and a lifelong Russophobe, had been on service in Victoria in August 1881. He had been formally invited to inspect the *Afrika* and did so on the morning of the fifteenth with a mixed party of naval and militia officers. His subsequent remarks, it is important to observe, were made when relations between Russia and Great Britain were again becoming tense and many Englishmen were troubled by the armaments already stockpiled by Russia, France, and Germany in obvious anticipation of a European war to be fought over the Balkans. There was therefore some temptation to make much of Russian military strength and past belligerence. Laurie possibly succumbed to it to some extent: he was a "plausible" and ready speaker and responded to the jingoistic spirit of the day in a "self-asserting" manner that Sir Edward Selby Smyth disliked.[55] Nevertheless, Laurie was not merely fantasizing in April 1883 when he said of Russian military preparations in the northeastern Pacific:

It is quite clear that these preparations are not made as against the United

States. . . . The conclusion therefore forces itself upon one, that but one antagonist is regarded as possible, the only other great Power with large interests and large possessions in that ocean, that is, Great Britain. I am the more confirmed in this from the tone of the Russian officers with whom we were brought in contact during a visit paid to Victoria (or rather to Esquimalt) by the Russian flagship "Africa," one of the converted merchant steamers. We were courteously shown over her, her armament pointed out, the expenses of conversion and strengthening discussed, a small matter of $272,000 or £55,000; she carried guns equivalent to our converted 32–64 pounders and was, of course, stated to be satisfactory; but the whole tenor of the conversation was that she was intended to be used against us. . . . She was in every way associated in their minds with a possible, almost a probable, war with "you English," and decently masked but hardly concealed expressions of regret fell from them that war had not resulted, as they felt they were in a position to do us much damage. I stood it for a time, but . . . looked up at the ensign, the St. Andrew's cross, and remarked that . . . I had not seen it since it was flying in the harbour of Sevastopol.[56]

Unconscious of, or at least untroubled by, such feelings on the part of officers long settled in or serving Canada, but whose experience of the Crimean War or more contemporary Anglo-Russian crises led them to consider Russia as the natural and worldwide rival of Great Britain in the future,[57] Aslanbegov left Esquimalt on 18 August. Winds were gentle and the sea was still. The *Afrika* was out of sight by noon.[58]

NEW ANGLO-RUSSIAN STRAINS AND THEIR PROVINCIAL IMPLICATIONS (1882–83)

Simmering through the 1870's and 1880's, Anglo-Russian problems more than once came to the boil. When they did so, steam was visible on the Pacific rim of Canada; and geographical remoteness, which had once prevented colonists from seeing them, now magnified the clouds that hung by Europe. 1881 brought news of Russian victory at Geok Teppe on the Afghan borderland and of continuing expansion in the south of Central Asia. From the far side of the world, it seemed inevitable that a Russian army would advance, sooner or later, to the Khyber Pass and so put pressure on the British Raj in India. It was an attitude that partly sprang from, and itself enhanced, a consciousness of military setbacks that together seemed to indicate a serious decline in British fortunes. In southern Africa, there had been routs (Isandlhana, 1879) and large defeats (Majuba Hill and Laing's Nek, 1881) that had sapped morale and undermined British prestige in Europe and America. In Asia, there had been the general withdrawal from Kabul (1879), followed by carnage that was widely held in London to have triggered off the latest

Russian effort in or by Afghanistan. To balance Wolseley's welcome victory in Egypt (Tel-El-Kebir, 1882), defeats were imminent. Above all, there was recognition in Great Britain and her colonies that half-a-dozen European states were on collision path and that, if war broke out over Bulgaria and Serbia between the European powers, it was probable that Britain would be drawn into the fray — and not on Russia's side.[59]

As was their duty, the provincial press and government of British Columbia assessed the likely implications of a war that pitted England against Russia. By and large, they doubted neither that the Russians would use their fast cruisers as commerce-raiders in the North Pacific, nor that the Macdonald government in Ottawa would turn a deaf ear to new requests to strengthen the militia and the coastal batteries. This being so, discussion of the impact of a war revolved essentially around the issues of the dry-dock and the C.P.R., to which Macdonald, paradoxically, was pointing as Canadian responses to immediate as well as longer-term imperial and west coast problems, that is, as responses to the Russian naval threat in the Pacific, if in fact there was one.[60] Even those who approved the work stoppage of April 1882 — in their outrage at the escalating cost — could see that the Esquimalt naval base could not develop fully till the dry-dock was complete. Only by rail could supplies and troops be sent quickly enough in an emergency to be of military significance. But it was here that provincial unanimity gave way to partisan contention. Was it wise to have the railway terminus at Burrard Inlet, as was planned at one point, and not at, say, Port Moody, which was more defensible? Was it strategically correct to have that terminus, the naval depot, and the vital source of coal (Nanaimo) at three separate points? If not, why should the C.P.R. not be extended to Esquimalt, or the naval base removed to Burrard Inlet? Who should pay for what? Hardly surprisingly, the *Mainland Guardian* threw its weight behind the C.P.R. and argued for its swift completion (at Port Moody) in the context of an imminent major Anglo-Russian clash. No less predictably, the *Daily Colonist* spoke for Victoria-Esquimalt. Colomb's thought was reconsidered in a changed context of continental rail-links and growing Russian confidence at sea.[61] Coincidentally, but symbolically, a visit to the province by the new governor general, the Marquis of Lorne, and the resultant understanding between province and Dominion regarding the Esquimalt dock (November 1882) precisely marked an upswing in explicit anti-Russian items in the local press.[62] Here, to illustrate the partisan debate then being carried on between Victoria-Esquimalt and New Westminster and a resurgent, cruiser-centred, Russophobia, are extracts from the *Mainland Guardian* editorial for 18 November 1882:

> Russia and France are on the eve of war; where and on what pretext the war will begin, it would be difficult to decide . . . but the opportunity will arise when the preparations are complete. They have both boundless resources in men and money: Russia is richer than the world would fain believe. . . . The

fleets of both Powers are being rapidly strengthened and war material is being piled up in limitless quantities. All this points to a terrible war. . . .

The policy of attacking a nation at her extremities was clearly brought home to Russia by the Crimean War. It is needless to say that she will attempt to inflict the same experience on England, and will doubtless launch her cruisers . . . on British Columbia, Australia and New Zealand. In Australia, the proper precautions are being taken, and we will doubtless be equally favoured in course of time. This Province will always be the refitting station for the fleet in the North Pacific, and will be the great depot for prizes. . . .

How about the Esquimalt Graving Dock that the *Colonist* and its clique have done everything to put a stop to? The dock . . . should most certainly be constructed, without a moment's delay. We need hardly say that not only the rivalry of the North Pacific, but the Imperial Government through the federal authorities, are spurring the C.P.R. Co. to complete their line. . . . Our readers may have some idea of the importance of Port Moody in the near future, and the absurdity of constructing the terminus of a great railway such as the Canadian Pacific in such an exposed position as English Bay or Coal Harbour.[63]

Thus were notes struck ten years earlier by Colomb, de Horsey, and Mackenzie[64] struck again, with disharmonious effect, by a provincial press more conscious now than earlier of the financial weight of local vested interests. As more than once before, it was to take more than the *prospect* of a war to halt such sniping, let alone to rouse the government in Ottawa to action where the west coast and its Russian bogey were concerned.[65] Such matters hardly figured in Macdonald's "National Policy."

Among the British officers most vexed by the Macdonald government's insouciance towards the weak state of west coast's defences[66] and most dissatisfied with the apparent lack of progress in the talks between the British and dominion authorities about their future by the early weeks of 1883 were those whom Navy or Militia duty had at some time taken to Vancouver Island. Representative of older naval officers who now attended meetings of the Royal United Service Institution and the Royal Colonial Institute in London and who strove to draw public attention to the naval and imperial potential of Esquimalt were Sir Henry Codrington and Captain Bedford Pim. Militia officers, and those who had completed special military assignments at Victoria for the imperial and/or dominion authorities, were represented by such men as Majors-General Laurie and Crossman.[67] At his own suggestion, Laurie read a paper in the R.U.S.I., on 6 April 1883, entitled "The Protection of Our Naval Base in the North Pacific."[68] Pim and Crossman were among the audience.

Laurie, who had fought in the Crimean War and was a lifelong Russophobe,[69] had only recently retired from the post of deputy adjutant-general of the Canadian

Militia. Like Crossman, he had paid a lengthy visit to Victoria in 1881, and he had discussed Esquimalt's weaknesses and strengths both with Dupont and with the officers of *Triumph*, Rear-Admiral F. Stirling's flag-ship. He was known to have politically important friends in Ottawa, including Sir Charles Tupper, and he was eloquent.[70] For all four reasons, he was listened to attentively even by men who smiled at his argument for the abandonment of the Esquimalt naval yard.

That argument revolved around three points. Esquimalt base was virtually indefensible against attack by foreign ships. Even to make it relatively safe, as it should obviously be as Britain's sole Pacific base and depot, would require an immense expenditure from which the Lower Mainland might not benefit. And even if the Esquimalt base were properly defended, the Nanaimo coal mines and the Burrard Inlet railway terminal would be exposed to hit-and-run attacks:

> We thus, by retaining Esquimalt as our naval station, expose ourselves to one of two alternatives: for by leaving it in its present open and unprotected state, it is certain to be destroyed at the outbreak of a war, but by undertaking a very heavy charge in permanent works and garrison, we . . leave our coal and railway communications unguarded. . . . It is from consideration of all this that I am led to recommend that our naval depot at Esquimalt be abandoned, and that one be established at Burrard Inlet.[71]

Burrard Inlet, noted Laurie, was "immediately opposite" Nanaimo. Not only would a Russian raider be observed while in the Strait of Georgia and before he reached the coal supply, therefore; he would also be attacked by British ships from Burrard Inlet. True, Victoria would suffer temporary losses from the move. But even *its* security and longer term prosperity would be increased by a secure naval base and railway terminal. There was no justice in the current condemnation of the works quickly put up by Colonel Irwin or the subsequent report by Colonel Lovell, since both had had instructions that removed "the power of recommending that Esquimalt was practically indefensible with the means at command, or likely to be furnished, and that another site . . . might be substituted."[72] Irwin's earthworks, added Laurie, had reminded him of hill forts on the Indian sub-continent. Attacked head-on, and at the gate, they were quite strong, but if attacked at *any* other point they fell at once because their walls were so dilapidated. By analogy, why should a Russian not "betake himself behind Clover Point or to Ross Bay," thus avoiding the coastal batteries to storm Victoria? No guns covered its rear — though, indeed, the batteries that were to cover the Esquimalt Harbour front would cover its approaches more effectively than they could cover shipping in Esquimalt roads:

> And vessels lying in the harbour, instead of in any way being able to cover the dockyard . . . would have it between them and their assailants and would

actually have to fire over or through the dockyard in order to assist in its defence. . . . Any hostile cruizer lying off at such a distance as would expose it to small risk of injury from the 9-ton gun at Brother's Island, could put shell into the naval yard and utterly destroy it. . . . Yet . . . the efficiency of the squadron stationed so far from the home dockyards must largely depend on its depot.[73]

For the speaker and his listeners, it went almost without saying that the "hostile cruizer" would be Russian. So convinced was Laurie of the fact that he inclined to look on even the Canadian Pacific Railway as a contributory factor to the likelihood of future Russian raids. It was a curious reversal of Macdonald's argument that the completion of a continental rail-link, by which supplies and ammunition could be poured to the west coast in a crisis, would decrease the danger of such raids. And yet, it apparently struck his audience as no less logical than his assertion that the shift of Russia's naval and imperialist efforts from the Black Sea region to the Far East was itself a pledge of coming confrontation between Russia and Great Britain in the North Pacific, where the Royal Navy was already at a dangerous strategic disadvantage. In an international atmosphere of nervous expectation and manoeuvring ("the nations," as the *Mainland Guardian* put it, "are becoming *fidgety* under their heavy loads of armour"),[74] even sober men saw trouble lurking behind every bush and headland:

The Canadian Pacific Railway . . . will at present rate of progress be completed in 1885, and if but a tithe of the expectations it has aroused are realized, an enormous trade from the so-called Far East will be carried on in British ships, and throughout over British territory, thus multiplying our responsibilities in that quarter. Every act points to the intention of Russia to remove her chief naval depot from the land-locked Euxine and Baltic . . . to Vladivostock, on what is practically an open coast, whence her fleets can run out as opportunities offer and work untold mischief. . . .

We often describe our increase of empire by the following process: first the missionary, then the trader, and lastly the man-of-war to protect the interests thus created; but Russia has struck another line, at least in her settlements in Eastern Asia. There, the man-of-war came first, and so far the trader has not followed; in other words, those settlements are exclusively military and . . . they can only be created for aggression.[75]

Laurie spoke *à thèse*. Though not a scholar like Sir John Colomb and certainly no student of the early growth of Russian influence in the Far East like Ravenstein, he fully realized that his analysis of the position in the North Pacific basin was simplistic.[76] So, to judge by their responses to his lecture, did the naval officers who heard him out, notably Bedford Pim and Admiral Sir Leopold M'Clintock,

F.R.S.[77] The point, however, is that widely though the speaker and his audience might differ on the matter of establishing a base at Burrard Inlet and on various related points, they were at one in the presumption that the enemy was Russia and was likely to remain so. "Russia cannot *exist* without war, and her armaments are now on such a scale that she must use them, or they will be turned upon herself.").[78] To illustrate, here are extracts from the comments made on Laurie's talk by Captain Pim and the geographer and Orientalist, C. Pfoundes:

> With regard to moving the strategical point from Esquimalt to Burrard's Inlet, I am hardly prepared to go with him there. . . . But I quite agree that the position of the forts is simply absurd. . . . I think it was in February 1877 that I brought a question before the House of Commons with regard to eleven Russian vessels. . . . From San Francisco last year, upwards of a million tons, not quarters, of grain came to this country. With light and active cruisers, nothing could be easier than to cut that supply.[78]

Pfoundes, too, had reservations about giving up Esquimalt base for Burrard Inlet. His solution to the problem was impractical perhaps, or would at best have been a palliative, temporary measure; but at least it was original, even prophetic, and addressed itself to the approaching day when Britain would, in Pim's own words, "really not have the command" of the Pacific:

> Some bond of unity with Japan, if our authorities could see fit to enter into a treaty of offence and defence against the Russians, would be of immense advantage. . . . I believe they would make splendid auxiliaries, or allies, both ashore and afloat. . . . Japan is a nation of nearly 40,000,000 of people, who have at their disposal, at the present moment, very valuable resources . . . important machinery, several large and well-appointed docks and arsenals . . . and are likely to have some of still more importance, so that if we will only protect them from the Russians the day may come when they will be very valuable to us.[79]

Representing Canada on the occasion of the Laurie talk, albeit unofficially, was Sir Alexander Galt. As he believed he should, Galt saw that Ottawa received a copy of the printed text of an "extremely able paper" by a general with influence in London as in Canada.[80] The gesture was fruitless. Like the Lovell and the Strange reports, Colonel Crossman's memoranda, and Carnarvon's volumes, Laurie's work was promptly shelved by the Macdonald government. Laurie himself was shortly afterwards passed over for G.O.C. of the Canadian Militia. As a consolation, he was sent with Middleton, who beat him out for the post, to crush the 1885 North-West Rebellion.[81]

THE GENERAL OFFICER COMMANDING THE MILITIA

Discussions and events of the early 1880's made it obvious that Canada and Britain viewed the question of the west coast's defence against external enemies quite differently. In particular, Esquimalt was the focus of their differences. British politicians thought it just that the Canadians should help defend the place, which was in Canada and of significance to the Dominion as well as the Empire. The very fact of British interest in the Victoria-Esquimalt region, on the other hand, and the imperialist sentiments of most Canadian militia officers who had connections with the west coast during that period, disposed most members of the House in Ottawa to treat the question of defences there as expediently British in its scope, and so not Canada's responsibility. British Columbia thus paid for Britain's presence at Esquimalt in the currency of federal neglect, the sacred C.P.R. apart.

This unfortunate division of responsibility was duplicated, far more dangerously for dominion security, in the Militia. British G.O.C.'s were in a practically impossible position, serving two masters at the overall expense of the efficiency, morale, and very future of their corps. Holding a Queen's commission as well as an appointment under Ottawa, such men as Middleton had periodically to choose between their duty to the Crown (and to their own career prospects) and to Canada. Among the awkward issues that arose between the G.O.C. and ministers of the Militia, not a few of whom were French Canadian and so the representatives of a profoundly *un*imperialist part of the Canadian electorate, were disciplining of Canadians, the shortfall of appropriations for militia use, and patronage of a distastefully political variety. Macdonald personally, it was widely known, regarded the militia funds as bribery, reward, and hustings money. But such problems overlaid the more essential and more dangerous divergence between British G.O.C.'s and their political superiors' objectives. Always in the background was the question whether Canada was contributing as she could, or should, to the Dominion's security and to the military power of the Empire.

Broadly speaking, British G.O.C.'s in Ottawa's employ may be said to have concerned themselves more genuinely with Victoria's defence concerns than any cabinet in Ottawa. That fact was not to the immediate or longer-term advantage of Victoria.

FACING UP TO INTERNATIONAL CRISIS (1884–85)

Russia's occupation of the Merv oasis near the Afghan borderland early in 1884 and the resultant heightening of Anglo-Russian tensions were reported in the British Columbia press, over the next three months at least, in very much the same imperialist, lofty tones that had been used eight years before in accounts of Balkan military and diplomatic strife.[82] Russian advances in that quarter of the globe, the

Daily Colonist and *Mainland Guardian* both asserted bluntly, were a logical response to Gladstone's "Little England" policies, of which the recent fate of Gordon in Khartoum had proved the underlying danger. "If Lord Beaconsfield were now Prime Minister," both newspapers and a majority in the provincial government believed, "Russia would be summoned not to stop at Merv, but to leave it."[83] Even so, there was no danger of a Russian occupation of Afghanistan, still less of an advance on India, "because it is there that England is strongest. . . . But she might foment rebellion and revolt in Afghanistan, in order to cause annoyance and expense to England."[84] Russia's game, in other words, was to distract John Bull in Central Asia while pursuing her traditional designs against the Porte. In the end, both west coast newspapers supposed, war might erupt over the Balkans once again: it seemed impossible that England would be "hood-winked" by the tsar as Mr. Gladstone was and that "the Muscovite's wily diplomacy" would triumph.[85] But was war so terrible a thing? British Colum-bians, to judge both by the press and by debates being conducted in the legislature at the time, were not disposed to think so in the early part of 1884.[86] During the pleasant summer months, they shared the Ottawans' unwillingness to think at all about such things, unless a foreign raid was actually looked for as in June 1878. An Anglo-Russian Boundary Commission was at work in "Turkistan," doing its best to reach agreement on respective zones of influence and so avert an armed collision. Gladstone's Liberals were under fire from *The Times* and from an Opposition strengthened by the news from Central Asia. There was little to be done until the fall or till "the next move on the European chessboard" seemed to place British Columbians themselves at risk[87] beyond attacking Gladstone's "inca-pacity and blundering abroad." The *Mainland Guardian* in particular relished the task. The Lower Mainland was Disraeli territory:

It often surprises us that the English people are so infatuated as to *allow* a senile, garrulous statesman like Gladstone to wield the destinies of an empire such as that of Great Britain. His ridiculous utopian notions of humanity are doing a great deal of mischief. . . . From the idiocy of Gladstone, Russia has been allowed to advance to within striking distance of India. . . . Imbecile ideas. . . . Radical poltroonery.[88]

In mid-September, in delayed response to the accumulated sombre news of months, a change came over *Mainland Guardian* editorials and letters where the Central Asian problem was concerned. The lofty tone and grandiose analyses of world events were not abandoned, certainly. Unlike the *Daily Colonist*, which had remained ever alive to the inadequacy of Victoria's defences and the likelihood that Russia would attack Vancouver Island, not the mainland, if she struck at all, the *Mainland Guardian* could still assert in March and April 1885 that, if an Anglo-Russian war *were* fought, it would "eventually" be a "blessing for humanity" since, letting poison out of "many ugly sores," it would enable them to heal and society to grow "upon a healthy basis."[89] What was changing by September was the willingness — encouraged by Sir John A. Macdonald's own approach to British ventures far from Canada and, more immediately, by the regional prosperity that the Canadian Pacific Railway had brought across the Rockies[90] — to regard the growing Central Asian problem as "imperial," yet lacking reference to the Esquimalt naval depot and the province or Dominion. It was a question of adjusting emphases, less in response to one specific piece of news than to collective commonsense. One might believe that "a great war would do much" to put Great Britain "in her former firm position at the head of nations";[91] but the fact remained that Russia could attack British Columbia more easily than Portsmouth — or Kabul. That being so, it seemed ridiculous towards the close of 1884 to claim, as the *Mainland Guardian* had in January, that an Anglo-Russian struggle would "do good in every respect." British Columbia would benefit from British dominance in Europe and from European "peace for many years," but it was not a part of Europe. Thus were lessons that had more than once been learned before, but rapidly forgotten, brought to mind by men whom Laurie and a dozen other writers had not interested in Amuria:

> Russia hates England because she is the only obstacle between the Muscovite and Constantinople. . . . O! if she could only strike England in some vital part, she would give almost anything but national existence. For this she is groping about, crawling through the grass in India. She has gone to enormous expense at Vladivostock, in the hope of one day pouncing upon Australia or Vancouver Island.[92]

Crisis broke on British Columbia, as on Great Britain, in the early spring of 1885. Russians moved into Afghanistan, challenging the value of the British protectorate. The Anglo-Russian Boundary Commission ceased its work. Russians and tribesmen skirmished, while the British government sent troops towards Herat. For thirty days, war seemed almost unavoidable. New Westminster was gripped by apprehensions as acute as those on the Victoria-Esquimalt coastline. As so often in the past, even the lieutenant-governor and the provincial cabinet had no idea of the whereabouts or strength of what was still thought of as Aslanbegov's squadron, and New Westminster was conscious of, and vexed by, its dependence on Victoria's ability and readiness to help it:

> Very proper attention is being paid to Victoria, Burrard Inlet and Nanaimo, in order to protect *them* from a possible attack of an enemy's war vessels, but nothing has yet been done, or even suggested, for the defence of New Westminster.
>
> Our present artillery consists of one gun and a half, which might be useful

to frighten the crows, but to oppose the landing of an invader would be productive of amusement. With proper defensive works, our volunteers — in the absence of regulars — would doubtless distinguish themselves; but in the absence of the needful artillery the best thing they could do would be to receive the enemy with bows instead of bullets. We hope . . . that the necessary precautions will be taken without delay, and render impossible the disagreeable contingency of having our beautiful city laid in ashes.[93]

On the Lower Mainland and Vancouver Island, the war scare reached its climax in the latter part of April. Of emergency precautions gladly taken by the ordinary colonists who, while they might not think a Russian shelling likely, fully recognized that one could burst upon them any day, suffice to mention practice charges with the bayonet; the forming of a temporary "Scottish home-guard" at Victoria; a doubling of telegraphic messages to Ottawa and San Francisco; and the installation of machine-gun posts behind Victoria, by a retired army colonel, with a view to keeping off the sudden overland attack described by Laurie two years before.[94] It was perhaps inevitable that the crisis should awaken latent fears of a Russo-American alliance to be sealed to the detriment of Canada in general and British Columbia especially. Such fears, after all, were a traditional ingredient of the Pacific Russian scare:

> Russia is ruled by the military — a horrible vampire which must be fed on foreign conquests. . . . While Gladstone has been chopping trees and indulging in some Homeric dream, Russia has been secretly burrowing in order to undermine the British Empire. . . . With a fair face and soft words, she has been stealing on like a deadly snake to reach striking distance, and so far as she has been able, to buy allies to assist her. . . . There is no part of the world where her largesse will be more lavishly distributed than in the United States, for two reasons: she can buy material of war and pay for the fitting out of privateers. . . . And she can strike England, or she thinks so, in her tenderest point by using the United States as her armory and as a means of destroying British commerce.[95]

By the end of April 1885, items of war news covered pages of the *Daily Colonist* and *Mainland Guardian*. Their tenor is reflected accurately by the following few lines from an article entitled, simply, "War":

> Those who wish to keep the peace and protect themselves should be always ready for war. . . . To arms! is not a foolish cry; but it would be a very silly sound tomorrow if a Russian frigate happened to be anchored in the river. To the citizens we say — Prepare for war. And remember the shame that would rest on you forever if you were forced to acknowledge that you are unfit to

defend yourselves. We are informed by good authority that in this city [New Westminster], there are not a hundred rounds of ammunition for the Volunteers.[96]

Well indeed might members of the Seymour Battery be sharpening their bayonets, while journalists exhorted their commander to look out his bow and arrows.

RESPONSES TO THE "AFGHAN" SCARE (1885–86)

The governments of British Columbia and Canada were two of many in the worried British Empire of April 1885 that cabled London for immediate advice about, and help with, new defence measures against the Russian men-of-war and privateers that were thought to be about to launch attacks upon colonial shipping or seaports.[97] Few had better reason to anticipate a cool response to their appeals. British Columbia had, after all, experienced a comparable threat within the past few years, yet was barely even manning guns, on crumbling defence works, that the British government had given it as loans or gifts, while the dominion authorities had paid no heed to numerous attempts by Britain to resolve the arguments that had surrounded the Esquimalt naval depot and Vancouver Island's southern coast defences since the later 1860's. The Dominion was not impoverished by war or famine, as some portions of the Empire might claim to be; yet it had skimped on its defences, on its coasts especially, because it counted on Great Britain, on the navy that the taxpayers of Britain had maintained, in such a crisis as had come.[98]

At least politically, the crisis proved Macdonald to have been correct in counting on the British in a British and imperial collision with a European naval power. Though frustrated by Canadian unwillingness to reinforce Vancouver Island's batteries, the British government conceded that its North Pacific interests were such as to necessitate immediate reaction to the messages from Canada. Accordingly, the new Colonial Defence Committee — a committee struck expressly for the purpose of considering imperial defence questions within the contexts of the present Russian and of future crises — sent an urgent memorandum on the matter of Esquimalt to the Admiralty Board, the War Office, and two or three other departments.[99] In it, the committee drew attention to the sorrily exposed state of Esquimalt which, the Admiralty still contended through Sir Astley Cooper Key, was an essential naval base. It passed in silence over Admiralty notes to the effect that it might be abandoned in a war as a majority of the Carnarvon Commission had, in fact, also proposed.

Specifically, the new committee recommended that marine mining equipment should be sent out to Esquimalt base at once and that the Admiralty should lend appropriate support vessels. Twenty years had elapsed since Rear-Admiral the

Honourable Joseph Denman, then the Commander-in-Chief, Pacific, had proposed that mines be strung across the entrance to Esquimalt Harbour.[100] His proposal, it was noted, had unfortunately been untimely. Now, however, both the stationary mine which could be detonated from the shore by an electric current and the Whitehead "fish" torpedo with its secret depth-hold mechanism, were reliable and instantly available in England. As was obvious, whatever steps were to be taken should be taken swiftly. Mines could be installed in all main harbours in the province, under naval supervision and would not prove too expensive.[101]

Admiral Sir Astley Cooper Key lent his support to the Colonial Defence Committee's mines proposal and had little difficulty in convincing his fellow sea lords of the need to send two kinds of vessel to the waters of Vancouver Island both to complement the mines and to alleviate the pressures on the Commander-in-Chief, Pacific, whoever he might be. A new appointment was expected any week.[102] The two varieties of warship were the armed mercantile cruiser of the *Afrika*, ex-*Saratoga* type (for temporary duties on a distant station, leaves might be taken from the Russians' and Americans' own books) and the torpedo boat. The former would protect the merchant shipping off the Northwest Coast that Russians might attempt to sink or capture, while the latter kept the Russians at a distance from the province.

Thanks in part to Aslanbegov's cruises and in part to printed works, Russian and other, the imperial authorities knew pretty well the range and speed of the potential Russian raiders in the North Pacific area in 1885. Movements of Russian ships en route for the Pacific were routinely telegraphed to London by an ever-spreading telegraphic network.[103] Thus, it was possible to identify and make allowance for potential reinforcements for the Russian squadron which might have to be coped with on the Northwest Coast, presumably by fast cruisers at sea. No Russian warship that could raid British Columbia or North Pacific shipping in the next few months, the Admiralty calculated, had a speed of more than thirteen knots. The armed mercantile cruisers therefore needed to make fourteen knots or better. Admiralty agents made suggestions. On 25 June, the steamers *Coptic* and *Britannia* were commissioned. *Britannia*, a fast passenger steamer, was immediately taken to Coquimbo in Chile and equipped with heavy guns.[104]

Neither *Coptic* nor *Britannia* was sent to sea against the Russians or to shepherd merchantmen in the Pacific. Peace negotiations with Russia proved successful ("War Cloud Disappearing," wrote the *Mainland Guardian* even on 16 May, in a leader that prefigured the dramatically simplistic headline story of the modern tabloid), so they were not needed. But the Admiralty went ahead with the dispatching of torpedo boats and mines to the Esquimalt base. Two 40-ton, first-class torpedo boats were bought from Chile and sailed up the coast under the escort first of *Pelican* composite sloop to Acapulco, then of *Satellite*, an elderly corvette due for retirement. The two were known as Nos. 39 and 40 or, alternately, *Swift* and *Sure*. At Esquimalt, they were overhauled and exercised. Dummy targets were destroyed by their efficient spar-torpedoes with a violence that gratified spectators and went far to reassure the nervous colonists. Subsequent mining demonstrations also pleased.[105]

Meanwhile, the Colonial Defence Committee's memorandum of 1 May, "Defence of Vancouver Island," had been sent for the attention of the government of Canada.[106] Ottawa received it without enthusiasm, for the Anglo-Russian crisis was abating by the middle of that month. What the committee was proposing, the Macdonald cabinet perceived, was more or less what the Carnarvon Commission had proposed in 1882. Canadians should build and pay for permanent defence works at Esquimalt and Victoria and man the garrisons, thereby enabling the Royal Navy better to protect British Columbia, that is, Vancouver Island *and* the mainland, as a whole.[107] Adolphe Caron, as minister responsible for the Militia and dominion defences, felt obliged to take the memorandum seriously, but he could reasonably claim to be preoccupied with other issues: the rebellion led by Louis Riel was under way, the G.O.C., Frederick Middleton, was on the Prairies, five thousand troops at least were in the field.[108] Doubtless, the protection of Vancouver Island was important, as the British government had often said. But it would have to wait until Riel had been destroyed and the rebellion put down: the western Indians and disaffected Métis, after all, were not chimeras like the west coast's Russian bogey. Not till November 1885, in the event, was Middleton requested to examine the Colonial Defence Committee memorandum of 1 May, Caron's response to it, and a collection of related documents, including militia and imperial reports, many of which were more than ten years old. His comments, when at length he made some, simply echoed those of Rear-Admiral F. Stirling and Lieutenant-Colonel C. F. Houghton of 1879. It would be well to send a hundred regular marine artillerymen to Esquimalt and to keep them there at the expense, not of Canadians, but of the British government. It was unlikely, after all, that Ottawa would start a war with Russia — or with any other nation that could trouble the good people of Esquimalt. The committee of the Privy Council liked the argument. A note, "On the Defences of British Columbia," declining to assume financial burdens of the size that the Colonial Defence Committee wished to place on all Canadians and questioning a policy whereby Great Britain would not answer for a British naval base, was sent to London.[109] It, too, was received with disappointment.

How did British Columbians themselves, potential sufferers as they unquestionably were, react to this persistent footdragging and parsimony on the part of the dominion authorities? Did memories of panic and acknowledged impotence in April not cause rage in May? Two illustrations will suffice to show how short the local memory of Russian-centred crisis was, and how indeed a basic readiness to turn a blind eye to the naval wars and crises of the future, of which Ottawa itself might have been proud, verged upon folly in a province that was savouring prosperity — and hungrily anticipating more of it.

The British Commander-in-Chief on the Pacific Station in the spring of 1885, Rear-Admiral John Baird, responded to the Afghan crisis by reviewing the defences of Esquimalt and proposing to Lieutenant-Colonel Holmes, then the provincial deputy adjutant-general, that among other things the coastal batteries of the Victoria-Esquimalt region should be linked by telephone. Holmes supported the idea and immediately sought permission to construct the necessary line from Colonel Walker Powell, the Canadian adjutant-general, who was in Ottawa. The news that local batteries would be connected with each other by a telephone-line, was received with pleasure in Victoria. Powell sent permission to proceed with laying, on 5 May, adding however that "of course" it should be stalled "unless war is actually declared." A thousand dollars was too grand a sum to spend, even on measures that would heighten the efficiency of all the coastal batteries, unless the Russians were on hand to justify it.[111] In Victoria, there was no outcry at this cancellation of a measure which, if put into effect, would have increased its own security appreciably.

At New Westminster, meanwhile, even hints that there had been slight progress in the Anglo-Russian peace negotiations and that units of the Anglo-Russian Boundary Commission were to press on with their interrupted work had led the *Mainland Guardian* to look on present international tensions, and the Anglo-Russian crises of the future, in an altered light. Its attitude was myopically self-centred. Not only was the province to draw economic benefit from Anglo-Russian tensions that would keep the Royal Navy in its harbours; it was also to be socially embellished by the families of Royal Navy officers who were engaged in raids on Russia's Asian ports:

> During a war of the magnitude of a struggle between England and Russia, in which other nations were involved, this Province would form a great centre of attraction. It would be the greatest resort of vessels, not only British, for coals and provisions. The fact of its being such a rendezvous would induce numbers of people to come here to reside. . . . Our position here will be the best in the world. . . .
>
> In case of captures, the prizes will all be brought here and most of them sold. The prize money will be spent and our traders reap the harvest. . . . Troops and munitions of war will arrive [at Port Moody] for despatch on expeditions to the Russian ports on the Pacific, and residences for the officers and their families will soon adorn the beautiful environs of the port.[112]

In short, the Russian bogey was dismissed, and it was time to reinforce the British bogey in the northeastern Pacific. Such assertions no doubt boosted morale in a notoriously ill-defended region of a province whose militia was dependent on Esquimalt for its heavy ammunition and whose gun platforms and carriages were literally rotting.[113] In the context of contemporary naval and imperial realities, they were unconscionable nonsense, demonstrating ignorance not only of the rapid growth of Russian naval strength but also of the relative decline of British power on the high seas in relation to the hypothetically combined strength of the leading foreign navies. Gone already by the middle 1880's was the time when Britain could maintain her old "two-power standard," that is, run a navy stronger than the navies of the second and the third sea powers, without debilitating effort and expense. It was ridiculous, in fact, to shout that "Britain must be able not only to beat Russia, but to defy every Power in the world."[114] Even in 1884–86, Britain's dominion at sea was being probed, if not yet challenged, by the German high-sea fleet. Comparatively speaking, Russia posed a minor threat to the *Imperium Britannicum* and to its commerce overseas; but even Russia was continuously building up her navy, as the British Admiralty recognized but as the jingoistic daily press of British Columbia and ministers in Ottawa would not.[115]

STALLING ON DEFENCE INTO THE 1890'S

Affected by the same tensions and Anglo-Russian crises as Canadians, the representatives of Australasian colonies had been discussing naval defence among themselves since 1880. At a colonial conference in London in 1887, they were ready to commit their fellow-colonists to making monetary contributions to a Royal Navy squadron which would in effect be stationed on the coasts of New South Wales and Victoria for the protection of their shipping. (New Zealand, recognizing this, pulled out and went her own independent way.) Canada's representatives, who acted less like delegates than North American observers at the conference, made no such offer or initiative despite the fact that Canada's shipping and other trade was larger and more valuable than Australia's. The notion of a British squadron stationed permanently at Canadian expense in Canada was no more palatable in the late 1880's than in 1867. In the first place, the United States would be aroused, and in the second, the Dominion could not afford it.

Over the next several years, the Colonial Defence Committee did its utmost to encourage the authorities in Ottawa to strengthen the dominion defences and improve existing military co-operation. Sir Adolphe Caron, Macdonald's minister for the Militia, was urged to set up a permanent Canadian Defence Commission with the worrying events of 1885 in mind. He would not do so. Nor, in cabinet, would he exhort his colleagues to reform and build up the Militia. Absence of apparent foreign threats to Canada and concentration on the more absorbing and rewarding problems of expanding the economy drew force out of the arguments of militarists and imperialists for increased defence expenditure. Only in 1888 did Caron belatedly report to the House of Commons in response to a demand for information about government reaction to a half-a-dozen British queries, some dating back to 1880, about Canada's defences in the context of imperial defence.

Caron observed that the Dominion had spent some $27 million on defence since 1867, asserted that the sole naval defence Canada needed was the fisheries protection service, and dismissed the fact that European powers such as Germany and Russia were becoming stronger on the high seas every year. He conceded that torpedo weapons seemed to warrant study as an economical, efficient means of protecting the Atlantic and Pacific ports against bombardment by, say, Russian cruisers, but insisted that the matter be referred to a defence committee to consist of the G.O.C., inspector of artillery, adjutant-general, and commandant of the new college at Kingston. British officers, in other words, would not take part in a Canadian discussion. The committee met in 1888 and asked for terms of reference in writing. These were not forthcoming. The committee never met again. By shrewd procrastination, Caron personally and Macdonald's government at large thus buried the questions of the proper and acceptable dominion contribution to imperial defence and, more unfortunately in the longer term, the means of even building up Canadian defences.

These policies were no more unacceptable to the Canadians in general during the 1890's than they had been in other times. Imperialist sentiment was strong in certain quarters, certainly, and nowhere stronger than in Denison's Toronto and, inevitably, at Victoria-Esquimalt. Most Canadians, however, were by no means willing to abandon a traditional, profoundly liberal non-militarist attitude and genuine distaste for standing armies and the gathering of weapons, in the grand cause of imperial — or even national — unity. Stephen Leacock might elect to be an imperialist because he would not be a colonial, and hundreds more might see imperialism as a natural extension of Canadian awareness of Canada's great future in an Empire that she could ultimately dominate. But, for thousands of Canadians, the fact remains imperialist sentiment was militarist sentiment, and both were to be kept under control by application of Macdonald's National Policy — by economic growth, new industry, tariffs, and railways. The whole cause of defence on the Pacific Coast was compromised by its association, physically embodied by the Royal Navy vessels at Esquimalt, with imperialist objects and imperial defence. It therefore languished with Canadian imperialist propaganda — propaganda that was finally to leave so slight a mark on the emergent nationalism of the country. Russian naval strength thus made no impact on Canadians at large, who were determined not to be impressed.

To what extent they and the government in Ottawa were ready to *dismiss* the Russian factor in a new power equation in the North Pacific Ocean, and implicitly to recognize Vancouver Island's indefensibility against attack either by Russia or by Russia's likely allies, in the age succeeding all *Dreikaiserbunden*, Russo-German "kissing and embracing" and the like,[116] became apparent in the latter part of 1888. In that year, France and Russia deliberately moved towards economic, military, and naval understanding and collaboration. British apprehension grew apace when a successful Russian loan, floated in Paris with official French encouragement, was followed by a giant Russian order for French rifles. An alliance was emerging. It was time for stocktaking in naval armaments. The 1889 Naval Defence Act, argued Lord George Hamilton, the First Sea Lord, was an essential measure, an imperial necessity, a duty.[117] Viewed from Ottawa, it was of far less moment. Its provisions, and the Russo-French entente, were noted in the west coast press as in Ontario, but they provoked no controversy in Victoria or Ottawa. A. J. Balfour was no doubt right to observe that France and Russia would have launched 13 new battleships by 1896, if both adhered to their large shipbuilding programmes and that 30 of their cruisers might in due course find their way to the Pacific.[118] Russia's naval strength in Asia was undoubtedly increasing, France was certainly developing her base at Papeete, in Tahiti, and, as Rear-Admiral A. Heneage, then Commander-in-Chief, Pacific, had observed at the beginning of the Bering Sea Dispute with the United States in 1888, the British force in the Pacific was inadequate even to release a west coast schooner wrongly seized in open waters at the Bering Strait. It had no hope of thwarting the intentions or designs of the United States in the Pacific, let alone of the United States and Russia in collusion.[119] All were right, and all was clear. Even so, Canadian authorities elected not to think about "the god-Dagon white Czar," [120] whose ironclads were "always in the East" and always able to approach Vancouver Island. It was, after all, traditional to do so and provided a both popular and economical "solution" to an old dilemma. No Canadian had yet been shot at in his own country by Russian men-of-war, nor, away from the Pacific coast, did such eventualities seem worthy of discussion. In the new Dominion, old attitudes died hard.

CONCLUDING OBSERVATIONS: CANADIAN NON-MILITARISM AND THE SCARES

Canadian reaction to a Russian threat to west coast settlements and interests that was both genuine and serious in 1877–78 and again in 1882–85, and genuine in other periods, well illustrates the weakness of militarism in the nationalism of the nineteenth-century Dominion. It also serves to underline inherent weaknesses in the Canadian imperialist movement as aroused by William Foster, G. T. Denison, and other keen Canada Firsters in the years 1868–71[121] and strengthened in the 1880's and the 1890's by United Empire Loyalists, Canadian Defence League members, Navy Leaguers, and assorted (and invariably Russophobic) local politicians and militia officers. It also throws a useful light on the development of tensions and disputes between the west coast and the government in Ottawa, providing reminders that these did not invariably have to do with dollars and cents, but could stem from incompatible perceptions of the present needs and future strength of Canada.

The federal authority inherited from Britain a traditional reluctance to commit money or men to the defence of the Pacific rim of British North America. Even before the sale-and-purchase of Alaska, it was plain enough that British Columbia could not be held against a resolute American advance; and that awareness, together with the Treaty of Washington (1871) and the consequent improvement of relations between Britain and the U.S.A. (at maritime Canadian expense) went far towards determining Canadians' positions on the question of dominion defence. Within four years of Confederation, in the view of most Canadians, it had become apparent that a west coast game could not be worth the candle and that even the construction of defence works in the East was of uncertain value in a war with the United States. As G. F. G. Stanley justly notes, within a year of the signing of the Treaty of Washington Ottawa first publicly discussed improvement of communications and specifically the building of the future C.P.R. as a defence measure of greater national value and strategic worth than any fort or port.[122] Nor should American military policies — reduction of the U.S. Army's size after the Civil War, preoccupation with the western plains, and Indian resistance to the settler — be overlooked in an assessment of the crystallizing of these unassertive attitudes in Ottawa. In sum, Canadian non-militarism was encouraged by awareness of the United States' great military strength and of the indefensibility of certain parts of the Dominion, Vancouver Island, for example. Successive cabinets in Ottawa responded to these military realities by treating the defence of the Pacific coast at large as an imperial responsibility and by declining to work with Britain to render any prospect of a *Russian* raid, at least, extremely faint. The Russian naval threat was thus enhanced by U.S. military strength, throughout the 1870's and 1880's, as in 1853–55.

Such non-aggressive attitudes and policies were not, however, merely functions of Canadian perception of American political and military preponderance. As study of the west coast and dominion as well as British treatment of the west coast's Russian problem shows so well (it is because that problem could have been resolved, by the Canadians, that I have used it in this case-study of failure to accept proper[123] responsibility for federal defence), Canadian non-militarism of the sort so long resented in Victoria was rooted in traditional Canadian convictions and positions. These may be placed under four headings: 1. Manchester liberalism; 2. democratic acceptance of the "stake in society" theory; 3. isolationism; and 4. awareness of membership of the British Empire.

As Canadian imperialists and advocates of military efficiency themselves well recognized, they faced a problem on the west coast that was almost hopeless. "No country," they conceded, "exhibits a greater corporate indifference to her defence than does Canada."[124] Their appeals for action on Vancouver Island and the arguments of Russophobic fellow-travellers were consequently couched in terms of "waking up the country" to its self-delusion and to outside menaces. The "Russian scares" served them well; but Canadians en masse displayed an unmistakable indifference towards such matters that was mirrored by the policies of Ottawa. Lack of concern with international tensions and even forthright antimilitary feelings sprang from sources including French-Canadian antipathy towards involvement in a foreign country's (Britain's) wars, nationalism that would not condone continuation of the common military defence arrangements of the 1860's on the ground that it would undermine Canadian autonomy, belief that the Dominion's security had been ensured by the Monroe Doctrine, and a corresponding disbelief that foreign shells would ever land in Canada. Regardless of its source or ground, however (and imperialist Russophobes responded to the sources as they found them), protest against military preparations, on the west coast or in any other part of the Dominion, was usually phrased in the indignant language of contemporary liberalism.

Ideologically, liberalism was the main source of Canadian antimilitarism. Canadians had indeed made many compromises in the effort to accommodate the pristine doctrines of Cobden and Bright to the environment or, rather, the environments of British North America; but one part of the liberal belief that had been easily adopted and adapted and had flourished in Canadian society was a dislike of all things martial. In its classical formation, Manchester liberalism posited that once all artificial limits upon trade were ended, economic interdependence would evolve among the nations and historic rivalries and even war, which landowners and nobles had encouraged in the past, would fade away. The hope for universal peace, so gloriously celebrated at the Crystal Palace (1851), continued to be nurtured by Canadians in towns and on their farms throughout the century. It seemed a sensible, and not ignoble, attitude to take in building up a nation — or at least a farm or factory — in undeveloped country, far from foreign troops and ships. It was a widespread, bedrock attitude, imbued with commonsense and pragmatism, that the advocates of an increased defence expenditure and sound fortifications in the West, or for that matter in the East, were never to prevail against. Imperialist aspirations, never quite identified with military strength or capability by the Canadian electorate, were grounded on its reef.

So often favoured in egalitarian societies of other times, not even the Militia had the general and permanent support of the Canadians. It was the victim of democracy in North America. So Selby Smyth and later British G.O.C.'s were forced to recognize, after a struggle with the facts and with themselves.[125] It was an odd twist that the "stake in society" theory, so long espoused as justification for retaining full control of British troops by those with funds enough to purchase their commission from the king, took in the democratic colonies of North America. There, the volunteer tradition was enthusiastically espoused in the belief that only patriots were needed to defend the hearth and home. Like the Americans, Canadians inclined to look askance at the professional, committed army officer and to dislike all standing armies. As for warships, it was known that the imperial authorities had plenty of them and that some were at Esquimalt or at Halifax. "Canadians," insisted the Toronto *Globe* in William Jennings Bryan fashion, "can dispense with a standing army because they possess the best possible constituents for a defensive force in themselves."[126] Suffice to add to this General Selby Smyth's dispirited remarks about the casual, undisciplined "constituents" who, in a crisis, would attempt to beat off Russians or Americans or both: "Certainly there have *been* camps of exercise. Very pleasant holiday gatherings they must have been." [127]

Added to this attitude, at least by 1870, was an indigenous Canadian isolationism which made much of the supposed and real differences between life in North America and in the war-wracked, predatory Old World. It was a tendency most marked in anti-imperial but nationalistic demogogues and writers, J. N. Blake and G. E. Fenety for instance. ("Armaments everywhere! Military glory! The bane of the Old World.")[128] To men like this, as F. H. Underhill observes[129] in reference to Wilfrid Laurier (whose nationalism certainly contained a "strong strain of North American isolationism"), an effort to collaborate more energetically with Britain in imperial defence, in the Victoria-Esquimalt region, for example, was a species of contamination.

Paradoxically, this same awareness of Britain's lingering commitments at Esquimalt and, particularly, Halifax and of Canadians' position in the worldwide British Empire led both to efforts by imperialist nationalists like Denison, Foster, and Mair to improve the weak dominion defences and Militia, incidentally responding to the growing Russian challenge in the North Pacific Ocean and to overall rejection of those efforts by their fellow-countrymen. Canada Firsters' inability to bring Canadians to recognize the need for credible defences in the early 1870's well illustrates the workings of that paradox. The fostering of national consciousness in Canada, asserted Denison in his address, "The Duty of Canadians to Canada," would halt imperial disintegration and oblige Great Britain, then in "Little England" mood, to see the benefits of empire and not to view colonials as troublesome inferiors too costly to maintain. Canadians should concentrate on the material development of Canada, take pride in nationality, and recognize their full responsibilities as self-reliant people. Englishmen would then regard them as potentially important, and not merely loyal, allies. These ideas were developed logically in William Foster's celebrated speech of 1871, "Canada First: or Our New Nationality." Foster agreed with Denison that the British connection would in time evolve into an "alliance of nations" and that first it was essential that a national entity emerge in Canada. If it did not, then the imperial alliance of the future would not be a pact of equals, but a further formalizing of the colony-and-motherland relationship.[130] And obviously, the development of national pride, discharging of dominion responsibility to self and Empire, and just perception of Canadian importance in the future of that Empire demanded that Canadian defences and defensive capability, to landward and to seaward, be considerably strengthened. Literary manifesto though it was, and no political or party programme, Foster's speech coherently and forcefully expressed the argument later advanced, for other purposes and people, by Mahatma Gandhi: that "a nation that has no control over her own defence force and external policy is hardly a responsible nation." It was not that Foster, Denison, or the Canadian imperalist nationalists that followed them ("there is no antagonism between Canadianism and imperialism. The one is but the expansion of the other")[131] sought political autonomy from Britain. They simply recognized the meaning of a minimal defensive capability as a deterrent against would-be raiders and a source of pride in nationhood.

Canadians would not accept the argument. Immigration to the western plains, also promoted by the movement, was acceptable. So, to a point, were its attacks on "partyism" and insistence on refashioning the civil service. But a policy of building up Canadian armed strength, even to deal with acknowledged foreign threats, for example, from Fenians in the United States or Russians based in Nagasaki or Amuria, was something else. The movement failed. Those who spurned it threw their lot in with Macdonald's "National Policy" and turned their back on "foreign problems" of the sort that, intermittently until the First World War, returned to vex them — and to haunt British Columbia.

Study of Canadian responses to the west coast's Russian problem of another age partially justifies complaints by west coast residents that the authorities of Ottawa neglected their defence responsibilities on the Pacific littoral. British Columbians themselves transformed the growing Russian presence in Amuria, Japan, and California into a bogey by refusing to acknowledge it except in times of Anglo-Russian crisis. More significant, however, and of wider application to a Canada not yet extant when Russian ironclads alarmed Victoria, is one more point that has emerged here: that nationalism came of age in the Dominion without militaristic fervour, thanks essentially to a Canadian awareness of U.S. military superiority so deep and lasting that it numbed the national will to render Canada secure even against the slighter threat that tsarist Russia represented. That consideration has strategic and political significance today.

Notes

NOTES TO THE INTRODUCTION

1. See C. P. Stacey, *Canada and the British Army, 1846–71* (London, 1936), Chapter 6.
2. See G. R. V. Barratt, *Russia in Pacific Waters, 1715–1825* (Vancouver, 1980), pp. 221–37.
3. C. Berger, *The Sense of Power: Studies in the Ideas of Canadian Imperialism, 1867–1914* (Toronto, 1970), p. 239.

4. J. C. R. Colomb, "Russian Development and Our Naval and Military Position in the North Pacific," *JRUSI* 21 (1877): 671–80, and *The Defence of Great and Greater Britain* (London, 1880), passim.
5. For a fuller treatment of these matters, see D. M. Schurman's paper, "Esquimalt: Defence Problem, 1865–1887," *BCHQ* 19 (1955): 57–69.

NOTES TO CHAPTER ONE

1. Royal Commonwealth Society Library, London: North West Company Papers: W. McGillivray (?), "Some Account of the Trade Carried on by the North West Company," fol. 20; see also "Appeal of the North West Company to the British Government to Forestall John Jacob Astor's Columbian Enterprise," *CHR* 17 (1936): 304–11, esp. p. 306 (and supporting diplomatic material in PRO, FO 42/149), and Washington Irving's *Astoria, or, Anecdotes of an Enterprise Beyond the Rocky Mountains* (NY, 1861), pp. 30–42.
2. Appeal and subsequent correspondence in PRO BT, 1/61 (Apr.—Nov. 1812.)
3. John Franklin to Barrow, Admiralty Board, 26 Nov. 1823: copy in HBCA, A/8/1, fols. 224–28.
4. PAC, Q/113, pp. 216ff; PRO, CO 42/149 (Nor'Westers' and agents' correspondence with Bathurst and Goulburn); also G. C. Davidson, *The North West Company* (Berkeley, 1916), pp. 133ff.
5. The U.S. government did not recognize Great Britain's claim to sovereignty on the coast in question; see *American State Papers: Foreign Relations*, (Washington, 1833–58), 3: 731–32. On the history of these claims, United States Congress, Senate, *Alaskan Boundary Tribunal Proceedings* (Washington, D.C., 1904: hereafter referred to as *ABTP*), 2: 19–24, and F. Merk, *The Oregon Question: Essays in Anglo-American Diplomacy and Politics* (Cambridge, MA, 1967).
6. PRO, BT 1/70, no. 16: memorial dated 30 June, encl. in Chetwynd to BT, submitted 9 Nov. 1812.
7. PRO, Adm. 2/1380, pp. 358–79 (preparations for sending *Phoebe* frigate to the Northwest Coast, etc.); Irving, *Astoria*, pp. 444–48; F. W. Howay, W. N. Sage, H. F. Angus, *British Columbia and the United States* (New Haven, 1942), pp. 33–34.
8. A point made by the Earl of Selkirk in his *Sketch of the British Fur Trade in North America, with Observations relative to the North West Company of Montreal* (London, 1816); see also n. 1.
9. PRO, CO 42/149: McTavish, McGillivrays & Co. to McTavish, Fraser & Co. and Inglis, Ellice & Co.,

18 Aug. 1812; copy in Atcheson to Bathurst, 9 Oct. 1812; also, ibid, McTavish, Fraser & Co., and Inglis, Ellice & Co. to Privy Council, 1 Oct. 1812.

10. Ibid., Simon McGillivray to Goulburn, 29 Dec. 1812, with endorsement.

11. L. F. R. Masson, *Les Bourgeois de la Compagnie du Nord-Ouest . . . avec une esquisse historique et des annotations* (Quebec, 1889–90), 2: 48–53; E. Coues, ed., *The Manuscript Journals of Alexander Henry and David Thompson, 1790–1814: New Light on the Early History of the Greater North-West* (NY, 1897), 2: 760–66.

12. "Statement Relative to the Columbia River (1815)," encl. in McGillivray to Sir Charles Bagot, 15 Nov. 1817, with fur traders' demands of 7 May 1814, in PRO, FO 5/123.

13. PAC, Q/134–2, pp. 385–92: Inglis, Ellice & Co. to Goulburn, 25 and 28 July, 2 Aug. 1815.

14. Merk, *The Oregon Question*, chapters 1 and 2; A. L. Burt, *The United States, Great Britain, and British North America* (New Haven, 1940), pp. 371–72, 411–14.

15. P. 125 in the 1817 text.

16. PRO, FO 5/128: Commodore J. Yeo to Croker, 30 Aug. 1817, encl. in Barrow to Hamilton et al., 3 Sept. 1817.

17. Original text in P. Tikhmenev, *Istoricheskoe obozrenie obrazovaniia Rossiisko-Amerikanskoi Kompanii . . .* (St. P., 1861), 1: 26–28; English text in *ABTP*, 2: 24–25.

18. See Barratt, *Russia in Pacific Waters*, chap. 3.

19. *ABTP*, 2: 25.

20. Tikhmenev, *Istoricheskoe obozrenie*, 1: 27; *PSZRI*, 37: doc. 28, 756.

21. TsGADA, fond A. R. Vorontsova, op. 1, dela 754–55; AVPR, fond kantseliarii Ministerstva Vneshnikh Del: 1822, delo 3645; 1823, delo 8735; *Niles' Weekly Register*, 23 and 25 Jan., 5 and 24 April 1823 (John Quincy Adams's political necessities and the 1821 ukases); A. de Nesselrode, ed., *Lettres et papiers du chancelier comte de Nesselrode* (Paris, 1904), 2: 38ff.; PRO, FO 181/48 (Castlereagh to Bagot, 19 Jan. 1822); "Correspondence of the Russian Ministers in Washington, 1818–1825," *AHR* 18 (1913): 336–38.

22. *ABTP*, 2: 94–95 (Nicolay to Londonderry, 12 Nov. 1821), and PRO, FO 181/48 (Londonderry to Lieven, 18 Jan. 1822, encl. in Castlereagh to Bagot, no. 5, 19 Jan. 1822). See also P. Kennedy Grimsted, *The Foreign Ministers of Alexander 1* (Berkeley, 1969), pp. 196, 210, on K. R. Nesselrode's unhappy role in these developments.

23. PRO, FO 181/48: Castlereagh to Bagot, no. 5; see also *ABTP*, 5: 12.

24. *ABTP*, 2: 12–13.

25. Ibid., 2: 94–95.

26. 26 Jan. 1822, pp. 343–44.

27. *Niles' Weekly Register*, 22 and 27 July 1822 (extracts from British newspaper editorials re the sovereignty issue); also H. W. V. Temperley, *The Foreign Policy of Canning, 1822–1827* (London, 1925), pp. 104ff.

28. Those rights were asserted only in mid-October by the Duke of Wellington, then in Verona: *ABTP*, 5: 19.

29. HBCA, A/6/20: Gov. and Committee to Simpson, 27 Feb. 1822; see also E. E. Rich, *The Hudson's Bay Company, 1670–1870* (Toronto, 1959), 3: 608–10; Davidson, *North West Company*, pp. 164ff.; Burt, *United States, Great Britain and British North America*, pp. 422–26; and J. S. Galbraith, *The Hudson's Bay Company as an Imperial Factor, 1821–1869* (Toronto, 1957).

30. F. Merk, ed., *Fur Trade and Empire: George Simpson's Journal, 1824–25* (Cambridge, MA, 1931), p. 71.

31. Rich, *Hudson's Bay Company*, 3: 568–72; *Narrative of Occurrences in the Indian Countries of North America* (London, 1817), p. 125.

32. See also E. E. Rich, "The Hudson's Bay Company Archives," *PHR* 8 (1938).

33. Rich, *Hudson's Bay Company*, 3: 568–69.

34. *American State Papers: Foreign Relations*, 4: 861–63; *North American Review* 15 (Oct. 1822): 370–401 ("An Examination of the Russian Claims").

35. Rich, *Hudson's Bay Company*, 3: 610.

36. HBCA, A/8/1 (reel 50).

37. Merk, *Fur Trade and Empire*, p. 241 (Gov. and Committee to Cameron, 22 July 1824).

38. HBCA, A/8/1: Pelly-Barrow corresp.,

1823, esp. fol. 220; National Library of Scotland, Edinburgh, Melville Papers, MS 3845 (Barrow on the Northwest Passage, Nov. 1823); J. Franklin, *Narrative of a Journey to the Shores of the Polar Sea . . .* 1819–1822 (London, 1823), p. 292 (signs of the Russian presence in America among the Loucheux Indians at Fort Good Hope).

39. The Scott Polar Research Institute, Cambridge, holds Franklin's Letter Books, MS 248/281 (1823); see also J. E. Caswell, "Sponsors of Canadian Arctic Exploration: Part 3, 1800–1839," *The Beaver*, Outfit 300 (1969), and B. Gough, ed., *To the Pacific and Arctic with Beechey* (Cambridge, 1973), pp. 9–10.

40. HBCA, A/8/1, fols. 224–29 (Franklin to Barrow, 26 Nov. 1823: copy.); see also Otto von Kotzebue, *A New Voyage Round the World* (London, 1830), 1: 1–8.

41. Illuminating data in Horatio Lamb's "Notes on Trade with the North West Coast, 1790 to 1810," MS in the Baker Library, Harvard.

42. William Dane Phelps, "Solid Men of Boston," MS in Baker Library, box 33; also A. Ogden, *The California Sea Otter Trade, 1784–1848* (Berkeley, 1941), chaps. 1 and 2; S.B. Okun', trans. C. Ginsburg, *The Russian-American Company* (Cambridge, MA, 1951), and F. W. Howay, "An Outline Sketch of the Maritime Fur Trade," Canadian Historical Association, *Report of the Annual Meeting, 1932* (Ottawa, 1932), pp. 5ff.

43. The point is made by K. Bourne, D. C. Davidson, F. A. Golder, W. Kaye Lamb, F. V. Longstaff, A. G. Mazour, et al.

44. *Materialy dlia istorii russkikh zavedenii po beregam Vostochnago okeana* (St. P., 1861), pt.3: 7–9; Tikhmenev, *Istoricheskoe obozrenie*, 1: 93–95; A. Ogden, "Russian Sea–Otter and Seal Hunting on the California Coast, 1803–41," *CHSQ* 12 (1933): 217–39.

45. *Materialy*, 3: 13–14.

46. *Vneshniaia politika Rossii XIX veka: dokumenty Rossiiskogo Ministerstva Inostrannykh Del: seriia* 1 (M., 1960–), 6: 276–81; L. Dermigny, *La Chine et l'Occident: le commerce a Canton au XVIIIe siècle* (Paris, 1964), 3:1178ff.

47. PRO, CO 42/149, pp. 44–48 (S. McGillivray to Goulburn, Dec. 1812,

and related papers); PAC Q/113, pp. 229–30 (McTavish, McGillivrays and Co. to McTavish, Fraser and Co., Jan. 1810, etc.).

48. *Vneshniaia politika Rossii*, 5: 329–32, 478–80; *American State Papers: Foreign Relations*, 5: 439–43; N. N. Bolkhovitinov, *Stanovlenie russko-amerikanskikh otnoshenii, 1785–1815* (M., 1966), pp. 445–75; V. M. Golovnin, *Sochineniia i perevody* (St. P., 1864), 4: 425–28; 5: 71ff.; K. W. Porter, *John Jacob Astor, Business Man* (Cambridge, MA, 1931), 1: 178–207, and bibliography.

49. F. W. Howay, "A List of Trading Vessels in the Maritime Fur Trade, 1785–1825," *Proceedings of the Royal Society of Canada: 3rd series* 25 (1931): 117ff.; 26 (1932): 44ff.; S. E. Morison, *Maritime History of Massachusetts, 1783–1860* (Boston, 1921), pp. 53–56.

50. C. F. Adams, ed., *The Memoirs of John Quincy Adams* (Philadelphia, 1874–77), 2: 151–52; Bolkhovitinov, *Stanovlenie*, pp. 468ff.; also for a glance at the mechanics of Russo-American trade relations in 1800–10, J. D'Wolf, *A Voyage to the North Pacific and a Journey through Siberia* (Cambridge, MA, 1861), pp. 39–72. The Baker Library at Harvard University holds papers (box 33) relating to the Astor-Bentzon-Rumiantsev negotiations of 1810–12, i.e., to Astor's plan to supply the Russian settlements and halt the spread of arms among Northwest Coast Indians.

51. PRO, CO 42/149 (McGillivray-Goulburn correspondence re Anglo-Russian amity, letters of introduction, etc.); Tikhmenev, *Istoricheskoe obozrenie*, 1: 207–14; K. T. Khlebnikov, trans. C. Bearne, *Baranov, Chief Manager of the Russian Colonies in America* (Kingston, Ont., 1973), pp. 86–87; J. R. Gibson, *Imperial Russia in Frontier America* (NY, 1976), pp. 160–62.

52. T. Lavrischeff, ed., *Documents Relative to the History of Alaska* (College, Alaska, 1936–38), 3: 202–3; Washington Irving, *Astoria*, pp. 419–22; M. E. Wheeler, "Empires in Conflict and Cooperation," *PHR* 40 (1971): 430–31; K. W. Porter, "The Cruise of the Forester," *WHQ* 23 (1932): 262–69; F. W. Howay et al., *Brit-*

ish Columbia and the United States (New Haven, 1942), p. 33.

53. See Irby C. Nichols, Jr., "The Russian Ukase and the Monroe Doctrine: A Reevaluation," *PHR* 36 (1967): 13–26, and Nichols and R. A. Ward, "Anglo-American Relations and the Russian Ukase: A Reassessment," ibid. 41 (1972): 444–56.

54. J. Q. Adams, diary, cited by Nichols, "The Russian Ukase," p. 17.

55. *Fur Seal Arbitration*, 4: 144–45.

56. *ABTP*, 2: App., p. 126; preceding correspondence in PRO, FO 181/52 (Stratford to George Canning, nos. 43–47, 1823), and *ABTP*, 5: 22–26.

57. PAC, Bagot Papers, 2, pt. 3: Bagot to Canning, 5 Oct. 1823; *ABTP*, 2, App., pp. 120–21 (despatch, 3 May 1823).

58. Nichols, "The Russian Ukase," pp. 16–18.

59. *ABTP*, 2: 42–43 (Middleton to Adams, 20 Aug. 1822); and App., pp. 129–30.

60. See J. Bagot, *George Canning and His Friends* (London, 1909), 2: 215–16, 270–71.

61. PAC, Bagot Papers, 2, pt. 3: Bagot to Canning, 5 Oct. 1823; PRO, FO 181/52 (Canning-Bagot correspondence); *American State Papers: Foreign Relations*, 5: 447–48; S. Lane-Poole, *Life of the Right Honourable Stratford Canning, Viscount de Redcliffe* (London, 1888), 1: 335–36.

62. Further on this, see Richard Rush, *A Residence at the Court of London, 1819–1825* (London, 1845), 2, passim; also E. H. Tatum, Jr., *The United States and Europe, 1815–23: A Study in the Background of the Monroe Doctrine* (Berkeley, 1936), pp. 54–58.

63. "Russian Correspondence," pp. 336ff.; *American State Papers*, 5: 439–43; Tatum, *The United States and Europe*, pp. 56–57; Bolkhovitinov, *Stanovlenie*, pp. 450ff.

64. *Niles' Weekly Register*, no. 20, 29 Dec. 1821; Nichols, "The Russian Ukase," pp. 18–19.

65. *ABTP*, 2: App., p. 146 (Canning to Bagot, 15 Jan. 1824).

66. Tatum, *The United States and Europe*, pp. 273–85; PAC, Bagot Papers, 2, pt. 3 (Bagot to Canning, 5 Oct. 1823.)

67. *ABTP*, 2, App., pp. 172ff. suggest that Bagot did not make such remarks at the negotiating table, despite his feelings.

68. Ibid., 1: 31–32; also Galbraith, *Hudson's Bay Company as an Imperial Factor*, p. 123.

69. Ibid., 1: 33; *Niles' Weekly Register*, 23 and 25 Jan. 1823; 24, 5 Apr. 1823; *American State Papers: Foreign Relations*, 5: 448; S. R. Tompkins, "Drawing the Alaskan Boundary," *CHR* 26 (1945): 22–24.

70. PAC, Bagot Papers, 2, pt. 3 (letter of 29 Mar. 1824); also see *ABTP*, 2, App., pp. 141, 153–58 (British proposals, Russian counter-offer), 173–75 (need to have Russo-British frontier ratified by U.S., etc.).

71. *ABTP*, 1: 30; HBCA, A/8/1, reel 50 (Pelly to Canning re inland line, 19 Apr. 1824). On contemporaneous attitudes and arguments of Count de Lambert, Admiral N. S. Mordvinov, and the Russian-American Company towards the "frontier question," AVPR, fond kantseliarii Ministerstva Vneshnikh Del: 1827, delo 7316 (Mordvinov-Nesselrode exchanges, esp. 20 Feb. 1824, pp. 8–9); V. A. Bil'basov, ed., *Arkhiv grafov Mordvinovykh* (St. P., 1901–03), 6: 655–57; *ABTP*, 2, App., pp. 172–81; A. G. Mazour, "The Russian-American and Anglo-Russian Conventions, 1824–25: An Interpretation," *PHR* 14 (1945): 303–6.

72. *ABTP*, 2: 41.

73. Ibid., p. 42.

74. Ibid., 1: 158.

75. PAC, Bagot Papers, 2, pt. 3: Bagot to Canning, 29 Mar. 1824.

76. See Tompkins, "Drawing the Alaskan Boundary," pp. 22–23.

77. PAC, Bagot Papers, 2, pt. 3: Bagot to Canning, 24 Aug. 1824.

78. *ABTP*, 2, App., pp. 212–14.

79. See Barratt, *Russia in Pacific Waters*, chap. 9.

80. *ABTP*, 2: 15–16. The original French and Russian texts are given in Martens, *Receuil des traités*, 9: 316–22.

81. USNA, "Records of the Russian American Company," 4: 451–55; *Arkhiv grafov Mordvinovykh*, 6: 642–43, 655–56; Tikhmenev, *Istoricheskoe obozrenie*, 1: 340ff.; Okun', *Russian-American Company*, pp. 86–87.

82. USNA, "Records of the Russian-American Company," 4: 453–54.

83. AVPR, fond kantseliarii Ministerstva

Vneshnikh Del: 1824, delo 3717, Nesselrode to Mordvinov, pp. 23–24; sketch of Kankrin in K. K. Arsen'ev, ed., *Entsiklopedicheskii slovar'* (St. P., 1895), 27: 292–94.

84. See Okun', *Russian-American Company*, pp. 108–10, and nn., pp. 285–86.
85. AVPR, fond kants. Min. Vnesh. Del: 1824, delo 3650, pp. 5–6.
86. Ibid., delo 3717, pp. 20–21; Bil'basov, *Arkhiv grafov Mordvinovykh*, 6: 656–57, 674–79.
87. Gibson, *Imperial Russia*, p. 84, and Barratt, *The Russian Navy and Australia to 1825* (Melbourne, 1979) on the "Pacific-naval" aspect of Decembrism.
88. V. I. Semevskii et al., *Obshchestvennye dvizheniia v Rossii v pervuiu polovinu XIX veka* (St. P., 1905), 1: 378–79; D. I. Zavalishin, "Kaliforniia v 1824 godu," *Russkii vestnik* 61 (1865): 322–68, and "Delo o kolonii Ross," ibid. 62 (1866): 55–58; Okun', *Russian-American Company*, pp. 136–40.
89. P. Efremov, ed., *Sochineniia i perepiska K. F. Ryleeva* (St. P., 1874), pp. 308–14; M. Dovnar-Zapol'skii, *Memuary dekabristov* (St. P., 1906), pp. 164–65; letters of A. E. Izmailov in *Pamiati dekabristov* (L., 1926), 1: 242–43.
90. TsGIA, fond 48, op. 1, delo 78, pp. 6–8: V. P. Romanov's testimony of 1 Feb. 1826 re possible collaboration with Capt. Franklin, surveying in the American Arctic; M. N. Pokrovskii, ed., *Vosstanie dekabristov: materialy po istorii vosstaniia*, 3: 147–48, 250–52; T. G. Snytko, "Ryleev na sledstvii," *Literaturnoe nasledstvo* 59 (L., 1954), bk. 1, pp. 198, 232; Barratt, *Voices in Exile:*

The Decembrist Memoirs (Montreal and London, 1974), passim.
91. D. I. Zavalishin, *Zapiski dekabrista* (St. P., 1906), pp. 90–91; Dovnar-Zapol'skii, *Memuary dekabristov*, p. 165; N. I. Grech, *Vospominaniia o moei zhizni* (L., 1930), pp. 441–42; Barratt, *Voices in Exile*, pp. 139–42.
92. Bil'basov, *Arkhiv grafov Mordvinovykh*, 6: 655–61. S. Ikonnikov's *Graf N. S. Mordvinov* (St. P., 1873) remains very serviceable.
93. TsGADA, fond grafa E. F. Kankrina, delo 35, pp. 11–12.
94. HBCA, A/8/1, fols. 220–29; ABTP, 5: 19; editorials and articles in *The Globe*, 23 May 1822; *Morning Chronicle*, 24 and 28 May 1822; *The Times*, 23 Aug. 1822; USNA: "Records of the Russian-American Company," 4: 3–7; Gibson, *Imperial Russia*, pp. 163–64.
95. Nichols, "The Russian Ukase," pp. 24–25; Wheeler, "Empires in Conflict," p. 441; Okun', *Russian-American Company*, pp. 224ff.
96. Nichols makes this last point confidently (p. 24), but he does not pursue it. It merits further study.
97. ABTP, 5: 20 (Nesselrode to Wellington, 23 Nov. 1822).
98. See Barratt, *Russia in Pacific Waters*, chaps. 8 and 9.
99. For example, the establishing of Fort Kilmaurs in the Babine Country: HBCA, A/6/20: Gov. and Committee to Simpson, 27 Feb. 1822; see also Rich, *Hudson's Bay Company*, 3: 608–10; Davidson, *North West Company* pp. 164ff.; and Burt, *United States and British North America*, pp. 422–26.

NOTES TO CHAPTER TWO

1. USNA, "Records of the Russian-American Company," 4: 417 (Ianovskii on the dwindling sea-otter catch); 5: 103–4 (failure of the oceanic supply system, 1826); 30: 260–62 (Chistiakov elaborates).
2. *Materialy dlia istorii russkikh zaselenii*, 3: 90–91; USNA, 36: 51.
3. USNA, "Records of the Russian-American Company," 31: 70ff.

4. Ibid., 36: 52 (60% of colonial catch bartered, 1827– 30, etc.).
5. Ibid., 32: 45–47; 44: 54.
6. Tikhmenev, *Istoricheskoe obozrenie*, 1: 339–40; Gibson, *European Settlement and Development*, pp. 62–64; R. A. Pierce, "Alaska's Russian Governors: Chistiakov and Wrangel," *Alaska Journal* (1971), no. 4: 38–41.

7. See Galbraith, *Hudson's Bay Company as Imperial Factor*, p. 140.
8. E. E. Rich, ed., *Part of a Dispatch from George Simpson Esq., Governor of Rupert's Land, to the Governor and Committee of the Hudson's Bay Company, London, March 1 1829. Continued and Completed, March 24 and June 5 1829* (Toronto, 1947), pp. 101–2.
9. Ibid., pp. 85–86; B. B. Barker, ed., *Letters of Dr. John McLoughlin Written at Fort Vancouver, 1829–1832* (Portland, 1948), p. 17; USNA, "Records of the Russian-American Company," 7: 20–22, 25–26; HBCA, D. 4/123, pp. 19ff. (Chistiakov's dissatisfaction with California as a grain source, 1829).
10. The subject is touched on by E. E. Rich, J. S. Galbraith, and F. Merk.
11. E. E. Rich, ed., *The Letters of John McLoughlin from Fort Vancouver to the Governor and Committee, First Series, 1825–38* (Toronto, 1941), p. civ.
12. F. Vrangel', "O pushnykh tovarakh Severo-Amerikanskikh Rossiiskikh vladenii," *Teleskop*, 1835, pp. 496–518; *Statistische und ethnographische Nachrichten über die russischen Besitzungen an der Nordwestküste von Amerika* (St. P., 1839), passim.
13. *ABTP*, 2: 264–65.
14. Ibid., 2: 266–67; HBCA D. 4/99 (Geo. Simpson, Correspondence Books: Simpson to Gov. and Committee, 10 August 1832, re the Company's move on to Nass and the false Skeena River).
15. *ABTP*, 2: 267. On Etholen, Wrangel, Zarembo, and other Russian naval officers, see *Obshchii morskoi spisok* (St. P., 1885–1907, 14v.).
16. Peter Skene Ogden, "Report of Transactions at Stikine, 1834," in Rich, *Letters of John McLoughlin*, pp. 317–22.
17. "Declaration of Captain Alexander Duncan as to the Proceedings and Opposition of the Russian Government to the Governor and Committee of Hudson's Bay, Erecting an Establishment at Stikine River on the Northwest Coast of America," HBCA, reel 5–M50, Section F: "Russian-American Company, Miscellaneous Papers, 1824–1903."
18. Bancroft Library, MS P-C 23: "Notes and Extracts From the Journal of the Hudson's Bay Company at Fort Simpson, 1834–37," entry under 30 July

1834 ("the Tongass Incident"); HBCA, F. 29/2: Wrangel to Ogden, 19 Sept. 1834 (the Ogden visit to Novo-Arkhangel'sk, etc.).
19. HBCA, A/8/2; see also A/6/23, Gov. and Committee to McLoughlin, 28 Aug. 1835 re Company policy towards the Russians in the short term.
20. See C. K. Webster, "Urquhart, Ponsonby and Palmerston," *EHR* 62 (1947); and G. H. Bolsover, "David Urquhart and the Eastern Question, 1833–37," *Journal of Modern History* 8 (1863).
21. J. H. Gleason, *The Genesis of Russophobia in Great Britain* (Cambridge, MA, 1950), pp. 107–225, esp. 181–83; D. Ross, *Opinions of the European Press on the Eastern Question* (London, 1936), chaps. 1 and 2.
22. *Morning Chronicle*, 10 Apr.; *The Globe*, 10 Apr. and 6 Aug.; *The Herald*, 21, 22, and 23 Aug. 1833.
23. *The Times*, 16 Nov. 1835. The *Chronicle, Globe, Herald* and *Standard* all showered invective on Nicholas I personally in December 1835 and subsequently. See also "A Manchester Manufacturer's" (i.e., Cobden's) pamphlet, *Russia, 1836*, reprinted in *The Political Writings of Richard Cobden* (London, 1867), 1: 194ff., and John McNeill's tract, *The Progress and Present Position of Russia in the East* (London, 1836).
24. Urquhart Papers, Balliol College, Oxford: Taylor to Urquhart, 14 Nov. 1835; related material in PRO, FO 181/119, no. 12, 181/130, no. 16 (Palmerston-Durham exchanges during the Stikine River incident's diplomatic aftermath). See also *Hansard*, Commons, 4 and 19 Feb. 1836 (Lord Dudley Stuart and T. Attwood on Russia's growing might, etc.). On Taylor, *DNB*, 55: 413–14.
25. U.S. Government, Dept. of State Archives: Vail to Forsyth, no. 214, 28 Nov. 1835. On Aaron Vail, *DAB* 19: 136.
26. Bolsover, "Urquhart and the Eastern Question," pp. 457–58; PRO, FO 65/223, no. 8, Durham to Palmerston, 21 Jan. 1836; H. V. F. Bell, *Lord Palmerston* (London, 1936), 1: 280–82.
27. See *The Chronicle, Globe,* and *Standard* for 21 April 1836.
28. David Urquhart, *England and Russia: being a Fifth Edition of England, France, Russia, and Turkey* (London,

1835), pp. xi–xii; *DNB* 24: 252–53 (on Hamond); J. Bach, "The Maintenance of Royal Navy Vessels in the Pacific Ocean, 1825–75," *MM* 56 (1970): 259–336; also Bancroft Library, Berkeley, CA: G. B. Roberts (ex-*Dryad*), "Recollections," ms. (contemporaneous interpretations of the Stikine River incident).

29. See John Barrow, *Voyages of Discovery and Research within the Arctic Regions, from the Year 1818 to the Present Time* (London, 1846), pp. 12ff.

30. Admiralty Hydrographer's Office, Taunton: S.L. 21, no. 4: Beechey to Beaufort, 1 Nov. 1836; Miscellaneous File no. 15, folder 1, nos. 3–6 (the need for a better survey of the Northeastern Pacific, etc.). On Beechey's earlier work, see his *Narrative of a Voyage to the Pacific and Bering's Strait, to Cooperate with the Polar Expeditions, 1825–1828* (London, 1831).

31. E. Belcher, *Narrative of a Voyage round the World in His Majesty's Ship "Sulphur," during the Years 1836–1842* (London, 1843), 1: intro.

32. PRO, Adm. 1/48: Lt. A. Hamond to Mason, encl. in Hamond to Wood, 25 Aug. 1837.

33. PRO, Adm. 1/1586, cap. B, no. 101: Belcher to Wood, 28 Dec. 1837; 1/1587, cap. B, no. 223: same to same, 10 June 1839. Belcher's and Chief Factor Finlayson's private assessments of the true strength and naval potential of Novo-Arkhangel'sk were similar in several respects: cf. HBCA, B-223b/12: Duncan Finlayson to J. McLoughlin, 29 Sept. 1836.

34. Hawaii State Library, Admiral Richard Thomas Papers, G. 4, Art. VI, para. 1.

35. On Torrubia's *I Moscoviti nella California* (Rome, 1759) and comparable tracts of that period, see W. L. Cook, *Flood Tide of Empire: Spain and the Pacific Northwest, 1543–1819* (New Haven and London, 1973), pp. 45–46.

36. HBCA, A/8/2: Strangeways to Pelly, 13 Nov. 1835; Pelly to Palmerston, 18 Nov. 1835; Backhouse to Pelly, 6 Jan. 1836 (cited here).

37. Ibid., Pelly to Palmerston, 14 Jan. 1836.

38. Ibid., Backhouse to Pelly, 28 Jan. 1836.

39. Ibid., Pelly to Palmerston, 28 Jan. 1836.

40. Ibid., F.O. to Pelly, 26 Mar. and 30 July 1836; Pelly to FO 10 Dec.

41. Ibid., Nesselrode to Durham, 22 Mar. 1837.

42. *ABTP*, 2: 287–90.

43. Report in HBCA, B-223b (Fort Vancouver Correspondence Book/12: D. Finlayson to McLoughlin, 29 Sept. 1836). The Russian governor was by then Kupreianov, not Wrangel.

44. A. M. Johnson, ed., "Simpson in Russia," *The Beaver*, Outfit 291 (1960), p. 6, see also HBCA, D/4/23.

45. HBCA, F/29/2 (1838) and reel 5-M50: "Report by Governor Pelly"; also Galbraith, *Hudson's Bay Company as Imperial Factor*, p. 152.

46. PRO, CO 42/485: Pelly to Russell, 6 Feb. 1841.

47. Simpson's comments while at Novo-Arkhangel'sk in 1841 later emerged in W. Politkowski et al. to Hudson's Bay Company directors, 14 Feb. 1854, and were enclosed in Colvile to Clarendon, 28 Feb. 1854: in HBCA, A/8/19.

48. R. C. Mayne, *Four Years in British Columbia and Vancouver Island: an Account of their . . . Resources for Colonization* (London, 1862), p. 25. On the infant Esquimalt, see bibliography under Longstaff.

49. Admiral J. Moresby, *Two Admirals* (London, 1913), p. 103.

50. Bancroft Library, Roderick Finlayson, ms; "History of Vancouver Island and the Northwest Coast," pp. 12–21; Tikhmenev, *Istoricheskoe obozrenie*, 1: 269ff.; Rich, ed., *The Letters of John McLoughlin from Fort Vancouver to the Governor and Committee, Second Series, 1839–44* (Toronto, 1943), 2: 53–54, 125–26; R. Saw, "Sir John Pelly, Bart.," *BCHQ* 13 (1949): 23–32.

51. USNA, "Records of the Russian-American Company," 18: 100–03; 55: 149–50; *ABTP*, 3: 213–14; HBCA, A/10/23 (Pelly-Wrangel correspondence) and D/5/24 (Ogden to Simpson, 14 Mar. 1849 etc.).

52. HBCA, A/10/23–24; Galbraith, *Hudson's Bay Company as Imperial Factor*, pp. 283–91; P. Knaplund, "James Stephen on Granting Vancouver Island to the Hudson's Bay Company, 1846–48, "*BCHQ* 9 (1945): 259–71. See also nn. 11–13 of chap. 3 below.

NOTES TO CHAPTER THREE

1. Surveys in P. E. Mosely. *Russian Diplomacy and the Opening of the Eastern Question in 1838 and 1839* (Cambridge, 1934), H. W. V. Temperley, *England and the Near East, the Crimea* (London, 1936), and Gleason, *The Genesis of Russophobia*, pp. 227ff.

2. PRO, CO 6/14, Pelly to Palmerston, 26 February 1840 (re foreign expansion in the North Pacific); HBCA, A.8/1: Pelly-Londonderry letters, 1822. For insights into George Simpson's expansionist imperialism, in the Pacific world at least, see J. Schafer, ed., "Letters of Sir George Simpson, 1841–43," *AHR* 14 (1908): 86–93.

3. HBCA, F.29/2: Agreement (copy). See also *ABTP*, 3: 209–12, for the full and revised Hamburg text.

4. On these matters, HBCA, A.8/2, Backhouse-Pelly-Palmerston correspondence, January-March 1839.

5. See bibliography under Bourne, K., Merk, F., Sellers, C.

6. Temperley, *England and the Near East*, pp. 248–55; Gleason, *The Genesis of Russophobia*, pp. 272–73. E. G. Ravenstein's pioneering work, *The Russians on the Amur: Its Discovery, Conquest, and Colonization* (London. 1861) remains useful.

7. *The Times*, 29 Aug. 1840, 1 May, and 30 July 1841, editorials; *The Herald*, 27 and 30 Jan. 1841; D. Urquhart, *An Exposition of Transactions in Central Asia through which the Independence of States . . . has been Sacrificed to Russia* (London, 1841); F. S. Rodkey, "Anglo-Russian Negotiations About a 'Permanent' Quadruple Alliance in 1840," *AHR* 36 (1931).

8. The Pelly-Wrangel correspondence of Oct. 1847 to Apr. 1848 may be found, in part, in HBCA, A.10/23–24.

9. On these matters, F. A. Golder, *Russian Expansion on the Pacific, 1641–1850* (Cleveland, 1914), pp. 263ff., and D. Mitchell, *A History of Russian and Soviet Sea Power* (London, 1974), pp. 143–44.

10. P. Knaplund, "James Stephen on Granting Vancouver Island to the Hudson's Bay Company, 1846–48," *BCHQ* 9

(1945): 259–71; Galbraith, *Hudson's Bay Company as Imperial Factor*, pp. 283–91.

11. Great Britain, *Parliamentary Papers*: 1849, no. 103, p. 5.

12. Royal Grant and Letters Patent, in HBCA, A.37/1, 13 Jan. 1849; relevant papers (defence responsibilities, finances, etc.) in PRO, CO 305/1 (B. Hawes to Grey, Pelly, J. E. Fitzgerald, et al.).

13. See W. E. Ireland, "Pre-Confederation Defence Problems of the Pacific Colonies," Canadian Historical Association, *Annual Report, 1941* (Toronto, 1941): 43–45; and W. Kaye Lamb, "The Governorship of Richard Blanchard," *BCHQ* ness," etc.).

14. HBCA, A.10/23.

15. *ABTP*, 3: 214: "Agreement . . . Renewing (with Certain Modifications) the Agreement Between the Two Companies of 6th February 1839."

16. HBCA, D.5/24, Simpson-Pelly correspondence; Okun', *Russian-American Company*, pp. 115–17.

17. Okun', *Russian-American Company*, p. 234.

18. HBCA, A.8/19: W. Politkowski et al. to Directors, Hudson's Bay Co., encl. in Colvile to Clarendon, 28 Feb. 1854, fol. 24.

19. PRO, Adm. 116/857, circular to C.-in-C. and accompanying papers; Bodleian Library, Clarendon Deposit, C. 14, fol. 150 (Admiral Sir J. Graham on the Pacific implications of war, Jan.-Feb. 1854).

20. HBCA, A.8/19, fols. 24–25: Addington to Colvile, 22 Mar. 1854.

21. Ibid., Politkowski to Directors, H.B.C., 17 Apr. 1854; PRO, CO 410 1/12: Grey to Douglas, 5 Aug. 1854 (the adequacy of existing defence arrangements for the Island, etc.); Ireland, "Pre-Confederation Defence Problems," pp. 44–45.

22. Bodleian Library, Clarendon Deposit, C. 14, fols. 150ff.; PRO, Adm. 1/5629, cap. S, 64: Stirling to Sec. of Admiralty, 6 Mar. 1854 (re contingency orders for the Admiral, China Station, etc.).

23. See Ravenstein, *Russians on the Amur*,

pp. 116ff.; Golder, *Russian Expansion*, pp. 262–64.

24. Copy in PABC, Victoria; see Galbraith, *Hudson's Bay Company as Imperial Factor*, pp. 293, 302–5 on Douglas as governor-cum-company official.

25. PRO, CO 410 1/6.

26. PRO, Adm. 116/857, circular of 24 Feb. 1854; see also W. F. Reddaway, "The Crimean War and the French Alliance, 1853–58," in *Cambridge History of British Foreign Policy* (Cambridge, 1923), 2: 357ff; and *DNB* 46: 326, on Price.

27. See also, on these issues, D. C. Davidson, "The War Scare of 1854: The Pacific Coast and the Crimean War," *BCHQ* 5 (1941): 243–44.

28. PRO, CO 305 5/22, Douglas to Newcastle, 20 July 1854; also W. N. Sage, *Sir James Douglas and British Columbia* (Toronto, 1930), pp. 180–82 (the local significance of these delays).

29. PRO, CO 305 5/4: Douglas to Newcastle, 16 May 1854.

30. HBCA, A.8/19. Galbraith, *Hudson's Bay Company as Imperial Factor*, pp. 16–17 on Colvile.

31. See Ireland, "Pre-Confederation Defence Problems," pp. 43–45 and notes.

32. PRO, WO 1/551, fols. 143–47, Douglas to Newcastle; annotations by Col. G. C. Manby on fol. 148. Manby's remarks to J. Shepherd, H.B.C. deputy governor, on this topic, later found their way back to Douglas; see HBCA, A.8/7, fol. 139: Manby to Shepherd, 31 Aug. 1854 (copy).

33. PRO, WO 1/551, fol. 156; HBCA, A/8/6, fols. 149–51 on Captain W. C. Grant, together with M. A. Ormsby, *British Columbia: a History* (Toronto, 1958), pp. 99–100 (Grant's "flightiness," etc.).

34. PRO, WO 1/551, fol. 146.

35. See Davidson, "War Scare of 1854," p. 244.

36. HBCA, D.4/74: Simpson to Board of Management, Western Dept., 29 Mar.

37. PABC, encl. in Shepherd to F. Peel, 19 Aug. 1854.

38. PABC, E. O. Scholefield, ed., Memoir no. 11, "Minutes of the Council of Vancouver Island, 1851–1861" (Victoria, 1918), pp. 24–25; Ireland, "Pre-Confederation Defence Problems," pp. 44–45, nn. 13–16.

39. PRO, BT 1/470, no. 2506: draft of Grant in Order-in-Council, 4 Sept. 1848; PABC, Douglas to Newcastle, 17 Aug. 1854; HBCA, A.11/63, fol. 64, R. Clouston to Barclay, 3 June 1854 (H.B.C. agent in Honolulu reports on Russian movements, etc.).

40. Notably, *The Friend*, various issues for June-Aug.

41. PRO, Adm. 1.5656: Frederick to Osborne, 13 Nov. 1854, Y15.

42. PABC, Grey to Douglas, 18 Dec. 1854.

43. Ibid., W. Molesworth to Douglas, 10 Dec. 1854. On the belated sending and receipt of the news of the companies' neutrality pact, see PRO, CO 305/6, Russell to Douglas, 20 June 1855; CO, 410/1, Douglas to Russell, 21 Sept. 1855, and Davidson, "The War Scare of 1854," pp. 246, 251–52.

44. B. M. Gough, *The Royal Navy and the Northwest Coast of North America, 1810-1914* (Vancouver, 1971), pp. 114–21.

45. M. Lewis, ed., "An Eye-Witness at Petropaulovski, 1854," *MM* 49 (1963): 265–72; PRO, Adm. 1/5656: Frederick to Osborne, 15 Nov. 1854.

46. HBCA, A.8/6, fols. 149–51, Blanshard in Grey to Pelly, 25 Feb. 1851; PRO, CO 305/4, Douglas to Newcastle, 24 Oct. 1853; also Moresby, *Two Admirals*, pp. 103ff.

47. See Gough, *The Royal Navy*, p. 121.

48. PABC, Douglas-Barclay correspondence, Nov. 1854 to Mar. 1855; PRO, CO 305/6, Douglas to Grey, 1 Feb. 1855.

49. PRO, Adm. 50/308, "Journal of Rear-Admiral Henry Bruce, C.-in-C., etc.," various entries for February 1855.

50. PABC, Douglas to Barclay, 20 Dec. 1854.

51. PRO, Adm. 1/5630, Moresby to Sec. of Admiralty, 13 Oct. 1853; see also G. S. Graham, *The Politics of Naval Supremacy* (Cambridge, 1965), pp. 102–3.

52. PRO, Adm. 1/5656, encl. in Bruce to Osborne, 14 Sept. 1855, Y116.

53. PABC, Admiralty Correspondence, 1, Douglas to Bruce, 8 May 1855.

54. Ibid., Douglas to CO, 13 June 1855; see also Davidson, "War Scare of 1854," p. 249.

55. See bibliography under Longstaff, F. V., and Wolfenden, M.

56. See W. Kaye Lamb, ed., "Correspondence Relating to the Establishment of a Naval Base at Esquimalt, 1851–1857," *BCHQ* 6 (1942): 280; L. Burpee Robinson, *Esquimalt: "Place of Shoaling Waters"* (Victoria, 1948), pp. 39ff.

57. J. Wood, "Vancouver Island, British Columbia," *Nautical Magazine* 27 (December 1858): 664; F. H. Burns, "H.M.S. *Herald* in Search of Franklin," *The Beaver*, Outfit 294 (1963), pp. 3–13 (on Kellett and his visit to Esquimalt); also Gough, *The Royal Navy*, pp. 104–5.

58. PRO, Adm. 1/5656, Bruce to Osborne, 14 Sept. 1855, Y116; Mayne, *Four Years in British Columbia*, pp. 53ff.

59. PABC, Douglas to Bruce, 28 June 1855.

60. See W. Laird Clowes et al., *The Royal Navy: a History* (London, 1897–1913), 6: 429–32; Barratt, *Russia in Pacific Waters*, Chap. 12.

61. PABC, Douglas to Bruce, 3 Aug. 1855; PRO, Adm. 1/5656, Douglas to Barclay, 19 May 1855, encl. in Shepherd to Phinn, 24 July 1855; Adm. 116/857, Parker (Adm.) to Clarendon, 28 Sept. 1855; also HBCA, A.11/64, fol. 27d, Douglas-Barclay and Allan-Barclay letters, Nov. 1848 to Aug. 1850, re American expansionism.

62. Admiral Sir C. Bridge, *Some Recollections* (London, 1918), pp. 117–19: J. M. Tronson, *Personal Narrative of a Voyage . . . in H.M.S. Barracouta* (London, 1858), pp. 85–90; also n. 60.

63. Tronson, *Personal Narrative*, p. 94; PRO, Adm. 1/5656: Bruce to Osborne, 15 June 1855, Y95; 1/5657, Stirling to Sec. of Admiralty, 1 Oct. 1855 (cap. S, 141).

64. PRO, Adm. 172/2: Remark Book of Capt. Charles Frederick, no. 7; P. B. Whittingham, *Notes on the Late Expedition against the Russian Settlements in Eastern Siberia* (London, 1860), pp. 95–99.

65. Ravenstein, *Russians on the Amur*, pp. 116ff.; Golder, *Russian Expansion*, pp. 265–66.

66. PRO, Adm, 50/308, Bruce's Journal, June-July 1855.

67. Details in F. V. Longstaff, *Esquimalt Naval Base: A History of Its Work and Its Defences* (Victoria, 1941), pp. 16–17, 29–30.

68. PRO, Adm. 50/308, Bruce's Journal, 13 July 1855.

69. PABC, Douglas to W. G. Smith, Esq., printed in Lamb, "Correspondence Relating to Esquimalt," p. 284.

70. Bridge, *Some Recollections*, pp. 118–19; Wolfenden, "Esquimalt Dockyard's First Buildings," *BCHQ* 10 (1946): pp. 237–38.

71. J. Graham to Clarendon, 25 Oct. 1854, cited in R. W. van Alstyne, ed., "Anglo-American Relations, 1853–1857," *AHR* 42 (1937): 498; see also Chap. 6 below.

72. Gough, *The Royal Navy*, p. 128.

73. See *Nautical Magazine* 26 (February 1858): 96–98; Ravenstein, *Russians on the Amur*, Chap. 5.

74. PRO, Adm. 1/5656, Bruce to Osborne, 14 Sept. 1855, Y116; PABC, Douglas to Smith, 21 Sept. 1855.

75. PABC, Douglas to Smith, 10 Oct. 1855, encl. in Smith to Sec. of Admiralty, 22 Dec. 1855.

76. Gough, *The Royal Navy*, pp. 130–32, 134–36.

77. Major-General J. W. Laurie, "The Protection of Our Naval Base in the North Pacific," *Journal of the Royal United Service Institution* 27 (1884): 376, 359. See Chap. 7. below on Laurie's lecture, and responses.

78. See Barratt, "The Enemy That Never Was: The New Zealand Russian Scare of 1870–1885," *New Zealand Slavonic Journal* (1976): 13–33.

79. PABC, Douglas to Rev. E. Cridge, 16 May 1855.

80. Ibid., same to same, 7 Sept. 1855, and H. Gardiner Fishbourne (Royal Commission of the Patriotic Fund) to Douglas, 10 Dec. 1855.

81. Ibid., Douglas to Cridge, 19 May 1856.

82. On the Fraser River gold strikes, which substantially increased the threat posed by American subjects en masse, see A, Waddington, *The Fraser Mines Vindicated* (Victoria, 1858); on the Stikine gold-strike of 1861 and its significance, C. I. Jackson, "A Territory of Little Value: The Wind of Change on the Northwest Coast, 1861–67," *The Beaver*, Outfit 298 (1967), pp. 40–45, and A. S. Morton, *History of the Canadian West to 1870–71* (London, n.d.), pp. 771-75.

83. For interesting Australasian parallels,

see V. Fitzhardinge, "Russian Naval Visitors to Australia, 1862–1888," *JRAHS* 52 (1966), pt. 2: 129–58. Also n. 78 here.

84. PABC, Bruce to Douglas, 14 Feb. 1855; *San Francisco Herald*, 22 Aug. 1855 (arrival of *Amphitrite* from Sitka, etc.).

NOTES TO CHAPTER FOUR

1. PRO, CO 305/3; Douglas to Grey, 29 Jan. 1852 (re American designs on the Queen Charlotte (Islands); also HBCA, A8/7, fol. 22 (Moresby-Douglas-Admiralty correspondence on American expansionism on the Coast).
2. PRO, WO 1/551, p. 148.
3. On this consideration, see the Crampton-Clarendon correspondence, 1854–55, Bodleian Library, Clarendon deposit, C.25, 44; BL, Aberdeen Papers, no. 43189 (Aberdeen to Clarendon, 25 Sept. 1854); PRO, Adm.116/857, J. Parker to Clarendon, 28 Sept. 1855.
4. Further on this, K. Bourne, *Britain and the Balance of Power in North America, 1815–1908* (London, 1967), pp.170–72; also *The Times*, 8 Aug. 1854 (early reaction to the prospect of an American Alaska).
5. See R. W. van Alstyne, "Anglo-American Relations, 1853–57," *AHR* 42 (1936–37): 493–95; also, on London's far harder line toward Central America, the same writer's "British Diplomacy and the Clayton-Bulwer Treaty, 1850–60," *Journal of Modern History* 11 (1939): pp.175–76.
6. J. M. Callahan, *Cuba and International Relations* (Baltimore, 1899), pp.221–97; R. W. van Alstyne, "Great Britain, the United States, and Hawaiian Independence, 1850–1855," *PHR* 4 (1935): 15ff.
7. F. A. Golder, "Russian-American Relations During the Crimean War," *AHR* 31 (1926): 462; see also bibliography under Bolkhovitinov.
8. Hansard, *Parliamentary Debates*, 3rd series, 130 (31 Jan. 1854), p.43.
9. J. B. Moore, ed., *The Works of James Buchanan, Comprising His Speeches, State Papers, and Private Correspondence* (Philadelphia and London, 1908–11), 9: 345ff.
10. Details in C. O. Paullin's article in *DAB* 7: 486–89.

11. van Alstyne, "Anglo-American Relations," pp. 493–95.
12. See Gough, *The Royal Navy*, pp. 108–12 and notes; Okun', *Russian-American Company*, pp. 116ff.
13. Golder, "Russian-American Relations," p. 462.
14. Ibid., p. 463. On Aleksandr Bodisko (1786–1854), see *Cong. Globe*, 28: 247.
15. Sketch in *AHR* 26, pp. 454–63.
16. *Works of James Buchanan*, 9: 166; PRO, Adm.1/5656, Frederick to Osborne, 13 Nov. 1854 (Y15, nervousness of a Russian raider at Victoria).
17. Golder, "Russian-American Relations," p. 466.
18. Wheaton, *Elements of International Law* (London, 1864), p. 771.
19. Hansard, *Parliamentary Debates*, 3rd series, 136 (1854), pp. 255, 283; see also van Alstyne's "John F. Crampton, Conspirator or Dupe?," *AHR* 41 (1936): pp. 492–502; and, on Marcy's approach to the active Russo-American alliance at which Stoeckl hinted, the paper by H. B. Learned in S. F. Bemis, ed., *The American Secretaries of State and Their Diplomacy* (NY, 1928), 6: 237–62.
20. Hansard, *Parliamentary Debates*, 3rd series, 136, pp. 519–610; Hughenden Manor, Disraeli Papers, Malmesbury 99 (Malmesbury to Disraeli, 4 Nov. 1854 ("These two islands cannot *furnish* males . . ." etc.).
21. Bodleian Library, Clarendon deposit, C.25 (Crampton to Clarendon, 4 Dec. 1854, acknowledgement and survey).
22. Golder, "Russian-American Relations," pp. 469–70.
23. Bodleian Library, Clarendon deposit, C.43 (Crampton to Clarendon, 18 June 1855); PRO, Adm.50/308 (Bruce Journal), 18 Sept. 1855 (rumours, surveillance of Russian shipping at Sitka and San Francisco); also van Alstyne, "Anglo-American Relations," p. 498

(Sir James Graham on Russian activity in California, Oct. 1854).

24. Bodleian Library, Clarendon deposit, C.25, 44 (Crampton to Clarendon, 24 Oct. 1854, 29 Oct. 1855.)

25. Ibid., C. 44 (Crampton to Clarendon, 24 Sept. 1855).

26. Bourne, *Britain and the Balance of Power*, p. 189.

27. Ibid., p. 190 and n. 5: *Works of James Buchanan*, 9: 161ff.

28. See W. D. Jones, *The American Problem in British Diplomacy* (London, 1974), pp. 145–47.

29. Golder, "Russian-American Relations," pp. 470–71.

30. Bodleian Library, Clarendon deposit, C.44 (Crampton to Clarendon, 10 Sept. 1855).

31. Bourne, *Britain and the Balance of Power*, pp. 187–88.

32. See n. 19.

33. BL. Add. MSS 48579, Palmerston to Clarendon, 24 Sept. 1855.

34. Cited by Bourne, *Britain and the Balance of Power*, p. 187.

35. PRO, Adm.1/5656: Frederick to Osborne, Y15, 13 Nov. 1854; Adm.1/5672, Bruce to Osborne, Y106, 11 July 1856.

36. BL, Add. MSS 49565 (Halifax Papers), Wood to Bruce, private, 16 Feb. 1855.

37. PRO, Adm.50/308, Bruce Journal.

38. On these questions, see Gough, *The Royal Navy*, pp. 187–89, and J. P. S. Bach, "The Maintenance of Royal Navy Vessels in the Pacific Ocean, 1825–75," *MM* 56 (1970): 259–736.

39. BL, Add. MSS 49565, Wood to Clarendon, 2 Jan. 1856.

40. See Head's memorandum, "On the Defensible Condition of Western Canada," cited by D. G. G. Kerr in *Sir Edmund Head: A Scholarly Governor* (Toronto, 1954), pp. 131–32.

41. BL, Add. MSS 49565, Bruce to Wood, 22 Sept. 1856.

42. PRO, Adm.1/5969: Admiralty instructions to Baynes, draft, 10 Mar. 1859.

43. BL, Add. MSS 49565, Wood to Bruce, 16 Feb. 1856.

44. PRO, Adm.1/5969, minute of 17 Feb. 1859.

45. See Barratt, *Russophobia in New Zealand* (Palmerston North, NZ, 1981), Chap. 5, on reactions to the Russian ab-rogation of the "Black Sea clauses" of the 1856 Treaty of Paris, in 1870.

46. On de Cosmos, see R. Wild, *Amor de Cosmos* (Toronto, 1952). No study of the early policies and fortunes of *The British Colonist* has been written.

47. "The European War: How It Will Affect Us," in *The British Colonist* 25, July 1859, p. 1.

48. Ibid., no. 10, p. 3

49. Ibid., p. 3 (miscellaneous items).

50. Ibid., p. 1 ("The Population of Russia").

51. 4 Nov. 1859, p. 1 ("General Suttler, who was Intendant of the Russian Army in the Crimea").

52. 18 Dec. 1858, p. 3 ("Tremendous fires . . . at Orel in Russia"); 8 Sept. 1862 ("Fearful Incendiarism in Russia").

53. Galbraith, *Hudson's Bay Company as an Imperial Factor*, pp. 169–74; C. I. Jackson, "The Stikine Territory Lease and its Relevance to the Alaska Puchase," *PHR* 36 (1967): 289–306.

54. Further on these events, see Gough, *The Royal Navy*, pp. 146–47.

55. "Izvestiia o plavanii nashikh sudov za granitsei: Izvlechenie iz doneseniia nachal'nika eskadry v tikhom okeane, Svity E.V., kontradmirala Popova," *Morskoi sbornik* 64 (1863), 1: 12–13; A. Belomer, "Vtoraia tikhookeanskaia eskadra," ibid. 283 (1914), 1: 54–56.

56. *British Colonist*, 19 Sept. 1862 ("The Russian Sailors").

57. Ibid., 22 Sept. 1862 ("First Soirée of the Season").

58. *Morskoi sbornik* 64 (1863), 1: 14–16. See also F. A. Golder, "The Russian Fleet and the Civil War," *AHR* 20 (1915): 801–14, on Popov's visit to San Francisco in 1863.

59. Review in T. A. Bailey, *A Diplomatic History of the American People*, 6th ed. (NY, 1958), pp. 364–65.

60. "Gorod Nanaimo na ostrove Vankuvera, i ego Kamennyi ugol'," *Morskoi sbornik* 75 (1864), 12: 173–87. An even longer and more factually detailed essay on Vancouver Island was Charles Forbes's "Ostrov Vankuvera: istochniki bogatstva i proizvoditel' nye sily ego, kak kolonii," ibid. 55 (1863), 3: 107–56. Forbes had nothing to say of defences, however.

61. See Barratt, "The Enemy That Never Was: The New Zealand Russian Scares,"

New Zealand Slavonic Journal (1976): 13–33, and "The Visit of the Russian Cruiser *Afrika* to Auckland, 1881," ibid. (1978): 1–23.

62. Typical of many pro-Polish pieces in the *Daily British Colonist* was that of 8 Sept. 1863, "The Insurrection in Poland: The Russian Note."

63. R. W. Winks, *Canada and the United States: The Civil War Years* (Baltimore, 1960), p. 375.

64. F. W. Howay, W. N. Sage, and H. F. Angus, *British Columbia and the United States* (New Haven, 1942), pp. 183–84.

65. C. P. Stacey, *Canada and the British Army, 1846–1871*, 2d ed. (Toronto, 1963), pp. 215ff.

66. Details in Corday Mackay, "The Collins Overland Telegraph," *BCHQ* 10 (1946): 187–215, and J. S. Galbraith, "Perry McDonough Collins at the Colonial Office," ibid. 17 (1953): 210ff.

67. Seymour personally assisted men of the California State Telegraph Co. to lay a cable across the Fraser River on 21 Mar. 1865.

68. 2 Oct. ("Preparations on the Mainland").

69. PRO, FO 65/701, Buchanan to Stanley, no. 387, 12 Sept. 1866; also Winks, *Canada and the United States*, pp. 164–65.

70. See T. A. Bailey, "Why the United States Purchased Alaska," *PHR* 3 (1934): 49; C. Vevier, "American Continentalism: An Idea of Expansion, 1845–1910," *AHR* 55 (1960): 332–33; and the *British Colonist*, 16 May 1867, p. 3.

71. See the *British Colonist*, 25 Apr. 1867, "The Rumoured Proposition to Cede this Colony," and the expansionist editorials of various west coast (American) publications that substantiated, or seemed to support, that attitude, e.g., in the Sacramento *Daily Union* and the Seattle *Puget Sound Gazette* for 1 Apr. and Apr. respectively.

72. For a basic English-language bibliography, see Hunter Miller, "Russian Opinion on the Cession of Alaska," *AHR* 48 (1943): pp. 521–33.

73. *New York Herald*, 1 Apr. 1867.

74. *Washington Evening Star*, 21 Dec. 1867.

75. *New York Herald*, 1 Apr. 1867 [cited, together with several other illuminating newspaper editorials of the day, by Welch in "American Opinion and the Purchase," pp. 280–88].

76. W. E. Ireland, "Pre-Confederation Defence Problems of the Pacific Colonies," Canadian Historical Association, *Annual Report, 1941* (1941): 51ff.; Gough, *The Royal Navy*, pp. 210–11; W. C. B. Tunstall, "Imperial Defence, 1815–1870," *Cambridge History of the British Empire*, (Cambridge, 1940), 2: 833–35 (withdrawals of imperial troops to 1871).

77. *British Colonist*, 16 May 1867.

78. Ibid., 29 Apr. 1867.

79. Tunstall, "Imperial Defence," pp. 817–20, 832–36; D. C. Gordon, *The Dominion Partnership in Imperial Defense, 1870–1914* (Baltimore, 1965), pp. 55–56; Barratt, *Russophobia in New Zealand*, Chap. 5.

80. PRO, Adm. 1/5969: Denman to Adm., 14 July and 26 Aug. 1866 (defending a "united colony," coal fields, etc.); CO 880/5, confidential, no. 37 Seymour to Cardwell, 17 Feb. 1866; M. A. Ormsby, *British Columbia*, pp. 245–57; W. L. Morton, *The Critical Years: The Union of British North America, 1857–73* (Toronto, 1964), pp. 169ff.

81. Further on these matters, see D. M. Schurman, *The Education of a Navy: The Development of British Naval Strategic Thought, 1867–1914* (London, 1965), pp. 17–20; Tunstall, "Imperial Defence," pp. 817–25.

82. Relevant figures in *PPGB*, 1862, 36 (3061); 1865, 37 (3434); 1870, 42 (254); and Hansard, *Parliamentary Debates*, 3rd series, 176, pp. 373–78. See also Stacey, *Canada and the British Army*, pp. 225–27.

83. Winks, *Canada and the United States*, pp. 164–65, 375; Morton, *The Critical Years*, pp. 169–71 (Fenian scare of 1866); and R. H. Roy, "The Early Militia and Defence of British Columbia, 1871–1885," *BCHQ* 18 (1954): 2–6 (of 1871).

84. Clarendon expressed his feelings crisply to Queen Victoria on 1 May 1869, see G. E. Buckle, ed., *Letters of Queen Victoria*, 2nd series (London, 1926), 1: 594–95. Also Stacey, *Canada and the British Army*, pp. 215–17, 228.

85. Tunstall, "Imperial Defence," p. 825.

See also, on this crisis of national defence and strategic planning, J. C. R. Colomb's seminal work, *The Protection of our Commerce and Distribution of our Naval Forces Considered* (London, 1867), esp. pp. iii–vi; and G. Wrottesley, *The Life and Correspondence of Field-Marshal Sir John Burgoyne* (London, 1873), 1: 436–51.

86. PAC, Papers of the Deputy Minister of Militia and Defence, nos. 6278 (Trutch-Howe correspondence re Victoria's defencelessness); Macdonald Papers, vol. 278, pp 150–51 (Trutch to Macdonald, 4 Jan. 1872, on the same topic).

87. Cator to Trutch, 7 Jan. 1872, cited by Roy in "The Early Militia," p. 4.

88. Department of Militia and Defence, *Report on the State of the Militia of the Dominion of Canada . . . 1872* (Ottawa, 1873), p. cxxvi; *Militia General Orders*, 13 Feb., 11 Apr., 10 July 1874; also R. H. Roy, "The Colonel Goes West," *Canadian Army Journal* 8 (1954): 76–81.

89. Roy, "The Early Militia," p. 9, notes that New Westminster acquired only a pair of obsolete 24-pounder howitzers when, in 1874, its first battery of "garrison artillery" was established.

90. PAC, Papers of the Deputy Minister of Militia, no. 02638, Col. G. F. Blair,

"Memorandum on the Defence of British Columbia" (1875); *Report on the State of the Militia . . . 1875* (Ottawa, 1876), pp. vi–x.

91. 68-pounders from the corvettes *Clio* and *Tartar*, which Rear-Admiral Maitland had decided to mount on Duntze Head, Esquimalt, together with fourteen old 32-pounders, in 1862, had not been ready for service until 1865–66, but remained there ten years later, PRO, Adm. 1/5924: Denman to Adm., 24 Jan. 1865; 1/5790, Maitland to same, 1 Feb. 1862; PRO, 30/6/122, Carnarvon Papers, pp. 44–46: "Memorandum by Colonel Sir W. F. D. Jervois . . . on the Defenceless Condition," 7 Jan. 1875.

92. Roy, "The Early Militia," p. 12; Longstaff, *Esquimalt Naval Base*, pp. 43–44; PRO, Adm.116/744, fols. 241–43: "Report of a Committee of the Hon. the Executive Council, British Columbia, approved . . . on the 11th day of June 1877" (copy).

93. Details of reductions in C. F. Hamilton, "The Canadian Militia: The Dead Period," *Canadian Defence Quarterly* 7 (1929): 78–89. On Ottawa's persistent neglect of its defence responsibilities in British Columbia, R. A. Preston, *Canada and "Imperial Defense"* (Durham, NC, 1967), pp. 120–23, 336–40.

NOTES TO CHAPTER FIVE

1. "The European War: How It Will Affect Us," *British Colonist*, 25 July 1859, p. 1.

2. Howay et al., *British Columbia and the United States*, p. 183.

3. In Ottawa, by contrast, such attitudes were in 1869–70 overwhelmed by dismay at the departure of British regulars: Canada, *Sessional Papers* 4 (1871), vol. 5, no. 46, p. 66 (Cartier to Young, 19 May 1870); no. 146, *Returns to Addresses of the Senate and House of Commons Relative to the Withdrawal of the Troops from the Dominion*; also J. E. Tyler, *The Struggle for Imperial Unity, 1868–1895* (London, 1938), pp. 1–5.

4. The *British Colonist* took *The Times* to

task, on 27 Jan. 1870, for errors and wrong emphases in that issue.

5. Ormsby, *British Columbia*, pp. 170ff.

6. See bibliography, under Merk, Vevier, Winks.

7. Howay, et al., *British Columbia and the United States*, p. 182.

8. J. Gleason, *The Genesis of Russophobia in Great Britain* (Cambridge, MA, 1950).

9. As reflected in the provincial press, see chap. 6.

10. "The European Difficulty," 6 Dec. 1876.

11. On 24 January 1877, the *Mainland Guardian* gave equal attention to such local issues and "The Eastern Ques-

tion," though the latter was the subject of its editorial.

12. L. G. Beskrovnyi, *Russkaia armiia i flot v XIX veke* (M., 1973), p. 511.

13. Further on this, see Barratt, "The Visit of the Russian Cruiser *Afrika* to Auckland (1881)," *New Zealand Slavonic Journal* (1978): pp. 2–4.

14. Beskrovnyi, *Russkaia armiia*, p. 512.

15. Barratt, "The Enemy That Never Was"; Fitzhardinge, "Russian Naval Visitors," pp. 151ff.

16. Beskrovnyi, *Russkaia armiia*, p. 514.

17. "Zhurnal Osobogo Soveshchaniia Morskogo Ministerstva," (1882, report by S. S. Lesovskii), Saltykov-Shchedrin Public Library, Leningrad, *Otdel rukopisei*, fond 169, kart. 42, delo 32, pp. 11ff.

18. Vice-Admiral A. B. Aslanbegov, among other senior Russian officers of the period, sadly contrasted Russia's Pacific ports with those of California and Vancouver Island; see *Morskoi sbornik* 187 (1881), no. 11 (Aslanbegov to Grand Duke Aleksei Aleksandrovich from San Francisco, 24 Aug. 1881), p. 31.

19. U.S. Navy records for Mare Island Navy Yard provide details of Russian comings and goings in these years.

20. Barratt, "The Visit of the Russian Cruiser *Afrika*," pp. 4–7.

21. On 13 May, the Russian squadron left Mare Island and proceeded to the Golden Gate locality; Longstaff, *Esquimalt Naval Base*, pp. 42, 59.

22. Their effect was increased by the immediacy of telegraph news.

23. Further on these matters, D. M. Schurman, "Esquimalt: Defence Problem, 1865–87," *BCHQ* 19 (1955): 57–69; Roy, "The Early Militia," pp. 11–12.

24. Gough, *The Royal Navy*, pp. 187–89, 194–96.

25. PRO, Adm. 1/6414, de Horsey to Admiralty, from Valparaiso.

26. G. A. Ballard, "British Frigates of 1875; the 'Shah,' " *MM* 20 (1936): 305–15; Longstaff, *Esquimalt Naval Base*, p. 40.

27. PRO. Adm. 1/6414, de Horsey to Sec. of Adm., 25 June 1877, with Robinson's report no. 34, 10 May.

28. Longstaff, *Esquimalt Naval Base*, p. 42.

29. *British Colonist*, 1 May; editorial.

30. Having left Valparaiso only on 25 June; see n. 27.

31. Captain J. C. R. Colomb, "Russian Development and Our Naval and Military Position in the North Pacific," *JRUSI* 21 (1877): 671–80.

32. PRO, Cab. 7/1: "Reports of a Colonial Defence Committee on the Temporary Defences," secret, June 1878; Carnarvon Papers, 30/6/122, pp. 19–21, C. H. Nugent, "Memorandum on the Relative Importance of Coaling Stations."

33. On the Institution, R. Higham, ed., *Consolidated Author and Subject Index to the Journal of the R.U.S.I., 1857–1963* (Ann Arbor, 1964).

34. Colomb, "Russian Development," pp. 692, 701.

35. *The Gate of the Pacific* (London, 1863).

36. See Gough, *The Royal Navy*, p. 210 (Rear-Admiral Denman's view).

37. On this point, see Schurman, *The Education of a Navy*, p. 19.

38. Colomb, "Russian Development," p. 677.

39. The *British Colonist* had delighted in the corruption and inefficiency of the Russian general staff since the 1850's; see, for example, its use of comments attributed to General Suttler on 4 Nov. 1859, p. 1.

40. The new, wider perspective was encouraged both by local veterans of the Crimean War, notably Lt.-Col. C. F. Houghton, now deputy adjutant-general of the province (cf. Longstaff, *Esquimalt Naval Base*, p. 58; Roy, "The Early Militia," p. 7), and by the Venerable Archdeacon Wright, who gave lectures to provincial audiences on the warlike menacing growth of Russia (see The *British Colonist*, 15 Feb. 1878, "Mechanics' Literary Institute").

41. "Europe a Vast Military Camp," 17 May 1877.

42. The *Mainland Guardian* concurred, on 30 May, in its editorial, "The Vitality of Islam."

43. *British Colonist*, 19 Sept. 1877: "The War."

44. Ibid., 6 Oct. 1877: "The Eastern War."

45. See n. 26.

46. *Mainland Guardian*, 29 Sept. 1877, "New and Grave Complications in Europe."

47. Ibid., 13 Oct., "The Lesson of Plevna"; *British Colonist*, 14 Dec., "The Fall of Plevna."

48. See Gough, *The Royal Navy*, pp. 221–22, 234–35 (the Admiralty aspect).
49. 22 Dec. 1877.
50. *Mainland Guardian*, 2 Feb. 1878; see also A. T. Mahan, *The Influence of Sea Power upon History, 1660–1783* (London, 1890), p. 14.
51. PRO, Adm. 116/744, fols. 241–43: "Copy of a Report of a Committee of the Honourable the Executive Council, approved . . . 11th day of June 1877."
52. Canada, *Sessional Papers* 13 (1880), vol. 5, no. 8, p. xiv: "Militia Report for 1879"; PAC, Papers of Deputy Minister of Militia and Defence, Inward, no. 04441 (Selby Smyth to Jones, 3 May 1878); Roy, "The Early Militia," pp. 7–12; Hamilton, "The Canadian Militia," pp. 82ff.
53. Canada, House of Commons, *Debates*, 1876, p. 1099ff.
54. On this, see R. A. Preston, *Canada and "Imperial Defense,"* pp. 69–70.
55. Canada, Department of Militia and Defence, *Report on the State of the Militia of the Dominion . . . 1875* (Ottawa, 1876), pp. vi–viii; PAC, Papers of Deputy Minister, Militia, Inward, no. 02638 (Blair's military intelligence report); also Preston, *Canada and "Imperial Defence,"* pp. 75–76, 78–79.
56. Roy, "The Early Militia," p. 11–12.
57. Ormsby, *British Columbia*, pp. 245–57.
58. Preston, *Canada and "Imperial Defence,"* chaps 3 and 4, passim.
59. PRO, CO 807/7, no. 74, pp. 3–4 (Mackenzie on the need to "concede" a railway to serve Esquimalt, 19 Feb. 1874); PAC, Dufferin Papers, microfilm 1140, p. 215: Dufferin to Hicks-Beach, n.d.; PRO, Adm. 1/6460, Admiral A. Milne to CO, 1 Apr. 1878.
60. Further on these matters, F. W. Howay and E. O. S. Scholefield, *British Columbia, from the Earliest Times to the Present* (Vancouver, 1914). 2: 402ff.; also D. M. Schurman, "Esquimalt: Defence Problem," pp. 60ff.
61. PRO, Adm. 1/6056, Rear-Admiral G. F. Hastings to Sec. of Adm., 3 Dec. 1868; Mayne, *Four Years in British Columbia*, pp. 159–60; Longstaff, *Esquimalt Naval Base*, pp. 25–27.
62. PRO, Adm. 1/6414, fols. 171–78: de Horsey to Sec. of Adm., 9 Oct. 1877.
63. The province had declined to avail itself of Admiralty support under the 1865 Colonial Docks Loan Act, as de Horsey noted, because it would be hard pressed to repay any loan.
64. PRO, Adm. 1/6414, de Horsey to Sec. of Adm., various.
65. See Tunstall, "Imperial Defence," pp. 838–40 for a summary of these "Blue Water school" principles.
66. See H. D'Egville, *Imperial Defence and Closer Union* (London, 1913); and D. M. Schurman, *The Education of a Navy*, chap. 2.
67. Colomb, *The Protection of Our Commerce*, p. iv.
68. Ibid., pp. vi, 1–2; J. C. R. Colomb, *On Colonial Defence* (London, 1873), pp. 22–23 (on Canadian obligations to contribute to the upkeep of imperial bases important to Canadian commerce, etc.).
69. Gough, *The Royal Navy*, pp. 207–8; Preston, *Canada and "Imperial Defense,"* pp. 132–33.
70. PRO, Cab. 7/1: "Reports of a Colonial Defence Committee on the Temporary Defences," secret, June 1878.
71. Great Britain, Colonial Office, Lt.-Col. W. F. D. Jervois, *Report on the Defence of Canada . . . February 1864* (London, 1865); Preston, *Canada and "Imperial Defense,"* pp. 41–42, 218–20.
72. PRO, Carnarvon Papers, 30/6/122, pp. 44–46.
73. Ibid., pp. 19–21.
74. Preston, *Canada and "Imperial Defense,"* pp. 53–71, 80–82.
75. *JRUSI* 21 (London, 1877): 659–80; responses to Colomb's paper, pp. 680–707.
76. Seven individuals, besides the chairman, addressed the audience at some length, ibid., pp. 689–707.
77. Ibid., pp. 670, 672.
78. Ibid., p. 677.
79. Ibid., pp. 672–73.
80. Ibid., p. 677.
81. Ibid., pp. 674, 677, 678–79.
82. Ibid., p. 701.
83. Ibid., p. 699 (Captain Field's remarks).
84. Ibid., p. 701 (Lord Dunsany's remarks, answered on p. 702).
85. Ibid., p. 685 (Mr. Strangway's remarks).
86. Ibid., p. 707.
87. Ibid., p. 702.
88. "The Report of a Colonial Defence

Committee on the Temporary Defences of the Naval Station of Esquimalt and the Important Commercial Town and Harbour of Victoria" was completed by 4

Apr. 1878, PRO, Cab. 7/1, and PAC, G. 21, no. 165 (vol. 3), secret, Hicks-Beach to Dufferin, 11 May 1878, and related papers.

NOTES TO CHAPTER SIX

1. Only on 6 May 1867, in "Delayed Dispatches: Europe," was the *British Colonist* able to report — by courtesy of the *London Herald*'s St. Petersburg correspondent and the California State Telegraph Company — that Russian reactions to the Alaska cession treaty concluded on 30 Mar. were generally favourable. Further on the strategic meaning of improving communication systems, Great Britain, *Parliamentary Papers*, 1867–68 (House of Commons, vol. 48), pp. 7–8 ("Correspondence, Capital of British Columbia"); also Corday Mackay, "The Collins Overland Telegraph," *BCHQ* 10 (1946): 187–215, and chap. n. 66 here.
2. *British Colonist*, p. 3.
3. That is, officially confirmed by British sources.
4. Beskrovnyi, *Russkaia armiia*, p. 514.
5. *British Colonist*, 15 Feb. 1878, "The War."
6. Ibid, 14 Feb. 1878: "The War"; Canada, *Sessional Papers* 13 (1880), vol. 5 no. 8, pp. xiii–iv (Selby Smyth's earlier warnings); Roy, "The Early Militia," pp. 13–14.
7. *British Colonist*, 17 Feb. 1878, "The War".
8. *Mainland Guardian*, 18 Feb. 1878, "Victoria Letter."
9. Russian sources call *Kreiser* a corvette or second-class cruiser, contemporaneous British sources, a cruiser or iron clipper; the *British Colonist*, on 19 Feb. 1878, refers to her as a sloop-of-war.
10. Ibid., "Arrival of a Russian Man of War at Esquimalt."
11. *Mainland Guardian*, 18 Feb. 1878, "Victoria Letter."
12. See n. 10.
13. But see *Morskoi sbornik*, issues for 1878, for details of *Kreiser*'s and other cruisers' routes, personnel, armament, and missions.

14. PRO, Adm. 1/6454, Robinson's report at Esquimalt, 20 Feb., encl. in de Horsey to Sec. of Adm., 4 Apr. 1878.
15. *Mainland Guardian*, 21 Feb. 1878, "Victoria Letter."
16. *British Colonist*, 17 Feb. 1878, "A Mess of It."
17. See n. 15 and 1 above.
18. *British Colonist*, 19 Feb. 1878.
19. Pertinent royal letters cited by F. Hardie, *The Political Influence of Queen Victoria, 1861–1901*, 2d. ed. (London, 1938), pp. 160–62; see also Kingsley Martin, "The Victorian Monarchy," *Edinburgh Review* (April 1926), pp. 381–82.
20. PAC, R.G. 7, G. 21, vol. 76, no. 165/4, "Memorandum by the Hon. A. Campbell, Minister of Militia and Defence," 21 April 1880; Canada, *Sessional Papers* 13 (1880), vol. 5, no. 8, "Militia Report for 1879," pp. xliv–xlv.
21. PRO, Adm. 1/6454–55, de Horsey to Adm., various (squadron movements).
22. Details in L. I. Strakhovsky, "Russia's Privateering Projects of 1878," *Journal of Modern History* 7 (March 1935): pp. 25ff.; see also Barratt, "The Visit of the Russian Cruiser *Afrika*," pp. 4–5.
23. See S. P. Moiseev, *Spisok korablei russkogo parovogo i bronenosnogo flota s 1881 po 1917 god* (Moscow, 1947), introduction and pp. 72–89.
24. J. F. von Kronenfels, *Das schwimmende Flottenmaterial der Seemächte* (Vienna and Leipzig, 1883), pp. 201–2.
25. PAC, Papers of the Deputy Minister of Militia and Defence, Inwards, 1878, no. 04441, Selby Smyth to A. G. Jones, confidential, 3 May; J. W. King, *The Warships and Navies of the World* (Boston, 1882), pp. 331–32; *DAB* 4: 499–500 (on C. H. Cramp and his services to Russia).
26. PAC, Papers of the Deputy Minister of Militia, Inwards, 1878, no. 04441; R.G. 7, G. 21, vol. 75, no. 165/3(b), Report of

the Committee of the Privy Council, Dominion of Canada, 4 May 1878.

27. See Bourne, *Britain and the Balance of Power*, pp. 310ff., (latent anti-British sentiment in the U.S., reflected in Cramp's activity of 1878); and Mahan, *The Influence of Sea Power*, p. 14. Admiralty awareness of U.S. naval strength in the Pacific at this time (cf. R. E. Johnson, *Thence Round Cape Horn*, App. 3) was transmitted in a context of Anglo-Russian crisis to the War Office; PRO, Adm. 1/6460, Adm. to Under-Sec. of State for War, 1 June 1878, secret.

28. *Mainland Guardian*, 26 June 1878; Roy, "The Early Militia," p. 14; Longstaff, *Esquimalt Naval Base*, pp. 42-43 (*Kreiser* in San Francisco Bay, 24 June — 1 July 1878, etc.).

29. King, *Warships and Navies*, p. 331; also Russia, *Ministerstvo finansov: istoricheskii obzor glavneishikh meropriiatii, 1802–1902* (St. P., 1902), 2: 640–43, on the financial aspects of this and other measures.

30. See n. 26; also V. Fitzhardinge, "Russian Naval Visitors to Australia, 1862–1888," *JRAHS* 52 (1966), pt. 2, pp. 138ff., and Barratt, "The Visit of the Russian Cruiser *Afrika*," pp. 16–18.

31. *Morskoi sbornik* 58 (1862), no. 3, pp. 178–80; Kronenfels, *Das schwimmende Flottenmaterial*, pp. 206–7.

32. Relevant papers in the New Zealand National Archives, Wellington, Department of Defence, Records, C. 16/7, "Attack (Proposed) on Australia by Russia, 1878" (memorandum by Major-General E. Harding Steward of 17 Nov. 1884, with three appendices). Steward's belief that Vice-Admiral S.S. Lesovskii, the Russian commander-in-chief in the Pacific, and a certain Colonel Bodisco, then in Japan, had in 1877–78 planned such raids at least in general terms, was shared by Major-General J. W. Laurie, the deputy adjutant-general of the Canadian Militia, on the basis of his conversations with Russian naval officers at Esquimalt in 1881; J. W. Laurie, "The Protection of Our Naval Base in the North Pacific," *JRUSI* 27 (1884): p. 358. The matter deserves further study.

33. Kronenfels, *Das schwimmende Flottenmaterial*, p. 207.

34. King, *Warships and Navies*, p. 331.

35. The *Melbourne Australian Sketcher*, cited by Fitzhardinge, "Russian Naval Visitors," p. 145.

36. Barratt, "The Visit of the Russian Cruiser *Afrika*," pp. 6–7; also A. S. Beliaev, *Ocherk russkogo voennogo sudostroeniia* (St. P., 1885), chap. 5.

37. As it would for another six years; see the *Mainland Guardian*, 18 Nov. 1882, "The Effect of a War upon This Province"; 2 May 1885, "War: Those Who Wish to Keep the Peace."

38. "Militia Report for 1879," p. xiv.

39. See *The Journal of the Journey of His Excellency the Governor-General of Canada from Government House, Ottawa, to British Columbia and Back* (London, 1877); on Dufferin's Russian associations (visit to the Crimean battlefields in 1856, speeches of 1863, appointment as ambassador to St. Petersburg in 1879, etc.), see Sir A. C. Lyall, *The Life of the Marquess of Dufferin* (London, 1905).

40. PRO, CO 42/753: Dufferin to Hicks-Beach, no. 56, 11 Mar. 1878.

41. PAC, R.G. 9, IIA 6, vol. 1, p. 21: Hicks-Beach to Dufferin, Mar. 1878.

42. On these matters, see Preston, *Canada and "Imperial Defense,"* pp. 125–28.

43. See G. F. G. Stanley, *Canada's Soldiers: The Military History of an Unmilitary People* (Toronto, 1960), p. 246.

44. PAC, Papers of the Deputy Minister of Militia and Defence, Inwards, 1878: no. 04375, enclosure.

45. PAC, G. 21, no. 165, vol. 3, secret, "Report of a Colonial Defence Committee on the Temporary Defences of the Naval Station of Esquimalt and the Important Commercial Town and Harbour of Victoria," Apr. 1878.

46. A copy of the report was enclosed in Hicks-Beach to Dufferin, 11 May 1878; it was recopied in Ottawa, and sent on to Victoria at once.

47. The report itself arrived with Colonial Miscellany 35B, PAC, G. 21, no. 165, vol. 3 (b). The original, also in secret and confidential print, was bound with other "Reports of a Colonial Defence Committee on the Temporary Defences" and filed at the CO as Cab. 7/1(a).

48. PAC, Macdonald Papers, M.G. 21, A. 1(a), vol. 100, Summary Report of the Committee of the Privy Council's Pro-

ceedings, 4 May 1878; Great Britain, *Parliamentary Papers* 55 (1907), 139 (Cd. 3523), on the decommissioning of gunboats on the Great Lakes and St. Lawrence.

49. PAC, R.G. 7, G. 21, vol. 75, no. 165/3(b).

50. PAC, Dufferin Papers, A 411: Mackenzie to Dufferin, 11 May 1878.

51. *Ottawa Times*, 2 May 1870; D. C. Thomson, *Alexander Mackenzie: Clear Grit* (Toronto, 1960), pp. 115ff.; Preston, *Canada and "Imperial Defense,"* pp. 81–82.

52. PAC, Dufferin Papers, A 411, Mackenzie to Dufferin, 11 June 1878.

53. Details in J. Ehrman, *Cabinet Government and War, 1890–1940* (Cambridge, 1958), p. 9, and in D. M. Schurman, "Imperial Defence, 1868–1887," Ph.D. thesis, Cambridge University, 1955, pp. 96–103. The Milne Papers, now held at the National Maritime Museum, Greenwich, include memoranda to and from Sir Stafford Northcote and others which illuminate the committee members' work on Esquimalt and views of Russian menace.

54. Schurman, "Imperial Defence," pp. 103ff.

55. PAC, Dufferin Papers, A 411: microfilm 1140, p. 215.

56. PAC, Macdonald Papers, M.G. 26, A 1(a), vol. 100, Report of the Committee of the Privy Council, 23 Jan. 1879; Canada, *Sessional Papers* 13 (1880), vol. 5, no. 8, "Militia Report of 1879," p. xlvi, (the re-boring of smooth-bore guns in Canada to deter Russian raids).

57. Ibid., vol. 100, Summary Report, Committee of the Privy Council, June — July 1878.

58. See Preston, *Canada and "Imperial Defense,"* p. 71.

59. PAC, Papers of the Deputy Minister of Militia and Defence, 1878, nos. 04465ff., Selby Smyth-Irwin correspondence; also *British Colonist*, 6 Mar. 1878 (anticipation of a Colonel Irwin in Victoria).

60. Longstaff, *Esquimalt Naval Base*, pp. 43–44.

61. PAC, Papers of the Deputy Minister of Militia and Defence, Inwards, 1875, no. 02638: "Memorandum on the Defence of British Columbia . . . by Colonel G.

F. Blair, R.A."

62. Ibid., no. 04470: Selby Smyth to R. W. Scott, 29 June 1878; Canada, Department of Militia and Defence, *Militia General Orders*, 19 July 1878.

63. PRO, Adm. 1/6460: de Horsey to Sec. of Adm., 28 June 1878; Schurman, "Esquimalt: Defence Problem," pp. 60ff.; Longstaff, *Esquimalt Naval Base*, p. 44.

64. PAC, Papers of the Deputy Minister of Militia and Defence, 1878, no. 04470: Selby Smyth to Scott, 29 June and 20 July 1878.

65. Ibid., same to same, 29 June 1878.

66. PAC, M.G. 13, A 6, vol. 4, pp. 285–87, de Horsey to Sec. of Adm., 28 July 1878 (copy).

67. See n. 64 and J. F. Cummins, "Colonel D. T. Irwin, a Distinguished Artillery Officer," *Canadian Defence Quarterly* 5 (1928): 137–41.

68. On naval-militia co-operation in these weeks, PAC, M.G. 13, A 6, vol. 4, pp. 288–96, F. D. Bedford to de Horsey, 27 June 1878; also Longstaff, *Esquimalt Naval Base*, p. 44.

69. Canada, Department of Militia and Defence, *Report on the State of the Militia of the Dominion of Canada, 1878* (Ottawa, 1879), pp. 306–12.

70. PAC, Dufferin Papers, A 411, Mackenzie to Dufferin, 5 Aug. 1878; Preston, *Canada and "Imperial Defense,"* pp. 128–29.

71. PAC, Dufferin Papers, A 409: Dufferin to Mackenzie, 2 Sept. 1878.

72. Ibid., A 411: Mackenzie to Dufferin, 8 Aug. 1878; A 407, Dufferin to Hicks-Beach, 28 Sept. 1878; R.G. 7, G. 21, no. 165, vol. 4(c): "Defence of Canada," memorandum of 21 Apr. 1880 on the Esquimalt-Victoria defences.

73. PAC, M.G. 13, A 6, vol. 4, pp. 289ff., Bedford to de Horsey, 27 June 1878.

74. Canada, Department of Militia and Defence, *Report on the State of the Militia . . . 1878*, p. 214.

75. Houghton meant a Canadian marine company, for which there were certain precedents, but probably dreamt — as his capitals betrayed — of the British R.M.A.

76. *Militia General Orders*, 1 Aug. 1878.

77. He supported it in Canada and England alike; see Sir J. Pope, ed., *Correspondence of Sir John Macdonald* (Oxford,

n.d.), pp. 239–42: Macdonald to Stafford Northcote, 1 May 1878.

78. PAC, Dufferin Papers, A 407: Dufferin to Hicks-Beach, 12 Oct. 1878; R.G. 7, G. 21, no. 165, vol. 3(b): Hicks-Beach to Lorne, 3 July 1879.

79. Ibid., vol. 3(b): Hicks-Beach to Dufferin, 11 May 1878.

80. PRO, Adm.1/6416: de Horsey to Sec. of Adm., 13 May 1877; PRO, Carnarvon Papers, 30/6/122, pp. 19–21, C. H. Nugent, "Memorandum on . . . Coaling Stations"; Schurman, "Imperial Defence," pp. 100–103, 130.

81. PRO, Adm.1/6460, de Horsey to Sec. of Adm., 28 June 1878.

82. PAC, M.G. 13, A 6, vol. 4, pp. 286ff.; G. N. Tucker, The Naval Service of Canada: Its Official History (Ottawa, 1952), 1: 42–43; Preston, Canada and "Imperial Defense," pp. 86–87, 99.

83. See n. 81.

84. PAC, Dufferin Papers, A 407: Dufferin to Hicks-Beach, 12 October 1878; Macdonald Papers, M.G. 26, A 1(a), vol.100, Report of the . . . Privy Council, Canada, 16 May 1879.

85. Ibid., R.G. 7, G. 21, no. 165, vol. 3(b): Hicks-Beach to Lorne, 3 July 1879; T. B. Strange, "Report on the Defences of British Columbia, November 1879," in PAC, "Correspondence of the Committee on the Defences of Canada, 1886," vol.6, pp. 416–25; J. W. Lovell, "Report on the Defences of Esquimalt and Victoria, December 1879," ibid., pp. 428–38; on Lt.-Col. Strange, see DCB, p. 720.

86. Lovell was based at Halifax in 1879.

87. PAC, Lovell, "Report," p. 437.

88. Surveys in Gordon, The Dominion Part-

nership, pp. 61–62, Preston, Canada and "Imperial Defense," pp. 90–91.

89. See nn. 30, 43; and PRO, 30/6/52, Hicks-Beach to Carnarvon, 12 Aug. 1879.

90. National Maritime Museum, Milne Papers, memorandum by Stafford Northcote, May-June 1878; Milne to Carnarvon, 11 Aug. 1879.

91. PRO, 30/6/52: Hicks-Beach to Carnarvon, 26 July 1879.

92. Ibid., same to same, 12 Aug. 1879.

93. Ibid., same to same, 12 Sept. 1879.

94. A. R. Stewart, "Sir John A. Macdonald and the Imperial Defence Commission of 1879," CHR 35 (1954): 132ff.

95. Earl of Carnarvon, Royal Commission to Enquire into the Defence of British Possessions and Commerce Abroad (London, 1880–83), 3: 30–32; T. Brassey, A Colonial Volunteer Force (London, 1878), intro.

96. Stewart, "Sir John A. Macdonald," p. 134.

97. Carnarvon, Royal Commission, 3: 23–25.

98. Ibid., 3: 32–33.

99. PRO, WO, Confidential Papers, A.66/1886: "Report of Committee on Colonial Garrisons"; Bourne, Britain and the Balance of Power, p. 314; Gordon, The Dominion Partnership, pp. 64–67.

100. But see J. Hyde Bennett, "In Retrospect," Selected Papers of the Canadian Officers' Club and Institute 41 (Toronto, 1946): 17–18; and T. C. Scoble, The Utilization of Colonial Forces in Imperial Defence (Toronto: Canadian Military Institute, 1879), on the patriotic mood of 1878–79 and the Militia Institute in Toronto.

NOTES TO CHAPTER SEVEN

1. HBCA, A.8/19, fols. 23–24, W. Politkowski and others to H.B.C., 2 Feb. 1854; PRO, WO 1/551, pp. 145–46: Douglas to Newcastle, 16 May 1854; E. G. Ravenstein, Russians on the Amur: Its Discovery, Conquest and Colonization (London, 1861), pp. 116ff.; A. R. Roche, A View of Russian America in

Connection with the Present War (Montreal, 1885).

2. Bodleian Library, Clarendon deposit, C. 15, fol.172: Palmerston to Clarendon, 29 Aug. 1854; see also Galbraith, The Hudson's Bay Company as an Imperial Factor, pp. 165–66, and PABC, Douglas-Russell correspondence, 20 June and 21 Sept. 1855.

3. For essential data on the growth of Russia's naval presence in the East, see S. F. Ogorodnikov, *Istoricheskii obzor razvitiia i deiatel'nosti Morskago Ministerstva za sto let ego sushchestvovaniia, 1802–1902* (St. P., 1902), *Statisticheskii vremennik Rossiiskoi Imperii; vtoraia seriia* (St. P., 1912), nos. 13–15, and Beskrovnyi, *Russkaia armiia*, index under "Nikolaevsk," "Vladivostok."

4. For example, Ravenstein, P. M. Collins, H. A. Tilley, T. W. Atkinson, B. W. Bax, details of their published works in bibliography; on Popov, see Mitchell, *History of Russian Sea Power*, Chap. 8; on Murav'ev(-Amurskii), naval expansion and supposed British threats to the northeastern Pacific shores, Golder, *Russian Expansion*, pp. 263–64 and P. F. Unterberger, *Primorskaia oblast'* (St. P., 1900), Chap. 2; on the Treaty of Aigun and its maritime implications, Bedford C. T. Pim, *The Gate of the Pacific* (London, 1863), pp. 132ff., and R. K. Quested, *The Expansion of Russia in East Asia, 1857–1860* (Kuala Lumpur, 1968), passim.

5. Ravenstein, *Russians on the Amur*, pp. 185ff.; A. I. Alekseev, *Spodvizhniki G. I. Nevel'skogo* (Iuzhno-Sakhalinsk, 1967); *Nautical Magazine* 26 (February 1858): 96–98 (British expectations of naval activity in Amuria); B. W. Bax, *The Eastern Seas; being a Narrative of the Voyage of H.M.S. "Dwarf" in China, Japan, and Formosa* (London, 1875), Chaps. 3 and 5 (their realization).

6. Details in F. A. Golder, "The Russian Fleet and the Civil War," *AHR* 20 (1915): 801–14.

7. "Izvestiia o plavanii nashikh sudov za granitsei," *Morskoi sbornik* 64 (St. P., 1863), no. 1, p. 13n.

8. *Melbourne Argus*, 25 March 1863: "The Volunteers and Our Defences"; see also *Sydney Morning Herald*, 28 Mar. 1863: "Look Out!" (on the *Bogatyr's* alleged spying in Port Phillip and Botany Bay).

9. *Melbourne Argus*, 6, 22, and 23 Jan. 1862 (the Royal Navy's weakness in Australia, the lack of ammunition in Port Phillip, etc.); also D. MacCallum, "The Alleged Russian Plans for the Invasion of Australia, 1864," *JRAHS* 44 (1958), pt. 5, pp. 301ff.

10. On Russian use of the treaty ports of Nagasaki and Yokohama (Kanagawa) as a wintering station, see H. Knollys, *Sketches of Life in Japan* (London, 1887); the *Japan Weekly Mail: A Review of Japanese Commerce, Politics, Literature and Art* (Yokohama, 1876–82, and esp. 29 Jan. 1881); and Alexander, Grand Duke of Russia, *Once a Grand Duke* (NY, 1932.) See Bax, *The Eastern Seas*, for a contemporary British reaction, H. S. Williams, *Foreigners in Mikadoland* (Tokyo, 1963), pp. 195–98, for an interpretation; also, on the matter of raids on British colonies, allegedly planned in and to have been launched from Japan, see Preston, *Canada and "Imperial Defense,"* p. 97 and Chap. 6, n. 32 here.

11. For example, in *The Statesman's Year-Book* (London, 1877).

12. Bax, *The Eastern Seas*, p. 72.

13. Beskrovnyi, *Russkaia armiia*, pp. 511–12; Mitchell, *History of Russian Sea Power*, Chaps. 8 and 9; PRO, Adm. 1/6414: de Horsey to Sec. of Adm., 25 June 1877 (encl. Captain F. C. Robinson's criticisms of units of Pauzino's squadron).

14. *Obzor deiatel'nosti Morskago Vedomstva, 1881–1894* (St. P., 1901), pp. 90ff.; Beskrovnyi, *Russkaia armiia*, p. 514.

15. *New Zealand Herald*, 13 Dec. 1881, "Arrival of the Russian Cruiser 'Africa' "; Auckland *Evening Star*, same date, "Russian Fleet in the Pacific; the 'Africa's' Visit"; Kronenfels, *Das schwimmende Flotten material*, pp. 206–7.

16. Barratt, "Visit of the Russian Cruiser *Afrika*," pp. 7–8; see also no. 10.

17. Details in R. E. Johnson, *Thence Round Cape Horn*, App. 3, and Gough, *The Royal Navy*, pp. 257–58. Aslanbegov's small cruisers were matched, in 1882, by Rear-Admiral A. McLennan Lyons' cruiser *Champion* and four composite sloops, *Gannet, Kingfisher, Mutine*, and *Sappho*.

18. *Obzor deiatel'nosti*, pp. 55ff.

19. "Zhurnal Osobogo Soveshchaniia Morskogo Ministerstva," in Saltykov-Shchedrin Public Library, Leningrad, *rukopisnyi otdel*, f. 169, k. 42, *delo* 32, p. 12.

20. Beskrovnyi, *Russkaia armiia*, p. 518.

21. TsGAVMF, f. 1166, delo 4, pp. 71–72 (Aslanbegov burns two Turkish brigs on

the Black Sea); A. A. Samarov, ed., *Russkie flotovodtsy: P. S. Nakhimov: dokumenty i materialy* (M., 1954), pp. 654–60 (Aslanbegov on Nakhimov's end, etc.). Further career details in *Obshchii Morskoi Spisok*, by index.

22. Moiseev, *Spisok korablei*, pp. 72–89; *Japan Weekly Mail* (Yokohama), 29 Jan. and various issues for Aug.-Sept. 1881; also F. T. Jane, *The Imperial Russian Navy* (London, 1904).

23. Canada, Department of Militia and Defence, *Report on the State of the Militia . . . 1879* (Ottawa, 1880), pp. 214–18. Houghton's consciousness of the need to cope with possible Russian raids was doubtless heightened by his Crimean War experiences; Longstaff, *Esquimalt Naval Base*, pp. 45 and 58, n. 5.

24. *Militia General Orders*, no. 20, 15 Oct. 1880.

25. Canada, *Report on the State of the Militia . . . 1880* (Ottawa, 1881), p. 67.

26. Canada, *Report on the State of the Militia . . . 1881* (Ottawa, 1882), pp. 62–63.

27. *Mainland Guardian*, 29 Nov. 1882: "Militia Inspection."

28. See Preston, *Canada and "Imperial Defense,"* pp. 122–23.

29. PRO, Adm.116/744, fols. 241–43; CO 880/8, vol. 98, "Memorandum Respecting the . . . Esquimalt Graving Dock," Aug. 1878.

30. Details in F. W. Howay and E. O. Scholefield, *British Columbia, from the Earliest Times to the Present* (Vancouver, 1914), 2: 402–14.

31. Longstaff, *Esquimalt Naval Base*, p. 38; also A. H. Ives, "First Graving Dock" (typescript, n.d.), in the Maritime Museum of British Columbia.

32. I thank Captain A. Ignat'ev, Assistant Head of the Library, TsGAVMF, for this information.

33. On the origins of that responsibility, see Barratt, "The Russian Navy and New Holland: Part 1," *JRAHS* 64 (1979): 218–19; on its actual discharging, see issues of *Zapiski Uchonogo Komiteta Morskogo Ministerstva* (St. P., 1827–33).

34. "Neofitsial'nyi otdel: morskaia khronika," pp. 50–52. *Army and Navy Gazette* was incorporated in the *United Services Review*.

35. See Chap. 6, n. 60.

36. Full details of (acknowledged) defence expenditures in Russia, *Ministerstvo finansov: istoricheskii obzor glavneishikh meropriiatii, 1802–1902*(St. P., 1902), 2: 640–43 (naval). 296,728,000 roubles went on the Russian Navy in 1880–88, by the official accounting system.

37. See Barratt, *Russia in Pacific Waters*, Chaps. 7 to 10.

38. M. S. Anderson, "Great Britain and the Growth of the Russian Navy in the Eighteenth Century," *MM* 42 (1956): pp. 132–46; "Great Britain and the Russian Fleet, 1769–70," *SEER* 21 (1952): 148–64.

39. See C. V. Penrose, *A Memoir of James Trevenen, 1760–1790*, ed. R. C. Anderson, C. Lloyd (London, Navy Records Society, no.CI, 1959), pp. 86–94; I. F. Kruzenshtern, *Puteshestvie vokrug sveta v 1803, 1804, 1805 i 1806 godakh na korabliakh "Nadezhda" i "Neva"* (St. P., 1809), 1: intro.; Barratt, *Russia in Pacific Waters*, index under "Mulovskii, G.I.," "Trevenen, J."

40. Barratt, "Visit of the Russian Cruiser *Afrika*," pp. 7–8, 20; *Russkii invalid* (St. P., 1868), no. 32.

41. Barratt, "Russian Warships in Van Diemen's Land: the "Kreyser" and the "Ladoga" by Hobart Town, 1823," *SEER* 53 (1975): pp. 566–78; Samarov, *Russkie flotovodtsy: P. S. Nakhimov*, p. 655 (Aslanbegov hearing Nakhimov's recollections of Lazarev and *Kreiser* in 1822–24).

42. A. B. Aslanbegov, *Zhizneopisanie admirala Alekseia Samuilovicha Greiga* (St. P., 1873); A. G. Cross, "Samuel Greig, Catherine the Great's Scottish Admiral," *MM* 60 (1974): pp. 251–65.

43. F. F. Veselago, *Kratkaia istoriia russkogo flota*, 2d. ed. (M., 1939), Chaps. 7 and 8; P. Martin, *Australia and the Empire* (Sydney, 1889), pp. 64–5; also nn. 38 and 42.

44. Further on this, see Barratt, *The Russian Navy and Australia to 1825: The Days Before Suspicion* (Melbourne, 1979).

45. Barratt, "Early Russian Knowledge of New Zealand," *New Zealand Slavonic Journal* (1980); *Bellingshausen: A Visit to New Zealand, 1820* (Palmerston North, N.Z., 1979).

46. *Morskoi sbornik* 188 (1881), no. 11, pp. 26–34; 190 (1882), no. 5, pp. 1–26.

47. Ibid., pp. 28–32.
48. Ibid., 192 (1883), no. 10, "Otchot Kommissii; ob osmotre kreisera "Afrika" po vozvrashchenii ego iz zagranichnego plavaniia."
49. On this, see his private secretary's comments later on the tour, "Our Admiral . . . liked to see the world. He himself sketched out the route. . . . We must have visited about sixty ports," etc.), in the *Melbourne Argus*, 24 Mar. 1882.
50. *Morskoi sbornik* 188 (1881), no. 11, p. 28.
51. Ibid., p. 31.
52. Ibid., p. 32.
53. See the *Daily Colonist* for 14–19 Aug. 1881. For comparative British colonial responses to the *Afrika's* wanderings, *New Zealand Herald* and *Auckland Evening Star*, 13–15 Dec. 1881, *Melbourne Age* and *Argus* for 1–22 Mar. 1882, and the *Adelaide Advertiser* for 28 Feb. 2 Mar.
54. PAC, Macdonald Papers, M.G. 26, A. 1(a), vol. 200: Adolphe Caron to Macdonald, 25 Apr. 1884.
55. See Preston, *Canada and "Imperial Defense,"* p. 156; on Laurie's earlier military career, in the Crimea and India, *DCB*, p. 395.
56. J. W. Laurie, "The Protection of Our Naval Base in the North Pacific," *JRUSI* 27 (1884); 358.
57. On the Crimean War experiences of two other Canadian Militia officers, Lt.-Col. Houghton and Col. P. Robertson-Ross, both of whom had been active in British Columbia in the 1870's (cf. Roy, "The Early Militia," p. 7), see respectively Longstaff, *The Esquimalt Naval Base*, pp. 45 and 58 and *Army and Navy Gazette*, 28 July 1883.
58. *Morskoi sbornik* 187 (1881), no. 11, p. 32.
59. Turnstall, "Imperial Defence, 1870–1897," pp. 242–48; C. K. Ensor, *England, 1870–1914* (Oxford, 1936), pp. 60–63, 69.
60. Stewart, "Sir John A. Macdonald, 1879," pp. 133ff.
61. See *A Memorandum in Reference to a Scheme for Completing a Great Inter-Colonial and Inter-Continental Telegraph System . . . by Sandford Fleming, 20 November 1882* (London, 1882), pp. 7–9; also Schurman, "Esquimalt: De-

fence Problem" pp. 64–69 and J. M. Jones, "The Railroad Healed the Breach," *Canadian Geographical Journal* 73 (1966): 98–100.
62. Longstaff, *Esquimalt Naval Base*, p. 38; *Daily Colonist*, 11–30 Nov. 1882.
63. "The Effect of a War Upon this Province," p. 2.
64. See Chap. 7 here.
65. PAC, R.G. 7, G. 21, no. 165, vol. 4(c): CO to Governor General, 27 July 1882 (Lovell's report and its chances of use); Macdonald Papers, M.G. 26, A. 1(a), vol. 100: Walker Powell-Macdonald and Macdonald-Lorne correspondence re Canadian participation in Britain's wars, Apr.-Aug. 1882; Stanley, *Canada's Soldiers*, pp. 247, 264 (neglect of the militia).
66. As stressed by Captain Dupont in 1880–82, *Report on the State of the Militia . . . 1881* (Ottawa, 1882), pp. 62–63, and revealed by Macdonald's own comments before the Carnarvon Commission, PRO, 30/6/126.
67. On Crossman, an old hand in Canada, see Preston, *Canada and "Imperial Defense,"* pp. 40,164.
68. It was printed in *JRUSI* 27 (1884): 357–73.
69. See n. 55.
70. Preston, *Canada and "Imperial Defense,"* p. 156, n. 95.
71. Laurie, "The Protection of Our Naval Base," pp. 365–66.
72. Ibid., p. 361.
73. Ibid., pp. 359, 362, 358.
74. 6 June 1883 (editorial).
75. Laurie, "The Protection of Our Naval Base," pp. 357–58.
76. Ibid., pp. 379–80 (replies to Curtis and Pim).
77. Ibid., pp. 375–76, 378–79.
78. Ibid., pp. 375–76.
79. Ibid., p. 374. Pfoundes was developing ideas that had come to him earlier, when studying Russo-Japanese relations; see his "Notes on the History of . . . Foreign Intercourse with Japan," *Transactions of the Royal Historical Society* 10 (1882): 82–92.
80. It was handed to Viscount Melgund, chairman of the new Canadian Defence Commission, and remained among his papers; PAC, Minto Papers, pt.3, CDC, 1884–85.

81. PRO, CO 42/777, Lansdowne to CO, 26 May 1884 and PAC, M.G. 26, A. 1(a), vol. 84, same to Macdonald, 2 Sept. 1884 (Laurie passed over); C. P. Stacey, "The North-West Campaign, 1885," in *Introduction to the Study of Military History for Canadian Students* (Ottawa, 1955), pp. 75ff.

82. See Chap. 7, n. 41–44.

83. *Mainland Guardian*, 13 Mar. 1884, "Will Russia Hoodwink Gladstone?"

84. Ibid., 4 June 1884, "The Eastern Question."

85. Ibid., and 17 Sept. 1884, "Our Indian Empire."

86. Ibid., 30 Jan. 1884: "Affairs In Europe"; *Sessional Papers, Parliament of the Province of British Columbia: Session 1884*, passim.

87. *Mainland Guardian*, 10 Sept. 1884: "The Next Move on the European Chessboard;" also 2 July, "The Central Asian Question" (fluid alliances).

88. Ibid., 17 Sept. 1884, "Our Indian Empire."

89. Ibid., 14 Mar. 1885, "European Complications."

90. C. P. Stacey, "John A. Macdonald on Raising Troops in Canada for Imperial Service, 1885," *CHR* 38 (1957): 37–40; Preston, *Canada and "Imperial Defense,"* pp. 145–47; Ormsby, *British Columbia*, pp. 265ff.

91. *Mainland Guardian*, 30 Jan. 1884, "Affairs in Europe."

92. See n. 87.

93. *Mainland Guardian* 21 Mar. 1885, "New Westminster in Case of War." On the reality of Nanaimo's and Burrard Inlet's weak defences in 1885 and the official discouragement given to would-be volunteer mounted infantry, see *Report on the State of the Militia . . . 1885* (Ottawa, 1886), pp. 54–57.

94. PAC, Papers of the Deputy Minister of Militia and Defence, Inward, no. A 1518, Baker to Caron, 2 May 1885; *Weekly Colonist* (Victoria), 17 Apr. 1885 (the need for Gatling guns at the posts behind the city).

95. *Mainland Guardian*, 22 Apr. 1885, "England and Russia."

96. Ibid., 2 May 1885.

97. PAC, G. 21, no. 168, 1897: "History of the Colonial Defence Committee"; N. H. Gibbs, *The Origins of Imperial Defence* (Oxford, 1955), pp. 6–10.

98. PAC, R.G. 9, II B.2 (71), vol. 32: Viscount Melgund to Campbell, 17 Jan. 1885, Campbell to Melgund, 27 Feb. 1885; PRO Cab 11/27, Colonial Defence Committee Minutes, draft memoranda (1 and 2M), by H. Jekyll et al.

99. PRO, Cab. 11/27, CDC Minutes, 2M, 1(4) May 1885

100. See Gough, *The Royal Navy*, pp. 209–10.

101. That is, to the British taxpayer, not the Canadian.

102. Rear-Admiral Sir Michael Culme-Seymour was appointed on 4 July. On his earlier career, in the Crimean and Baltic campaigns of 1854–55 and on the China station in the 1860's, where also he had been very conscious of Russian ambitions, see Longstaff, *Esquimalt Naval Base*, p. 59.

103. For example, from Singapore and Galle in Ceylon. See the *Auckland Weekly News*, 29 Apr. 1871, p. 15, "The Mission of the 'Haydamack,' " and n. 61 here, in this connection. Also *Mainland Guardian*, 22 Apr. 1885, p. 3.

104. PRO, Adm.1/6762, Y.121 and enclosures, Rear-Admiral J. K. Baird to Sec. of Adm., 25 June 1885; also, on the naval potential of fast steamers based in British Columbia, CO 880/9, vol. 119, p. 21: memo. by Maj-Gen. A. Clarke of 16 Apr. 1886, re C.P.R.'s proposed service to Hong Kong and Yokohama.

105. PRO, Adm.1/6762: Culme-Seymour to Sec. of Adm., 8 Sept. 1885; *Daily Colonist*, 5 June 1886.

106. PAC, R.G. 7, G. 21, no. 165, vol. 4(b), 1880–87, papers received (Caron).

107. PRO, Cab.11/27, CDC Minutes, Confidential Memorandum no. 2M, p. 2.

108. See n. 81.

109. PAC, R.G. 7, G. 21, no. 165, vol. 4(b), Privy Council Order 1050F, 25 Nov. 1885. London's reaction, as voiced by a frustrated Committee on Colonial Garrisons, may be found in PRO, CO 323/366, no. 23204, Confidential Report, 1886, p. 11.

111. PAC, Adjutant-General's Correspondence, letters inward, no. 09577, Baird to Holmes, 4 Apr. 1885; letters sent,

vol. 46, p. 683, Powell to Holmes, 5 May 1885.

110. Roy, "The Early Militia," pp. 23–24.

112. 2 May 1885, "The Effects of the War on British Columbia."

113. Canada, Department of Militia and Defence, *Report on the State of the Militia . . . 1885* (Ottawa, 1886), pp. 51–56; also Stanley, *Canada's Soldiers*, pp. 263–64.

114. *Mainland Guardian*, 23 Dec. 1885: "The Eastern Question."

115. C. Wentworth Dilke and S. Wilkinson, *Imperial Defences* (London, 1892), pp. 57–60, 88–89.

116. *Mainland Guardian*, 19 Sept. 1884: "The Next Move on the European Chessboard."

117. Great Britain, *Parliamentary Papers: Third Series*, 333. p. 1170, Committee, 7 March 1889.

118. Ibid., *Fourth Series*, 19, pp. 1770–72, 1809–10.

119. PRO Adm.1/6914: Rear-Admiral Heneage to Adm., 9 June 1888, etc.; see also Gough, *The Royal Navy*, pp. 235–36.

120. *Mainland Guardian*, 22 Apr. 1885, "England and Russia."

121. Survey in C. Berger, *The Sense of Power: Studies in the Ideals of Canadian Imperialism, 1867–1914* (Toronto, 1970), pp. 49–63.

122. G. F. G. Stanley, *Canada's Soldiers* pp. 234, 250.

123. That is, constitutional, by the terms of the British North America Act (1867) and the Militia Act (1868), as well as moral.

124. *Canadian Military Gazette* 17 (4 Nov. 1902), p. 9.

125. See Gordon, *The Dominion Partnership*, pp. 42–43; Stanley, *Canada's Soldiers*, pp. 259–65; Roy, *The Early Militia*, pp. 13ff.

126. *Weekly Globe*, 26 Aug. 1870.

127. Canada, *Sessional Papers*, 1875, Paper no. 6, p. xvi.

128. J. N. Blake, *The True Commercial Policy for Greater Britain: an Address Delivered . . . before the Commercial Union Club at Association Hall, Toronto, April 5th, 1888* (Toronto, 1888), p. 26; see also *"Imperial Federation,:* by George Edward Fenety, Queen's Printer (Fredericton, 1888), pp. 12–13.

129. F. H. Underhill, *In Search of Canadian Liberalism* (Toronto, 1960), p. 220.

130. W. A. Foster, *Canada First: A Memorial of the Late William A. Foster, Q.C.,* with introduction by Goldwin Smith, D.C.L. (Toronto, 1890), pp. 13–47. ("The Canadian Confederacy," in *Westminster Review* [Apr. 1865] in some respects prefigures Foster's 1871 address.)

131. See Berger, *The Sense of Power*, p. 259.

Selected Bibliography

ARCHIVAL MATERIALS

United Kingdom

Public Record Office, London: Official Correspondence and Records

Adm.1 (In-letters from Admirals, Captains, Departments). /498 (Geo. Murray, 1794); /1586 (Belcher, 1837); /5656 (Frederick, 1854; /5629 (Stirling, 1854); /5630 (Morseby, 1853–54); /5656 (Bruce, 1854–55); /5672 (Bruce, Stirling, 1856); /5969 (Baynes, 1859); /5924 (Denman, 1864–65); /5790 (Maitland, 1862); /6414–16 (de Horsey, 1877–78); /6460 (Milne, 1878); /6454 (de Horsey, 1878); /6762 (Culme-Seymour, 1885); /6914 (Heneage, 1888).
Adm.2 (Out-letters and Instructions).2/13; 2/1380; 2/1442
Adm.7 (Reports on foreign navies and miscellaneous documents)
Adm.50 (Admirals' Journals). 50/308 (Bruce, 1855)
Adm.116 (Reports on Esquimalt naval base). /744 (Executive Council Committee Report, B.C., June 1877, re Esquimalt graving-dock and defences); /857 (Circular to commander-in-chiefs, Feb. 1854, re Russian aggression, French co-operation)
Adm.172/1–2 (Pacific Station records). Remark Book of Commodore C. Frederick, No. 7
BT 1/70/16 (Memorial from Chetwynd re North-West Company, Nov. 1812); 1/61/12-17 (papers from or concerning the company); 1/470/2506 (draft of Vancouver Island Grant, 1848)
Cab.7/1 (Colonial Defence Committee Reports on Temporary Defences for B.C., June 1878): 11/27 (C.D.C. Minutes, memoranda on Vancouver Island defences, May 1885)
CO 6 (Boundary Questions). /14 (Pelly on Russian expansionism, esp. in the North Pacific, 1840)
CO 42 (Original Correspondence, Canada). /149 (McGillivray-Goulburn-Bathurst correspondence, 1812, re North-West Co. grant claims, Russian activity, etc.). /485 (Pelly on H.B.C.-Russian-American Co. relations, 1840–41); /777 (Lansdowne on G.O.C., Canadian Militia, 1884, and Maj.-Gen. Laurie)
CO 62 (Sessional Papers, British Columbia). (1870–85)
CO 305 (Original Correspondence, Vancouver Island. 1/6 (Terms of grant, 1849); 5/4–22 (Vancouver Island during the Crimean War: Douglas-Newcastle letters.); /6/12–22 (Douglas-Russell letters, 1855)
CO 410 (Out-letters). /1/2ff (Grey and Russell to Douglas)
CO 323 (Colonial Garrisons and Defences). /366/23204 (report on the defence needs of Vancouver Island, 1886)
CO 807/7/74 (Alexander Mackenzie and a railway for Vancouver Island, 1874)
CO 880/5/37 (The Pacific colonies' weakness, 1866, amalgamation benefits); /8.98 (Esquimalt graving-dock, need for, 1878)
FO 65 (Russia). /18 (Catherine II's pro-Spanish leanings, 1790); /138 (Northwest Coast boundary negotiations, 1822–23; Canning-Bagot letters); /223 (David Urquhart and Anglo-Russian tensions, 1833–36); /701 (Russo-American entente)
FO 181/48 (Castlereagh-Bagot correspondence re Northwest Coast Boundary, 1822); /119/12–16 (the Stikine River affair, Palmeston-Durham exchanges)
WO 1/551/143–56 (defence plans for Vancouver Island, 1854, and cool responses)

PRO 30/6/52–126. Carnarvon "Private" Papers, re his commission.

British Library, London: Additional Manuscripts and Papers

Aberdeen Papers
Chatham Papers
Halifax Papers
Add. MSS. 28066 (Burges, 1790); 48579 (Palmerston, 1855)

Royal Commonwealth Society Library, London

North West Company papers re the need to forestall Americans and Russians on the Northwest Coast; "Some Account of the Trade Carried on by the North West Company," with responses

Balliol College Library, Oxford

Urquhart Papers (Taylor-Urquhart letters, 1834–35)

Bodleian Library, Oxford

Clarendon Deposit, c.14/150 (Admiral J. Graham on war in the Pacific, Jan.-Feb. 1854); c.25, 44 (Clarendon-Crampton letters, 1854–55, re recruiting in the U.S. and American Russophilia)

Hughenden Manor Library, Bucks

Disraeli Papers, Malmesbury no.99 (Problems of recruiting for a lengthy war against Russia, Nov. 1854)

Hydrographer's Office, Taunton, Somerset

S.L.21/4; Miscellaneous File 15, folder 1/3 (Beechey and plans to examine the Northeastern Pacific, including Russian outposts, at Sitka and on the Farallones Islands, 1831–35)

National Library of Scotland, Edinburgh

Melville Papers. MS. no.3845 (Barrow and the Northwest Passage, Nov. 1823; consciousness of Russian activities, etc)

Canada

Public Archives of Canada, Ottawa

Q/113/229ff (North West Company papers, 1810); /134/385–92 (ditto, 1815: awareness of Russian activity on Northwest Coast)
Bagot Papers, Vol.2, pt.3 (Northwest Coast Boundary negotiations 1823–24)
Dufferin Papers: Microfilm 1140 (the "Russian scare" of 1878); A.411, 409, 411 (Dufferin-Mackenzie-Hicks-Beach letters, re same)
Macdonald Papers, 1879–85. M.G.21, A.1(a), vol.100 (Privy Council on defences, May 1878, etc.); vol.200 (Caron on same, April 1884); vol.84 (Lansdowne on same, Sept. 1884.); M.G.13, A.6, vol.4 (de Horsey on Esquimalt and foreign cruisers, July 1878)
R.G.7, G.21: Papers and reports re the defences of B.C. and Esquimalt (1878–85)
R.G.8, IIIB: Pacific Station Records, 39 vols.
R.G.9, IIA 6, vol.1 (C.O. on Esquimalt, 1878); IIB 2, vol.32 (Viscount Melgund re same, 1885)

Militia and Defence Department Papers: Deputy-Minister's Papers, inward: 1872–86. Outward, 1878–80

Hudson's Bay Company Archives, Winnipeg and London

A.8/1 (Pelly-Barrow correspondence, 1823, keeping the Russians at bay beyond the Rockies, etc.: fols.220–29, reel 50)
A.8/2 (Diplomatic background to 1839 H.B.C.-Russian-American Company agreement)
A.8/6/149–51 (Captain W. C. Grant and Vancouver Island's security against attack, 1854)
A.8/7/139 (W.O. to H.B.C. re the same, 1854)
A.8/19 (Discussion of a neutrality pact, C.O., F.O. views)
A.6/23–25 (Governor and Committee to John McLoughlin re the competition of Russians, 1835–41)
A.10/23–24 (Pelly-Wrangel letters, 1847–48, trade, friendly co-operation on Northwest Coast)
A.11/64 (Correspondence, San Francisco). /27d
A.37/1 (Vancouver Island, Royal Grant and Letters Patent)
A.12/2/292 (winding up Puget's Sound Agric. Co., comments)
B.223/12 (Fort Vancouver Correspondence Books, 1836)
D.4/123/19 (Chistiakov's grain needs, 1829); 4/66/52, 4/99 (Russian requirements, Simpson's Correspondence Books, 1835–42)
D.5/24 (renewal of the Companies' Agreement, 1849)
F.29/2 (Ogden at Novo-Arkhangel'sk, 1834; 1839 pact) F. "Russian-American Co.: Miscellaneous Papers," Micro. reel 5-M50 (Captain Alexander Duncan's testimony re the Stikine River affair, 1833)

Provincial Archives of British Columbia, Victoria, B.C.

Admiralty Correspondence, 6 vols.
James Douglas Papers: Douglas-Grey and Douglas-Bruce letters, 1854–55; Douglas to Cridge, 16 May 1855; Douglas-Newcastle-Russell exchanges, 1854–55, re defence against Russian warships, plans to take Sitka Island

United States

United States National Archives, Washington, D.C.

"Records of the Russian-American Company, 1802–1867: Correspondence": 4/4–6, 98–99, 417, 451–54; 5/103–4; 7/20–26; 18/100–3; 30/260–1; 32/45–47; 36/51–52; 44/54; 55/150–51
Department of State Archive: Vail to Forsyth, no.214 (28 Nov. 1835, re British reaction to the Stikine River affair and Urquhart's propagandist fervour)

Baker Library, Harvard Graduate School of Business Administration, Boston

William Dane Phelps, "Solid Men of Boston": MS. Astor Papers, Box 33 (1809–10, Astoria: 1810–12, Bentzon-Rumiantsev talks re supplying Russian settlements, etc.)

Bancroft Library, Berkeley, California

MS P-C.23, "Notes and Extracts from the Journal of the Hudson's Bay Company at Fort Simpson, 1834–37."
G. B. Roberts, "Recollections": MS. (Voyage of *Dryad*)
Roderick Finlayson, "History of Vancouver Island and the Northwest Coast," MS.

Hawaii State Library, Honolulu

Admiral Thomas Papers, G.4, Article 6 (from Articles of Command, Office of the Lord High Admiralty)

Beinecke Library, Yale University, New Haven

Coe Collection of Western Americana, no.355 (Antonio Muro's anti-Russian plans of 1789)

U.S.S.R.

Tsentral'nyi Gosudarstvennyi Arkhiv Drevnikh Aktov

fond A. R. Vorontsova, delo 754 (official Russian interest in the North Pacific fur-trade since 1800)
Arkhiv grafa E. F. Kankrina, delo 35 (K. F. Ryleev's efforts to reinforce Russia's failing position on the Northwest Coast, February 1825)

Tsentral'nyi Gosudarstvennyi Istoricheskii Arkhiv

fond 48, op. 1, delo 78 (Lieutenant V. P. Romanov on his 1822–23 plans for Russian expansion in Arctic North America.)

Tsentral'nyi Gosudarstvennyi Arkhiv Voenno-Morskogo Flota SSSR

fond 7, op. 1, dela 3–5 (V. M. Golovnin to Kozodavlev, de Traversay, re naval collaboration with the Russian-American Company in the Pacific)
fond 203, delo 1123 (M. P. Lazarev on the situation at Novo-Arkhangel'sk in 1823)
fond 315, delo 476 (Otto von Kotzebue and I. F. Kruzenshtern on a proper Russian response to British Arctic exploration, 1818–19)
fond 1166, delo 9 (P. S. Nakhimov on Novo-Arkhangel'sk in 1823)
fond 1214, delo 1 (Preparation of the Billings expedition, the correct attitude towards foreign subjects met off North American shores, etc.)

Arkhiv Vneshnei Politiki Rossii

fond 1 Otdela Ego Velichestva Sobstvennoi kantseliarii: 1802, 152 (N. P. Rezanov on southward expansion down the Northwest Coast, 1806)
fond Rossiisko-Amerikanskoi Kompanii, dela 284–85 (Navy criticism of the Russian-American Company, 1816)
fond Kantseliarii Ministerstva Vneshnikh Del 1823, dela 3645–46, 8735 (relations with Spaniards in California, the status of Ross, development of trade)
1824, dela 3717, 3650 (Mordvinov, Nesselrode, and the Russo-American and Anglo-Russian Conventions of 1824–25)
1827, delo 7316 (Mordvinov and minimal territorial and trade concessions, 1824)

Arkhiv Geograficheskogo Obshchestva SSSR, Leningrad

fond G. IV 1, item 92 (G. I. Shelikhov's plans, Navy pilots and midshipmen; problems associated with them)
razriad 99, op. 1, no. 29: anon., "Kratkaia istoricheskaia zapiska o sostoianii Rossiisko-Amerikanskoi Kompanii"
razriad 99, op. 1, no. 111: K. T. Khlebnikov, "Zapiski o koloniiakh v Amerike Rossiisko-Amerikanskoi Kompanii"

Akademiia Nauk SSSR: Institut Istorii

"Materialy po istorii Rossiisko-Amerikanskoi Kompanii," documents 44-49. (Company difficulties, 1815–18)

Saltykov-Shchedrin Public Library, Leningrad

Otdel rukopisei: fond 169, karton 42, delo 32: "Zhurnal Osobogo Soveshchaniia Morskago Ministerstva . . . 1880–82" (S. S. Lesovskii on the Pacific squadron's requirements for the future, Japanese naval plans plans, etc.)

Spain

Archivo General de Indias, Seville

Estado 10–20 (Grimaldi-Arriaga-Bucareli correspondence, 1774); Estado 23–27 (Branciforte-Godoy-Varela papers, 1795–7); Estado 28–39 (Manuel Rodriguez-Urquijo papers, 1799)

NEWSPAPERS AND WEEKLY PUBLICATIONS CONSULTED

Advertiser (Adelaide)	1881–82
Age (Melbourne)	1864, 1882
Argus (Melbourne)	1863–64, 1878–82
Auckland Evening Star	1880–82
Auckland Weekly News	1871, 1877–78
British Colonist (Victoria)	1859–88
(London) *Chronicle*	1822, 1833–35
(Sacramento) *Daily Union*	1866–67
(London) *Globe*	1833–35
(London) *Herald*	1833
Japan Weekly Mail (Yokohama)	1878–82
London Gazette	1795–99
Mainland Guardian (New Westminster)	1877–87
New York Herald	1866–68
New Zealand Herald	1878–82
Niles' Weekly Register	1821–25
(London) *Post*	1822–25
Puget Sound Gazette (Seattle)	1867, 1877
Russkii invalid (St. P.)	1866–68
San Francisco Herald	1854–55
(London) *Standard*	1833–34
Sydney Morning Herald	1863–64, 1882
(London) *Times*	1822–25, 1854–81
Washington Evening Star	1867–69

UNPUBLISHED WORKS

Bach, J. P. S. "The Royal Navy in the South Pacific, 1826–1876," Ph.D. thesis, University of New South Wales, 1964

Finlayson, R. "History of Vancouver Island and the Northwest Coast," copy in Archives of British Columbia, n.d.

Mackinnon, C. S. "The Imperial Fortresses in Canada: Halifax and Esquimalt, 1871–1906," Ph.D. thesis, University of Toronto, 1965

Schurman, D. M.   "Imperial Defence, 1868–1887," Ph.D. thesis, Cambridge University, 1955
Trubetzkoy, A. S.   "Extracts from the Esquimalt Naval Establishment Records, 1862–1881," PABC, n.d.
Johnson, S.   "Baron Wrangel and the Russian-American Company, 1829–49," Ph.D. thesis, University of Manitoba, 1978

GOVERNMENT PUBLICATIONS

Canada, Department of Militia and Defence. *Report on the State of the Militia of the Dominion of Canada . . . 1872*, and annually to 1885 (Ottawa, 1873–86)
————————· *Militia General Orders*
————————· *Parliament Commons Debates* (1876–78)
————————· *Sessional Papers* (1871, 1878–81, 1885)
————————· Department of the Interior. *Certain Correspondence of the Foreign Office and the Hudson's Bay Company* (Ottawa, 1899), pts. IV–V
————————· British Columbia, Legislative Council
Journals. 21 January 1864 to 28 March 1871.
Debate on the Subject of Confederation with Canada (1870)
————————· Archives Department. *Memoir no. 11*: "Minutes of the Council of Vancouver Island, 1851–61," ed. E. O. S. Scholefield (Victoria, 1918)

Great Britain, Parliament, *Hansard*

————————· *Parliamentary Papers*
————————· "Correspondence between the Hudson's Bay Company and the Secretary of State for the Colonies Relative to the Colonization of Vancouver's Island," 1847–48 (XLII) (619)
————————· "Report of the Committee on the Expense of Military Defences in the Colonies," 1860 (XLI) (282)
————————· "Papers Relative to the Affairs of British Columbia. Pts. I–IV: 1859–62 (Cd. 2476, 2578, 2724, 2952, 1st series.)
————————· "Despatches and Other Papers Relating to Vancouver's Island," 1849 (CIII) (H. of Commons)
————————· "Papers on the Union of British Columbia with the Dominion of Canada," 1869 (CCCXC) (H. of Commons)
————————· "Return Showing the number of Her Majesty's Ships and Vessels on the Various Stations . . . 1847–67," 1868 (XLV) (H. of Commons)
————————· Lt.-Col. W. F. D. Jervois. *Report on the Defence of Canada, 10 November 1864* (London: Colonial Office, 1865)
————————· (Earl of Carnarvon). *Royal Commission to Enquire into the Defence of British Possessions and Provinces Abroad*. 3 vols. (London: War Office, 1880–83)
————————· Foreign Office. *British and American Joint Commission for the Final Settlement of the Claims of the Hudson's Bay and Puget's Sound Agricultural Companies* (London, 1865–69, 14 vols.)

Spain, Kingdom of

Convencion entre el Rey Nuestro Senor y el Rey de la Gran Bretana, transigiendo varios puntos sobre pesca, navegacion y comercio en el Oceano Pacifico y Los Mares del Sur, firmada en San Lorenzo el Real a 28 de octubre de 1790 (Madrid, 1790?)

United States, Congress

American State Papers, Foreign Relations (Washington, 1833–59: 6 vols.)

———·——— Senate. *Journal of the Executive Proceedings of Senate of the United States of America, 1789–1905* (Washington, 1828–1948, 90 vols.)

———·——— *Alaskan Boundary Tribunal Proceedings* (Washington, 1904, 58th Congress, 2nd session, 7 vols.)

———·——— *Treaties, Conventions, International Agreements between the United States of America and Other Powers, 1776–1909* (Washington, 1910, 2 vols.)

———· *Fur Seal Arbitration: the Proceedings of the Tribunal of Arbitration Convened at Paris, 1893* (Washington, 1895)

———· Congress. *Congressional Globe.* Various nos.

Russia, Ministerstvo finansov. *Istoricheskii obzor glavneishikh meropriiatii, 1802–1902* (St. P., 1902)

———· *Statisticheskii vremennik Rossiiskoi Imperii: vtoraia seriia* (St. P., 1912, nos. 13–15)

———· *Polnoe sobranie zakonov Rossiiskoi Imperii: pervaia seriia* (St. P., 1830)

———· Morskoe Ministerstvo. *Obzor deiatel'nosti Morskago Vedomstva, 1881–1894* (St. P., 1901)

———· Morskoe Ministerstvo. *Zapiski Uchonogo Komiteta Morskago Ministerstva* (St. P., 1833–38)

U.S.S.R., Glavnoe arkhivnoe upravlenie MVD USSR. TsGAVMF.

Materialy po istorii russkogo flota. Russkie flotovodtsy: M. P. Lazarev. ed. A. A. Samarov (M., 1952)

———· *Voenno-istoricheskii zhurnal* (1959–66)

DOCUMENTARY COLLECTIONS

Adams, C. F., ed. *The Memoirs of John Quincy Adams* (Philadelphia, 1874–77)

Andreev, A. I., ed. *Russkie otkrytiia v Tikhom Okeane i Severnoi Amerike v XVIII–XIX vekakh* (M., 1944)

Azadovskii, M. K. *Pamiati dekabristov* (L., 1926)

Barker, B. B., ed. *Letters of Dr. John McLoughlin Written at Fort Vancouver, 1829–1832* (Portland, 1948)

Barratt, G. R. V., trans & ed. *Voices in Exile: The Decembrist Memoirs* (London and Montreal, 1974)

Bil'basov, V. A., ed. *Arkhiv grafov Mordvinovykh* (St. P., 1901–3)

Blinov, A. I., ed. *K istorii Rossiisko-Amerikanskoi Kompanii: sbornik dokumental'nykh materialov* (Krasnoiarsk, 1957)

Boyd, J. P., ed. *Papers of Thomas Jefferson* (Princeton, 1950–65)

Buckle, G. E. ed. *Letters of Queen Victoria* (London, 1926, 2nd series)

Coues, E., ed. *The Manuscript Journals of Alexander Henry and of David Thompson, 1790–1814: New Light on the Early History of the Greater North-west* (New York, 1897)

Dovnar-Zapol'skii, M., ed. *Memuary dekabristov* (St. P., 1906)

Krenov, D., trans. and ed., *Supplement of Some Historical Documents to the Historical Review of the Formation of the Russian-American Company* (of P. Tikhmenev) (Seattle, 1938)

Efremov, P., ed. *Sochineniia i perepiska K. F. Ryleeva* (St. P., 1874)

Lavrischeff, T., ed. *Documents Relative to the History of Alaska* (College, Ala., Alaska History Research Project, 1936–38)

Masson, L. F. R. *Les Bourgeois de la Compagnie du Nord-Ouest . . . avec une esquisse historique et des annotations* (Quebec, 1889–90)

Materialy dlia istorii russkikh zaselenii po beregam Vostochnago okeana (St. P., 1861: suppl. to *Morskoi sbornik*)

Moore, J. B., ed., *The Works of James Buchanan, Comprising His Speeches, State Papers, and*

Private Correspondence (Philadelphia and London, 1908–11)

Nesselrode, A. de, ed. *Lettres et papiers du chancelier comte de Nesselrode* (Paris, 1904)

Nicolas, Sir N., ed. *The Despatches and Letters of Vice-Admiral Lord Nelson* (London, 1844)

Pokrovskii, M. N., ed. *Vosstanie dekabristov: materialy po istorii vosstaniia dekabristov: Dela Verkhovnogo Ugolovnogo Suda i Sledstvennoi Kommissii* (M., 1925–)

Pope, Sir J., ed. *Correspondence of Sir John Macdonald* (Oxford, n.d.)

Rich, E. E., ed. *The Letters of John McLoughlin from Fort Vancouver to the Governor and Committee, First Series, 1825–38.* (Toronto, 1941, Hudson's Bay Company Series, Champlain Soc., no. 4)

————————— *Second Series, 1839–1844* (Toronto, 1943, Hudson's Bay Company Series, Champlain Soc., no. 6)

Semevskii, V. I., comp. and ed. *Obshchestvennye dvizheniia v Rossii v pervuiu polovinu XIX veka* (St. P., 1905)

Tikhmenev, P., comp. *Istoricheskoe obozrenie obrazovaniia Rossiisko-Amerikanskoi Kompanii i deistvii eio.* (St. P., 1861–63)

Wallace, W. S., ed. *Documents Relating to the North West Company* (Toronto, 1934, Champlain Soc. no. 21)

U.S.S.R. *Vneshniaia politika Rossii XIX veka: dokumenty Rossiiskago Ministerstva Inostrannykh Del: seriia 1* (M., 1960–78)

PRIMARY PRINTED SOURCES, SELECTED

Aslanbegov, A. B. *Zhizneopisanie admirala Alekseia Samuilovicha Greiga* (St. P., 1873)

————— "Izvlecheniia. . . ." *Morskoi sbornik* 187 (1881), no. 11, pp. 28–32 (on Vancouver Island in 1881); 190 (1882), no. 5, pp. 1–26 (on New Zealand in 1881)

Atkinson, T. W. *Travels in the Regions of the Upper and Lower Amoor and the Russian Acquisitions on the confines of India and China* (London, 1860)

Barrow, Sir J. *Voyages of Discovery and Research within the Arctic Regions, from the Year 1818 to the Present Time* (London, 1846)

Bax, Captain B. W. *The Eastern Seas: being a Narrative of the Voyage of H.M.S. "Dwarf" in China, Japan, and Formosa* (London 1875)

Beechey, F. W. *Narrative of a Voyage to the Pacific and Beering's Strait, to co-operate with the Polar Expeditions, 1825–28* (London, 1831)

————— *Voyage of Discovery towards the North Pole in H.M.S. "Dorothea" and "Trent," under the command of Captain D. Buchan in 1818; with a summary of all the early Attempts to reach the Pacific by way of the Pole* (London, 1843)

Belcher, Sir E. *Narrative of a Voyage round the World, performed in Her Majesty's Ship "Sulphur," during the Years 1836–1842* (London, 1843)

Bellingsgauzen, F. *Dvukratnye izyskaniia v Iuzhnom Ledovitom Okeane i plavanie vokrug sveta, v prodolzhenie 1819, 1820, i 1821 godov, sovershennye na shliupakh Vostoke i Miriom.* (St. P., 1831). English version by Frank Debenham, as *The Voyage of Captain Bellingshausen to the Antarctic Seas, 1819–1821* (London, 1945, Hakluyt Soc., 2nd series, no. 92)

Berkh (Berg), V. N. *Khronologicheskaia istoriia otkrytiia Aleutskikh ostrovov* (St. P., 1823)

Brassey, Lord T. *A Colonial Volunteer Force* (London, 1878)

————— *The British Navy* (London, 1882)

Bridges, Adm. Sir. C. *Some Recollections* (London, 1918)

Burges, Sir J. B. *A Narrative of the Negotiations Occasioned by the Dispute Between England and Spain in the Year 1790* (London, 1791?)

————— *Letters Lately Published in the Diary on the Subject of the present Dispute with Spain Under the Signature of Verus* (London, 1790)

Butakov, Capt. G. "Izvlecheniia," *Morskoi sbornik* 57 (1862), no.2, pp. 65–66; 58 (1862), no.3, pp. 178–82 (on *Svetlana* frigate in Southeast Asia and Australia, 1862)

Campbell, Archibald. *A Voyage Round the World, from 1806 to 1812, in which Japan, Kamchatka, the Aleutian Islands, and the Sandwich Islands were Visited* (Edinburgh, 1816)

Choris, M. L. *Voyage pittoresque autour du monde* (Paris, 1822)
Cobden, Richard. *Russia, 1836* (London, 1836); reprinted in *The Political Writings of Richard Cobden* (London, 1867, 1: 194–97)
Collins, Perry M. *A Voyage down the Amur* (NY, 1860)
Colomb, J. C. R. *The Protection of Our Commerce and Distribution of Our War Forces Considered* (London, 1867)
————· *On Colonial Defence* (London, 1873)
————· "Russian Development and Our Naval and Military Position in the North Pacific," *JRUSI* 21 (London, 1877): 671–80
————· *The Defence of Great and Greater Britain* (London, 1880)
Cook, Capt. James. *A Voyage to the Pacific Ocean* (London, 1784)
————· Ed. J. C. Beaglehole. *The Journals of Captain James Cook on his Voyages of Discovery: The Voyage of the "Resolution" and "Discovery," 1776–1780* (Cambridge, 1967, Hakluyt Soc.)
Corney, Peter. *Voyages in the North Pacific. Narrative of several trading voyages from 1813 to 1818, between the North West Coast of America, the Hawaiian Islands and China, with a Description of the Russian Establishments on the North-West Coast* (Honolulu, 1896: reprinted from the *London Literary Gazette*, issues for 1821)
Cox, Ross. *Adventures on the Columbia River, including the Narrative of a Residence of Six Years on the Western Side of the Rocky Mountains* (London, 1831)
Craufurd, H. W. *The Russian Fleet in the Baltic in 1836* (London, 1837)
Coxe, William. *An Account of the Russian Discoveries between Asia and America* (London, 1780)
Dalrymple, A. *A Plan for Promoting the Fur-Trade, and Securing It to This Country, by Uniting the Operations of the East-India and Hudson's-Bay Companys* (London, 1789)
————· *The Spanish Pretensions Fairly Discussed* (London, 1790)
————· *The Errors of the British Minister in the Negotiation with the Court of Spain* (London, 1790)
Davydov, G. I. *Dvukratnoe puteshestvie v Ameriku morskikh ofitserov Khvostova i Davydova* (St. P., 1810)
de Groot, Henry. *British Columbia. Its Condition and Prospects, Soil, Climate and Mineral Resources Considered* (San Francisco, 1859)
Dilke, Sir Charles and Wilkinson S. *Imperial Defences* (London, 1892)
Dixon, Captain Geo. *Remarks on the Voyages of John Meares, Esq., in a Letter to that Gentleman* (London, 1790). Facsimile, F. W. Howay, ed. *The Dixon-Meares Controversy* (Toronto and New York, ca. 1929)
D'Wolf, John. *A Voyage to the North Pacific and a Journey through Siberia* (Cambridge, MA, 1861)
Ellis, William. *An Authentic Narrative of a Voyage Performed by Captain Cook.* (London, 1782)
Examination of the Russian Claims to the Northwest Coast of America. *North American Review* 15 (1822): 370–401
[Etches, John]. *An Authentic Statement of All the Facts Relative to Nootka Sound: Its Discovery, History, Settlement, Trade, and the Probable Advantages to be Derived from It. In an Address to the King* (London, 1790)
Fleming, Sandford. *Memorandum in Reference to a Scheme for Completing a great Inter-Colonial and Inter-Continental Telegraph System, by establishing an Electric Cable across the Pacific* (London, 1882)
Forbes, Charles. *Vancouver Island, its Resources and Capabilties, as a Colony* (Victoria, 1862)
Franklin, Sir John. *Narrative of Journey to the Shores of the Polar Sea . . . 1819–1822* (London, 1823)
Geimbruk, Lt.-Col. A. "Gorod Nanaimo na ostrove Vankuvere, i ego kamennyi ugol'." *Morskoi sbornik* 75 (1864), no. 12: 173–87
Gillesem (Gilsen), K. "Puteshestvie na shliupe Blagonamerennom dlia issledovanii beregov Azii i Ameriki za Beringovym prolivom s 1819 po 1822 god." *Otechestvennye zapiski* 66 (St. P., 1849), sect. 8.
Golovnin, V. M. *Memoirs of a Captivity in Japan during the years 1811–1813* (London, 1824)
————· "Zapiska o sostoianii Rossiisko-Amerikanskoi Kompanii v 1818 godu" (St. P., 1819).

Reprinted in *Materialy dlia istorii russkikh zaselenii, 1:48–115. Sochineniia i perevody* (St. P., 1864)

Grant, W. C.   "Description of Vancouver Island." *Journal of the Royal Geographical Society* 27 (1857): 268–320

Irving, Washington.   *Astoria* (Portland, n.d.)

James W.   *Naval History of Great Britain from the Declaration of War by France* (London, 1822–26)

Jervois, Sir W. F. D.   *The Defence of Great Britain and Her Dependencies* (Adelaide, 1880)

Khlebnikov, K. T.   *Zhizneopisanie Aleksandra Andreevicha Baranova* (St. P., 1835). Translated in shortened form by C. Bearne as *Baranov* (Kingston, Ont., Limestone Press, 1973)

Khrushchev, S. P.   "Plavanie shliupa Apollona . . . v 1821–1824 godakh," *Zapiski Admiralteiskago Departamenta* (St. P., 1826, pt. X, pp. 200–216)

King, J. W.   *The Warships and Navies of the World* (Boston, 1882)

Knollys, H.   *Sketches of Life in Japan* (London, 1887)

Kotzebue, Otto von.   *A Voyage of Discovery into the South Sea and Beering's Straits* (London, 1821)

Kronenfels, J. F. von.   *Das schwimmende Flottenmaterial der Seemächte* (Vienna and Leipzig, 1883)

Kruzenshtern, I. F.   *Puteshestvie vokrug sveta* (St. P., 1813). Trans. by R. B. Hoppner as *A Voyage Round the World, in the Years 1803, 1804, 1805 & 1806.* (London, 1813)

Langsdorf(f), G. H.   *Voyages and Travels in Various Parts of the World. During the Years 1803, 1804, 1805, 1806 and 1807* (London, 1813–14)

Lamb, W. Kaye, ed.   "Correspondence Relating to the Establishment of a Naval Base at Esquimalt, 1851–57." *BCHQ* 6 (1942): 277–94; *Journal of a Voyage to the North West Coast of North America during the Years 1811, 1812, 1813 and 1814, by Gabriel Franchère* (Toronto, 1969, Champlain Soc., no. 45)

Laurie, J. W.   "The Protection of Our Naval Base in the North Pacific," *JRUSI* 27 (1883): 357–81

Lazarev, Aleksei P.   *Zapiski o plavanii voennogo shliupa Blagonamerennogo v Beringov Proliv i vokrug sveta v 1819–1822 godakh* (M., 1950)

Lazarev, Andrei P.   *Plavanie vokrug sveta na shliupe "Ladoga" v 1822, 1823 i 1824 godakh* (St. P., 1832)

Lisianskii, Iu. F.   *Puteshestvie vokrug sveta* translated by the author as *A Voyage Round the World, in the Years 1803, 4, 5 & 6, performed . . . in the Ship "Neva"* (London, 1814)

Mackenzie, Alexander.   *Voyages from Montreal, on the River St. Lawrence, Through the Continent of North America to the Frozen and Pacific Oceans, in the years 1789 and 1793* (London, 1801)

McNeill, John.   *The Progress and Present Position of Russia in the East* (London, 1836)

Mayne, R. C.   *Four Years in British Columbia and Vancouver Island: An Account of Their Forests, Rivers, Coasts, Gold Fields, and Resources for Colonization* (London, 1862)

Meares, John.   *Authentic Copy of the Memorial to the Right Hon. William Wyndham Grenville, One of His Majesty's Principal Secretaries of State, by Lieutenant John Mears, of the Royal Navy; Dated 30th April 1790, and Presented to the House of Commons, May 13 1790. Containing Every Particular Respecting the Capture of the Vessels in Nootka Sound* (London, 1790)

Moresby, J.   *Two Admirals* (London, 1913)

Napier, C.   *A Letter to His Grace the Duke of Wellington upon the Actual Crisis of the Country in Respect to the State of the Navy* (London, 1838)

Nesselrode, K. R.   Letters to Baron de Tuyll et al. given in "Correspondence of the Russian Ministers at Washington." *AHR* 18 (1913): 336ff

Ogden, Peter Skene.   "Report of Transactions at Stikine, 1834." In E. E. Rich, ed., *The Letters of John McLoughlin from Fort Vancouver* (Toronto, 1941, pp. 317–22)

On the Ambitious Projects of Russia in Regard to North West America, with Particular Reference to New Albion and New California (London, 1830) (Reprinted and ed. by G. P. Hammond, Kentfield, CA 1955)

Pemberton, J. D.   *Vancouver Island and British Columbia* (London, 1860)

Penrose, Adm. C. V.   *A Memoir of James Trevenen, 1760–1790.* Ed. C. Lloyd and R. C. Anderson (London, 1959, Navy Records Soc., no. 101)

Pfoundes, C.   "Notes on the History of . . . Foreign Intercourse with Japan." *Transactions of the Royal Historical Society* 10 (1882): 82–92.
Pim, Bedford C. T.   *The Gate of the Pacific* (London, 1863)
————· *The Eastern Question, Past, Present and Future* (London, 1877)
Popov, A. A.   "Izvlechenie iz doneseniia nachal'nika eskadry v Tikhom Okeane, Svity E. V. kontr-admirala Popova." *Morskoi sbornik* 64 (1863), no.1: 12–13
————· "Izvlechenie." Ibid. 69 (1863), no.9: 35–40 (the *Bogatyr'* corvette in Australia)
Portlock, Capt. N.   *A Voyage Round the World; but More Particularly to the North West Coast of America; performed in 1785, 1786, 1787 and 1788 in the King George and Queen Charlotte, Captains Portlock and Dixon* (London, 1789)
Ratmanov, M. I.   "Vyderzhki iz dnevnika krugosvetnogo puteshestviia na korable 'Neva'." *Iakhta* (St. P., 1876), no.22, pp. 28–33
Ravenstein, E. G.   *The Russians on the Amur: Its Discovery, Conquest, and Colonization* (London, 1861)
Rezanov, N. P.   *The Rezanov Voyage to Nueva California in 1806.* Trans. T. C. Russell (San Francisco, 1926)
Roche, A. R.   *A View of Russian America in Connection with the Present War* (Montreal, 1885)
Rush, Richard.   *A Residence at the Court of London, 1819–1825* (London, 1845)
Sauer, Martin.   *An Account of a Geographical and Astronomical Expedition to the Northern Parts of Russia.* (London, 1802)
Scoble, T. C.   *The Utilization of Colonial Forces in Imperial Defence* (Toronto, 1879)
Selkirk, Earl of.   *Sketch of the British Fur Trade in North America, with Observations Relative to the North West Company of Montreal* (London, 1816)
Shabel'skii, A. P.   *Voyage aux colonies russes de l'Amérique fait à bord du sloop de guerre l'Apollon, pendant les années 1821, 1822 et 1823* (St. P., 1826)
Shelikhov, G. I.   *Rossiiskago kuptsa imenitago rylskago grazhdanina Grigor'ia Shelikhova pervoe stranstvovanie s 1783 po 1787 god* (St. P., 1791). Extracted and trans by William Tooke as "The Voyage of Gregory Shelekhof." *Varieties of Literature* (1795), pp. 1–42
Shemelin, F. I.   "Istoricheskoe izvestie o pervom puteshestvii Rossiian krugom sveta." *Russkii invalid* (St. P., 1823), nos. 23, 28, and 31
Simpson, Sir Geo.   *Narrative of a Journey round the World during the Years 1841 and 1842* (London, 1847)
Schafer, J., ed.   "Letters of Sir George Simpson, 1841–1843." *American Historical Review* 14 (1908): 70–94
Tilley, Henry.   *Japan, the Amoor, and the Pacific; with Notices of other Places comprised in a voyage of circumnavigation in the Imperial Russian Corvette "Rynda," in 1858–1860* (London, 1861)
Torrubia, José.   *I Moscoviti nella California, o sia dimostrazione della verita' del passo all' America Settentrionale nuovamente scoperto dai Russi, e di quello anticamente practicato dalli popolatori, che vi transmigrarono dall' Asia* (Roma, 1759)
Tronson, J. M.   *Personal Narrative of a Voyage . . . in H.M.S. Barracouta* (London, 1859)
Urquhart, David   *England and Russia; being a Fifth Edition of England, France, Russia and Turkey* (London, 1835)
————· *An Exposition of the Transactions in Central Asia, through which the Independence of States . . . have been Sacrificed to Russia* (London, 1841)
Vancouver, J., ed.   *A Voyage of Discovery to the North Pacific Ocean . . . under the command of Captain George Vancouver* (London, 1798)
Veniaminov, I.   *Zapiski ob ostrovakh Unalashkinskago otdela* (St. P., 1840)
Waddington, A.   *The Fraser Mines Vindicated* (Victoria, 1858)
Wheaton, Henry.   *Elements of International Law* (London, 1864)
Whittingham, Paul.   *Notes on the Late Expedition against the Russian Settlements in Eastern Siberia; and of a Visit to Japan and the Shores of Tartary* (London, 1856)
Wolseley, Garnet.   "England as a Military Power in 1854) and 1878." *Nineteenth Century* 22 (1878): 433–56
Wood, James.   "Vancouver Island — British Columbia." *Nautical Magazine* 27 (1858): 663–66
Wrangel(1), F. von.   *Statistische und ethnographische Nachrichten über die russischen Be-*

sitzungen an der Nordwestküste von Amerika (St. P., 1839)
————' and Baronin E. von Wrangell. "Briefe aus Sibirien und den russischen Niederlassungen in Amerika." *Dorpater Jahrbücher für Litteratur, Statistik and Kunst, besonders Russlands* (Dorpat, 1833–34), 1: 169–80, 353–74; 2: 179–86, 356–64
Zavalishin, D. I.   "Kaliforniia v 1824 godu." *Russkii vestnik* (1865): 322–68
————· "Krugosvetnoe plavanie fregata "Kreiser" v 1822–25 godakh, pod komandoiu Mikhaila Petrovicha Lazareva." *Drevniaia i novaia Rossiia* (St. P., 1877), nos. 5–7, 11
————· *Zapiski dekabrista* (St. P., 1906)

SELECTED SECONDARY SOURCES

Alekseev, A. I.   *Spodvizhniki G. I. Nevel'skogo* (Iuzhno-Sakhalinsk, 1967)
Allen, H. C.   *Great Britain and the United States: A History of Anglo-American Relations, 1783–1952* (New York, 1955)
Anderson, M. S.   "Great Britain and the Growth of the Russian Navy in the Eighteenth Century." *MM* 42 (1956): pp. 132–46.
Andrews, C. L.   "The Wreck of the St. Nicholas." *WHQ* 13 (1922): 27–31.
Atherton, G.   "Nicolai Petrovich Rezanov." *North American Review* 189 (1909): 651–61.
Bach, J.   "The Maintenance of Royal Navy Vessels in the Pacific Ocean, 1825–1875.: *MM* 56 (1970): 259–336
Bagot J.   *George Canning and his Friends* (London, 1909)
Ballard, G. A.   "British Frigates of 1875: the "Shah." *MM* 20 (1936): pp. 305–15
Bailey, T. A.   "Why the United States Purchased Alaska." *PHR* 3 (1934): pp. 39–49
————· *A Diplomatic History of the American People* (NY, 1958)
Bancroft, H. H.   *History of Alaska* (San Francisco, 1886)
————· *History of British Columbia, 1792–1887* (San Francisco, 1887)
Barratt, G. R. V.   *Voices in Exile: The Decembrist Memoirs* (Montreal and London, 1974)
————· "The Russian Interest in Arctic North America: the Kruzenshtern-Romanov Projects, 1819–23." *SEER* 103 (1975): pp. 27–43.
————· "Russian Warships in Van Diemen's Land: *Kreyser* and *Ladoga* by Hobart Town, 1823." Ibid., pp. 566–78
————· "The Enemy that Never Was: The New Zealand Russian Scare of 1870–1885." *New Zealand Slavonic Journal* (1976): 13–33
————· "The Visit of the Russian Cruiser Afrika to Auckland, 1881." Ibid (1978): pp. 1–23
————· "The Russian Navy and New Holland: Part 1." *JRAHS* 64 (1979): 217–34
————· *The Russian Navy and Australia to 1825: The Days before Suspicion* (Melbourne, 1979)
————· *Russia in Pacific Waters, 1715–1825: The Origins of Russia's Naval Presence in the North and South Pacific* (Vancouver, 1980)
————· *Russophobia in New Zealand, 1838–1908* (Palmerston North, NZ, 1981)
Bartlett, C. J.   *Great Britain and Sea Power, 1815–1853* (Oxford, 1963)
Baxter, J. P.   *The Introduction of the Ironclad Warship* (Cambridge, MA, 1923)
Beliaev, A. S.   *Ocherk russkogo voennogo sudostroeniia* (St. P., 1885)
Bell, H. C. F.   *Lord Palmerston* (London, 1936)
Belomer, A.   "Vtoraia tikhookeanskaia eskadra." *Morskoi sbornik* 283 (1914), no. 1, pp. 54–68
Bemis, S. F., ed.   *The American Secretaries of State and Their Diplomacy* (NY, 1928)
Berkh, V. N.   "Izvestie o mekhovoi torgovle, proizvodimoi Rossiianami pri ostrovakh Kurilskikh, Aleutskikh i severozapadnom beregu Ameriki." *Syn otechestva*, 1823, pt. 88, pp. 243–64; pt. 89, pp. 97–106
Beskrovnyi, L. G.   *Russkaia armiia i flot v XIX veke* (M., 1973)
Bezobrazov, V.   *Graf F. P. Litke* (St. P., 1888)
Blok, T.   "The Russian Colonies in California — a Russian Version," *CHSQ* 12 (1933): 189–90
Blue, G. V.   "Vessels Trading on the Northwest Coast of America, 1804–14," *WHQ* 19 (1928): 294–95

————· "French Interest in Pacific America in the Eighteenth Century." *PHR* 4 (1935): 246–66
Bolkhovitinov, N. N. *Stanovlenie russko-amerikanskikh otnoshenii, 1785–1815* (M., 1966)
Bourne, K. *Britain and the Balance of Power in North America, 1815–1908* (London, 1967)
Bradley, H. W. "Hawaii and the American Penetration of the Northeastern Pacific, 1800–1845." *PHR* 12 (1943): 276–77
Buckingham, W. *The Honourable Alexander Mackenzie: His Life and Times* (Toronto, 1892)
Burt, A. L. *The United States, Great Britain and British North America from the Revolution to the Establishment of Peace after the War of 1812* (NY, 1961, 2d ed.)
Callahan, J. M. *Cuba and International Relations* (Baltimore, 1899)
Caswell, J. E. "Sponsors of Canadian Arctic Exploration: Part 3, 1800–1839," *The Beaver*, Outfit 300 (1969), pp. 26–35
Chittenden, H. M. *The American Fur Trade of the Far West* (N.Y., 1902)
Clark, D. E. "Manifest Destiny and the Pacific." *PHR* 1 (1932): 1–17
Cook, W. L. *Flood Tide of Empire: Spain and the Pacific Northwest, 1543–1819* (New Haven and London, 1973)
Clowes, W., et al. *The Royal Navy: A History* (London, 1897–1913)
Cross, A. G. "Samuel Greig, Catherine the Great's Scottish Admiral." *MM* 60 (1974): pp. 251–65
Cummins, J. F. "Colonel C. T. Irwin, a Distinguished Artillery Officer," *Canadian Defence Quarterly*, 5 (1928), pp. 137–41
————· "General Sir Edward Selby Smyth, K.C.M.G." Ibid., pp. 403–11
Davidson, D. C. "Relations of the Hudson's Bay Company with the Russian American Company on the Northwest Coast, 1829–1867." *BCHQ* 5 (1941): 33–51
————· "The War Scare of 1854: The Pacific Coast and the Crimean War." Ibid., pp. 243–54
Davidson, G. C. "The Tracks and Landfalls of Bering and Chirikof on the Northwest Coast of America." *Transactions and Proceedings of the Geographical Society of the Pacific*, 2nd ser., 1 (1901), pp. 1–44
————· *The North West Company* (Berkeley, 1918)
Day, Sir A. *The Admiralty Hydrographic Service, 1795–1919* (London, 1967)
D'Egville, H. *Imperial Defence and Closer Union: A Short Record of the Life-Work of the Late Sir John Colomb* (London, 1913)
de Kiewet, C. W., ed. *The Dufferin-Carnarvon Correspondence, 1874–1878* (Toronto, 1955, Champlain Soc., no. 33)
Dermigny, L. *La Chine et l'Occident: le commerce à Canton au XVIIIe siècle* (Paris, 1964)
Dodge, E. S. *Northwest by Sea* (NY, 1961)
————· *Beyond the Capes: Pacific Exploration from Captain Cook to the "Challenger," 1776–1877* (Boston, 1971)
Dulles, F. R. *The Old China Trade* (Boston, 1930)
Ehrman, J. *Cabinet Government and War, 1890–1940* (Cambridge, 1958)
Elagin, S. I. *Istoriia russkago flota* (St. P., 1875)
Essig, E. O. "The Russian Settlement at Ross." *CHSQ* 12 (1933): 191–209
Farr, D. M. L. *The Colonial Office and Canada, 1867–1887* (Toronto, 1955)
Farrar, V. J. "The Reopening of the Russian-American Convention of 1824." *WHQ* 11 (1920): 83–88
————· *The Annexation of Russian America* (Washington, 1937)
Fedorova, S. F. *Russkoe naselenie Aliaski i Kalifornii* (M., 1971)
Fitzhardinge, V. "Russian Ships in Australian Waters, 1807–1835." *JRAHS* 51 (1965), pt. 2
————· "Russian Naval Visitors to Australia, 1862–1888."
Ibid. 52 (1966), pt. 2, pp. 129–58
Galbraith, J. S. "Perry McDonough Collins at the Colonial Office," *BCHQ* 17 (1953): 207–14
————· "The Early History of the Puget's Sound Agricultural Company, 1838–1843," *OHQ* 55 (1954): 234–59
————· *The Hudson's Bay Company as an Imperial Factor, 1821–1869* (Berkeley and Los Angeles, 1957)
Gibson, J. R. "Russian America in 1833: the Survey of Kirill Khlebnikov." *PNQ* 63 (1972): 1–13
————· *Imperial Russia in Frontier America: The Changing Geography of Supply of Russian*

America, 1784–1867 (NY, 1976)

———· *Feeding the Russian Fur Trade: Provisionment of the Okhotsk Seaboard and the Kamchatka Peninsula, 1639–1856* (Madison, 1969)

Gibbs, N. H.   *The Origins of Imperial Defence* (Oxford, 1955)

Gleason, J. H.   *The Genesis of Russophobia in Great Britain: A Study in the Interaction of Policy and Opinion* (Cambridge, MA, 1950)

Golder, F. A.   *Russian Expansion on the Pacific, 1641–1850: An Account of the Earliest and Later Expeditions.* (Cleveland, 1914)

———· "The Russian Fleet and the Civil War." *AHR* 20 (1915): 801–14

———· "Russian-American Relations during the Crimean War." Ibid. 31 (1926): 462–76

———· "Proposals for Russian Occupation of the Hawaiian Islands." *Publications of the Archives of Hawaii* 5 (1930): 39–50

Gordon, D. C.   *The Dominion Partnership in Imperial Defence, 1870–1914* (Baltimore, 1965)

Gough, B.   "The Records of the Royal Navy's Pacific Station." *JPH* 4 (1969): 146–53

———· *The Royal Navy and the Northwest Coast of North America, 1810–1914: A Study of British Maritime Ascendancy* (Vancouver, 1971)

———· ed.   *To the Pacific and Arctic with Beechey* (Cambridge, 1973, Hakluyt Soc.)

Graham, G. S.   *The Politics of Naval Supremacy: Studies in British Maritime Ascendancy* (Cambridge, 1965)

Grenader, M. B.   "Istoricheskaia obuslovlennost' vozniknovaniia Severo-vostochnoi Ekspeditsii 1785–1795 godov" *Uchonnye Zapiski Petropavlovskogo Gosudarstvennogo Pedagogicheskogo Instituta* (1957), no. 2, pp. 25–35

Grimsted, P. K.   *The Foreign Ministers of Alexander I* (Berkeley, 1969)

Gronsky, P.   "L'Etablissement des Russes en Californie." *Revue d'Histoire moderne* 4 (1929): 401–15; 5 (1930): 101–23

Hamilton, C. F.   "The Canadian Militia: The Dead Period." *Canadian Defence Quarterly* 7 (1929): 78–89, 217–22, 383–89

Hardie, F.   *The Political Influence of Queen Victoria, 1861–1901* (London, 1938)

Hildt, J. C.   *Early Diplomatic Negotiations of the United States with Russia* (Baltimore, 1906)

Howay, F. W., and Scholefield, E. O. S. *British Columbia. From the Earliest Times to the Present* (Vancouver, 1914)

Howay, F. W.   "Early Days of the Maritime Fur-Trade on the Northwest Coast." *CHR* 4 (1923): 26–44

———· "A List of Trading Vessels in the Maritime Fur Trade, 1785–1794." *Proceedings of the Royal Society of Canada*, 3rd ser., 24 (1930): 111–34; 25 (1931): 117–49; 26 (1932): 43–86; 27 (1933): 119–47; 28 (1934): 11–49

———· "An Outline Sketch of the Maritime Fur Trade." Canadian Historical Association *Report of the Annual Meeting, 1932* (Ottawa, 1932): 5–14

———· and Sage, W. N., Angus, H. F. *British Columbia and the United States* (New Haven, 1942)

Huculuk, M.   *When Russia Was in America: The Alaska Boundary Treaty Negotiations, 1824–25* (Vancouver, 1971)

Innis, H. A.   *The Fur Trade in Canada* (New Haven, 1962)

Ikonnikov, S.   *Graf N. S. Mordvinov* (St. P., 1873)

Ireland, W. E.   "The Evolution of the Boundaries of British Columbia." *BCHQ* 3 (1939): 263–82

———· "James Douglas and the Russian American Company, 1840." Ibid. 5 (1941): 53–66

———· "Pre-Confederation Defence Problems of the Pacific Colonies," Canadian Historical Association, *Annual Report, 1941* (Toronto, 1941): 41–54

Ivashintsev, N. A.   *Russkie krugosvetnye puteshestviia s 1803 po 1849 god* (St. P., 1872)

Jackson, C. I.   "The Stikine Territory Lease and its Relevance to the Alaska Purchase." *PHR* 36 (1967): 289–306

———· "A Territory of Little Value: The Wind of Change on the Northwest Coast, 1861–1867." *The Beaver*, Outfit 298 (1967), pp. 40–45

Jane, F. T.   *The Imperial Russian Navy* (London, 1904)

Johnson, A. M.   "Simpson in Russia," *The Beaver*, Outfit 291 (1960), pp. 3–12

Johnson, R. E.   *Thence Round Cape Horn: The Story of the United States Naval Forces on Pacific Station, 1818–1923* (Annapolis, 1963)

Jones, J. M.   "The Railroad Healed the Breach." *Canadian Geographical Journal* 73 (1966): 98–101

Jones, W. D.   *Lord Aberdeen and the Americas* (Athens, GA, 1958)

———· *The American Problem in British Diplomacy* (London, 1974)

Jordon, M. E.   "H.M.C. Dockyard, Esquimalt." *Canadian Geographical Journal* 50 (1955): 124–32

Kashevaroff, A. P.   "Fort Ross: An Account of Russian Settlement." *Alaska Magazine* 1 (1927): 235–42

Kerner, R. J.   "Russian Expansion to America: Its Bibliographical Foundations." *Papers of the Bibliographical Society of America* 25 (1931): 111–29

Kerr, D. G. G.   *Sir Edmund Head: A Scholarly Governor* (Toronto, 1954)

Kerr, J. B.   *A Bibliographical Dictionary of Well-Known British Columbians* (Vancouver, 1890)

Kirwan, L. P.   *A History of Polar Exploration* (NY, 1960)

Knaplund, P.   "James Stephen on Granting Vancouver Island to the Hudson's Bay Company, 1846–48." *BCHQ* 9 (1945): 259–71

Kuykendall, R. S.   *The Hawaiian Kingdom, 1778–1854* (Honolulu, 1938)

Kuznetsova, V. V.   "Novye dokumenty o russkoi ekspeditsii k severnomu poliusu." *Izvestiia Vsesiuznogo Geograficheskogo Obshchestva* 50 (1968), no. 3, pp. 237–45

Lamb, W. Kaye   "The Founding of Fort Victoria." *BCHQ* 7 (1943): 71–92

———· "Correspondence Relating to the Establishment of a Naval Base at Esquimalt, 1851–1857." Ibid. 6 (1942): 277–96

———· "The Governorship of Richard Blanchard." Ibid. 14 (1950): 1–40

Lane-Poole, S.   *Life of the Right Honourable Stratford Canning, Viscount Stratford de Redcliffe* (London, 1888)

Lewis, M. A.   "An Eye-Witness at Petropaulovski, 1854." *MM* 49 (1963): 265–72

———· *The Navy in Transition, 1814–1864: A Social History* (London, 1965)

Longstaff, F. V.   "The Beginnings of the Pacific Station and Esquimalt Royal Naval Establishment." *Third Annual Report and Proceedings of the British Columbia Historical Association, 1925* (Vancouver, 1925)

———· "Notes on the Early History of the Pacific Station." *Canadian Defence Quarterly* 3 (1926): 309–18; 4 (1927): 292–309. (titles vary)

———· *Esquimalt Naval Base: A History of Its Work and Its Defences* (Victoria, 1941)

———· and Lamb, W. Kaye. "The Royal Navy on the Northwest Coast, 1813–1850." *BCHQ* 9 (1945): pp. 1–24, 113–28

Lyall, A. C.   *The Life of the Marquess of Dufferin* (London, 1905)

McCabe, J. O.   *The San Juan Boundary Question* (Toronto, 1964)

Mackay, Corday.   "The Collins Overland Telegraph." *BCHQ* 10 (1946): 187–215

Mahan, A. T.   *Sea Power in Its Relations to the War of 1812* (Boston, 1905)

Makarova, R. V.   *Russkie na Tikhom Okeane vo vtoroi polovine XVIII veka* (M., 1968)

Malkin, M. A.   *Grazhdanskaia voina v Soedinennykh Shtatakh i tsarskaia Rossiia, 1861–1865* (M., 1939)

Manning, W. R.   "The Nootka Sound Controversy." American Historical Association, *Annual Report, 1904* (1905): 279–478

Martin, K.   "The Victorian Monarchy." *Edinburgh Review* (April 1926): 366–84

Marder, A. J.   *The Anatomy of British Sea Power: A History of British Naval Policy in the pre-Dreadnought Era, 1880–1905* (NY, 1940)

Mazour, A. G.   "The Russian-American and Anglo-Russian Conventions, 1824–25: An Interpretation." *PHR* 14 (1945): 303–10

———· "Dimitry Zavalishin: Dreamer of a Russian-American Empire." Ibid. 5 (1936): pp. 26–37

Merk, F., ed.   *Fur Trade and Empire: George Simpson's Journal . . . 1824–1825* (Cambridge, MA, 1931, Harvard Hist. Studies, no. 31)

Merk, F.   *The Oregon Question: Essays in Anglo-American Diplomacy and Politics* (Cambridge, MA, 1967)

———· "The Genesis of the Oregon Question." *Mississippi Valley Historical Review* 36 (1950): pp. 583–612

Miller, D. Hunter   "Russian Opinion on the Cession of Alaska." *AHR* 48 (1943): 521–32

Mitchell, D. W.   *A History of Russian and Soviet Sea Power* (London, 1974)
Moiseev, S. P.   *Spisok korablei russkogo parovogo i bronenosnogo flota s 1881 po 1917 god* (M., 1947)
Morison, S. E.   *The Maritime History of Massachusetts, 1783–1860* (Boston and NY, 1921)
Morton, A. S.   *A History of the Canadian West to 1870–71* (London, 1939)
Morton, W. L.   *The Critical Years: The Union of British North America, 1857–1873* (Toronto, 1964)
Mosely, P. E.   *Russian Diplomacy and the Opening of the Eastern Question in 1838 and 1839* (Cambridge, 1934)
Nichols, I. C., Jr.   "The Russian Ukase and the Monroe Doctrine: A Re-evaluation." *PHR* 36 (1967): 13–26
————· and Ward, R. A.   "Anglo-American Relations and the Russian Ukase: A Reassessment," Ibid. 41 (1972): 444–56
Norris, J. M.   "The Policy of the British Cabinet in the Nootka Crisis." *EHR* 70 (1955): 562–80
Novakovskii, S.   *Iaponiia i Rossiia* (Tokyo, 1918)
Ogden, A.   *The California Sea Otter Trade, 1784–1848* (Berkeley, 1941)
Ogorodnikov, S. F.   *Istoricheskii obzor razvitiia i deiatel'nosti Morskago Ministerstva za sto let ego sushchestvovaniia, 1802–1902* (St. P., 1902)
Okun', S. B.   "K istorii prodazhi russkikh kolonii v Amerike," *Istoricheskie zapiski* 2 (1938): 209–39
————· *Rossiisko-Amerikanskaia Kompaniia* (M., 1939). Trans. by C. Ginsburg as *The Russian-American Company* (Cambridge, MA, 1951)
Oliver, E. H.   *The Canadian North-West* (Ottawa, 1915)
O'Neil, M.   "The Maritime Activities of the North West Company, 1813–1821," *WHQ* 21 (1930), pp. 243–67
Ormsby, M. A.   *British Columbia: a History* (Toronto, 1958)
Pierce, R. A.   *Russia's Hawaiian Adventure, 1815–1817* (Berkeley, 1965)
————· "Alaska's Russian Governors: Chistiakov and Wrangel." *Alaska Journal* 1 (1971): 38–41
Poniatowski, M.   *Histoire de la Russie d'Amérique et d'Alaska* (Paris, 1958)
Porter, K. W.   *John Jacob Astor, Business Man* (Cambridge, MA, 1931)
Preston, R. A.   *Canada and "Imperial Defense": A Study of the Origins of the British Commonwealth's Defense Organization, 1867–1919* (Durham, NC, 1967)
Quested, R. K.   *The Expansion of Russia in East Asia, 1857–1860* (Kuala Lumpur, 1968)
Reddaway, W. F.   "The Crimean War and the French Alliance, 1853–58." *Cambridge History of British Foreign Policy* (Cambridge, 1923), 2: 357–402
Rich, E. E.   *The History of the Hudson's Bay Company, 1670–1870* (Toronto and London, 1958–59)
Rodkey, F. S.   "Anglo-Russian Negotiations about a "Permanent" Quadruple Alliance, 1840–1841." *AHR* 36 (1931): 343–49
Robinson, L. B.   *Esquimalt: "Place of Shoaling Waters"* (Victoria, 1947)
Rose, J. H.   "Sea Power and the Winning of British Columbia." *MM* 7 (1921): 74–79
Ross, D.   *Opinions of the European Press on the Eastern Question* (London, 1936)
Roy, R. H.   "The Early Militia and Defence of British Columbia, 1871–1885." *BCHQ* 18 (1954): 1–28
————· "The Colonel Goes West." *Canadian Army Journal* 8 (1954): 76–81
Sage, W. N.   *Sir James Douglas and British Columbia* (Toronto, 1930)
Schurman, D. M.   "Esquimalt: Defence Problem, 1865–1887." *BCHQ* 19 (1955): 57–69
————· *The Education of a Navy: The Development of British Naval Strategic Thought, 1867–1914* (London, 1965)
Semevskii, V. I. et al.   *Obshchestvennye dvizheniia v Rossii v pervuiu polovinu XIX veka* (St. P., 1905)
Shur, L. A.   *K beregam Novogo Sveta* (M., 1971)
Sokolov, A. V.   *Tri krugosvetnykh plavaniia M. P. Lazareva* (M., 1951)
Sellers, C.   *James K. Polk: Continentalist, 1843–1846* (Princeton, 1966)
Snytko, T. G.   "Ryleev na sledstvii." *Literaturnoe nasledstvo*, 59 (M., 1954), bk. 1, pp. 196ff
Stacey, C. P.   "The North-West Campaign, 1885." *Introduction to the Study of Military History*

for Canadian Students (Ottawa, 1955)

———· "John A. Macdonald on Raising Troops in Canada for Imperial Service, 1885." *CHR* 38 (1957): 37–40

———· *Canada and the British Army, 1846–1871* (Toronto, 1963)

Stanislavskaia, A.   "Angliia i Rossiia v gody vtoroi turetskoi voiny, 1787–1791." *Voprosy istorii* (1948), no. 11, pp. 36ff

Stanley, G. F. C.   *Canada's Soldiers: The Military History of an Unmilitary People* (Toronto, 1960)

Stewart, A. R.   "Sir John A. Macdonald and the Imperial Defence Commission of 1879." *CHR* 35 (1954): 119–39

Strakhovsky, L. I.   "Russia's Privateering Projects of 1878." *JMH* 7 (1935): 22–40

Tatum, E. H., Jr.   *The United States and Europe, 1815–23: A Study in the Background of the Monroe Doctrine* (Berkeley, 1936)

Taylor, G. P.   "Spanish-Russian Rivalry in the Pacific, 1769–1820." *The Americas* 25 (1958): 109–27

Temperley, H. W. V.   *The Foreign Policy of Canning, 1822–1827* (London, 1925)

Thomas, B. P.   *Russo-American Relations, 1815–1867* (Baltimore, 1930)

Thomson, D. C.*Alexander Mackenzie: Clear Grit* (Toronto, 1960)

Tompkins, S. R., and Moorehead, M. L. "Russia's Approach to America. Part I, From Russian Sources, 1751–61." *BCHQ* 13 (1949): 55–66; "Part II, From Spanish Sources, 1761–75." Ibid., pp. 231–55

Tompkins, S. R.   "Drawing the Alaskan Boundary." *CHR* 26 (1945): 22–34

Tucker, G. N.   *The Naval Service of Canada: Its Official History* (Ottawa, 1952)

Tunstall, W. C. B.   "Imperial Defence, 1815–1870." *Cambridge History of the British Empire* (Cambridge, 1940), 2: 807–42; "Imperial Defence, 1870–1897," 3: 230–53

Tyler, J. E.   *The Struggle for Imperial Unity, 1868–1895* (London, 1938)

Unterberger, P. F.   *Primorskaia oblast'* (St. P., 1900)

van Alstyne, R. W.   "International Rivalries in the Pacific Northwest." *OHQ* 46 (1945): 185–218

———· "Anglo-American Relations, 1853–1857." *AHR* 42 (1936): 492ff

———· "Great Britain, the United States, and Hawaiian Independence, 1850–1855." *PHR* 4 (1935): 15–24

Vevier, C.   "American Continentalism: An Idea of Expansion, 1845–1910." *AHR* 65 (1960): 323–35

Veselago, F. F.   *Kratkaia istoriia russkogo flota, 1700–1801* (St. P., 1893, rev. ed. M., 1939)

———· *Ocherk russkoi morskoi istorii* (St. P., 1875)

Volkl, E.   "Das russische Pazifik-Imperium Aufbauversuche und Ruckzug." *Saeculum* 17 (1965): 357–88

Wagner, H. R.   "Fray Benito de la Sierra's Account of the Hezeta Expedition to the Northwest Coast in 1775." *CHSQ* 9 (1930): 201–8

———· "The Last Spanish Exploration of the Northwest Coast and the Attempt to Colonize Bodega Bay." Ibid. 9 (1931): 313–45

———· "Creation of Rights of Sovereignty through Symbolic Acts." *PHR* 7 (1938): 297–326

Webster, C. K.   "Urquhart, Ponsonby, and Palmerston." *EHR* 62 (1947): 327–51

Wheeler, M. E.   "The Origins of the Russian-American Company." *Jahrbucher für Geschichte Osteuropas* (1966): 485–94

Williams, G.   *The British Search for the Northwest Passage in the Eighteenth Century* (London, 1962)

Williams, W. A.   *American-Russian Relations, 1781–1947* (NY, 1952)

Winks, R. W.   *Canada and the United States: The Civil War Years* (Baltimore, 1960)

Wolfenden, M.   "Esquimalt Dockyard's First Buildlings." *BCHQ* 10 (1946): 235–40

Wrinch, L. A.   "The Formation of the Puget's Sound Agricultural Company," *WHQ* 24 (1933): 3–8

Wrottesley, G.   *Life and Correspondence of Field Marshal Sir John Burgoyne, Bart.* (London, 1873)

Ziugenkov, I. P.   *Morskoi flot v Krymskoi voine* (M., 1900)

Zubov, N. N.   *Otechestvennye moreplavateli-issledovateli morei i okeanov* (M., 1954)

Index

PLACE INDEX